THE NEW SAINT BASIL HYMNAL

THE NEW SAINT BASIL HYMNAL

COMPILED, ARRANGED AND EDITED
FOR UNISON OR
FOUR MIXED VOICES
BY THE

BASILIAN FATHERS

WILLIS MUSIC COMPANY
FLORENCE, KENTUCKY 41022-0548

Imprimi potest
George B. Flahiff, C.S.B.
Superior General

Nihil obstat
Hubert P. Coughlin, C.S.B.
Censor Deputatus

Imprimatur
✠ James C. Cardinal McGuigan
Archbishop of Toronto

Feast of St. Basil, June 14, 1958

Approved by
The White List Committee
of the Society of Saint Gregory
of America

PRINTED IN THE UNITED STATES OF AMERICA

FOREWORD

Be filled with the Spirit, speaking to one another in psalms and hymns and spiritual songs, singing and making melody in your hearts to the Lord." That is the way Saint Paul exhorted the first Catholics at Ephesus. And throughout the ages, the Holy Spirit has always filled the Church with hymns of praise. Today, like the Ephesians, we ourselves have been reminded of the role of Christian song. In the encyclical *Musicae Sacrae Disciplina*, Pope Pius XII tells us that Church music ought to contribute "more every day to greater splendor in the celebration of divine worship and to the more effective nourishment of spiritual life among the faithful."

The Church uses many arts in her worship, and although they are outside the essential stream of her sacramental life, these arts are no mere surface adornment unrelated to that life. "The purpose of the Christian religion," remarks Abbot Ildefons Herwegen, O.S.B., "is to bring us as transfigured Christians to the transfigured Christ . . . The idea of Christian transfiguration is the art-principle of the Liturgy. (*Liturgy's Inner Beauty*, p. 15.)" Thus Church architecture and sculpture and the graphic arts participate on the material level in restoring—transfiguring—all things into Christ. And music does this in a still closer way because of its part in the very texture of the Liturgy. Through sacred song, Saint Basil says, the Holy Spirit blends the delight of melody with doctrine. Music's role is to transfigure the text, to uplift the heart of the praying Church.

The sublime center of our worship is the Mass; it is the public and corporate sacrifice which the entire Mystical Body offers to God the Father. Because such worship must be external as well as internal, Pope Pius XII insists that "all the faithful should be aware that to participate in the Eucharistic Sacrifice is their chief duty and supreme dignity, *and that not in an inert and negligent fashion. (Mediator Dei, 80.)*" Such an active sharing of the laity in liturgical worship may be accomplished:

> when, for instance, the whole congregation, in accordance with the rules of the Liturgy, either answers the priest in an orderly and fitting manner, or sings hymns suitable to the different parts of the Mass, or do both, or finally in High Masses when they answer the prayers of the minister of Jesus Christ and also sing the liturgical chant. (*Mediator Dei*, 105.)

These words of our Holy Father and his encyclical on Sacred Music suggest an apostolate for the promotion of congregational singing. It is this apostolic spirit which has led to the compilation of *The New Saint Basil Hymnal*. The aim of the editors has been to provide a hymnal which will stir the faith and piety of the faithful to a more active and fruitful participation in the liturgical and extra-liturgical worship of the Church.

The singing of the chants and hymns is a form of divine worship which is essentially congregational. It is not meant simply to provide the right atmosphere for praying during Mass and extra-liturgical services; it actually serves to unite the congregation in one mind and one heart, one prayer. The communion which results is not only spiritual, but physical: each member of the congregation lends his voice as an element of the sacrificial offering of Christ; his voice becomes an offering, a part of the sacramental worship of the Church. Such a song can be likened to the hymn which our Lord and His eleven apostles sang around the first Eucharistic Table. To sing is thus a dignity for all and a means of holiness: for where the song is holy, the singer will be sanctified.

Since congregational hymnody invests the laity with an active role in the worship of the Church, it must be characterized by the holiness, beauty and universality which are consonant with the celebration of Christ's mysteries. The following criteria, therefore, have guided the compilers in the selection of hymns and melodies. The most important element is the text. In it must be found the character and spirit of the Church's public prayer: it should be objective, not subjective; communal, not individualistic. It should convey deep theological teaching in a manner which is both beautiful and inspiring, and express not so much the personal emotion of the individual as the universal mood of the praying Church.

As a complementary principle, the Hymnal Committee has also borne in mind that the primary function of Sacred Music is to clothe prayer with a suitable melody. Sacred Music is neither a mere entertainment, nor simply an ornamentation; for Saint Pius X states that:

> its proper aim is to add greater efficacy to the text, in order that through it the faithful may be more easily moved to devotion and better disposed for the reception of the fruits of grace belonging to the celebration of the holy mysteries. (*Motu Proprio*, 1.)

Because Gregorian chant, the official liturgical music of the Church, is most beautifully adapted to this purpose, a hymnal ought to contain a wide selection of its melodies—and it is hoped that a greater familiarity with, and use of the chants in this compilation will dispel the notion that Gregorian chant is a monotonous and mournful music, the peculiar property of monks, beyond the capabilities of a singing congregation. There should also be a rich representation of the music which is the legitimate expression of particular cultures; for example, the traditional melodies of English, French, German, Irish, Italian and Slavic congregations. Fine examples of these are to be found in the following pages, along with several contemporary tunes which we hope will be worthy additions to the treasury of Church music.

The New Saint Basil Hymnal is exactly what its name implies: it is not a mere revision of an older book; it is a new one. Only the best hymns and tunes have been retained from the old *St. Basil's Hymnal*, and these have been carefully re-edited and re-harmonized. The new publication is much broader in scope than the former and is designed to supply the musical needs of both large and small parishes and schools. In order to accommodate the different literary and musical standards of individuals, the contents have been intentionally made larger than the necessities of any one group would demand.

Many who have used the *St. Basil's Hymnal* in the past will look in vain for some of the "good, old hymns." These have been passed over by the Committee because, as has been observed, they are really neither *good*, nor *old*. The majority of them reflect the sentimental, individualistic piety of the late Victorian period. Too frequently their melodies are poor copies of the secular music of that era, while their texts unduly emphasize the human nature of the Savior, tending to bring God to a purely human level rather than to lift man's thoughts to God. Such hymns are more than dated; they are positively harmful in that they attempt to express a religious emotion which is exaggerated, over-familiar and, eventually, false—since they teach the singer to pray badly. In the present collection, then, they have yielded place to *better*, and in some cases *older* hymns of genuine piety and dignity.

Seventy years ago, the first *Saint Basil's Hymn Book* was published in order to promote congregational singing. Through the intervening years, it has undergone many editions and revisions, but it has always served that purpose. Today, the Basilian Fathers sincerely hope that the new hymnal dedicated to their patron, Saint Basil the Great, will continue to contribute to the greater splendor of God's worship.

EXPLANATORY NOTES

THE HYMNS

The hymnal is divided into two parts, a hymn section and a service section. The hymn section has been subdivided into convenient groups which may be noted in the Table of Contents. Within each group, the hymns are arranged in the following sequence: Latin hymns; Latin hymns with an English rendering set to the same tune; Latin hymns and their English translations on facing pages; English hymns in alphabetical order. Festal hymns in honor of Our Lady and the Saints are arranged chronologically. In order to avoid unnecessary turning of pages, this order has occasionally been set aside.

The names and obituary dates of the authors are given on the left above each hymn; where these are unknown, an attempt has been made to give the source and date of publication. No dates have been assigned, however, to living authors or translators. If the hymn is a translation, the title of the original is given, and the name of the translator, preceded by *Tr.*, follows the author's name. Initials have been employed in the case of translators who have contributed several translations or who have helped in the compilation of the hymnal. The names of these translators are listed in the *Index of Authors*. The abbreviation *alt* denotes alterations made by the compilers or others.

The service section provides especially for the needs of congregations and small choirs. The liturgical directions and the chants for High Mass, Funerals, Confirmation and the Forty Hours Adoration, will make possible correct and complete services for most occasions.

Throughout both sections, the acute accent (′) designates the stress of Latin words of three or more syllables. Latin words of two syllables are always accented on the first syllable.

THE MUSIC

The musical settings have been selected as suitable for congregational singing. They are in regular measures or in the free rhythm characteristic of Gregorian chant. Hymn-tunes in the first style have been generally so arranged that they can be sung in unison by a congregation and also in four voices by a mixed choir. The harmonizations are especially designed to provide simple and strong accompaniments, although more elaborate arrangements, such as those of J. S. Bach, have occasionally been introduced.

On the right, above each hymn, may be found the name of the composer and his obituary date or the source and date of publication where these are known. The names of composers who have harmonized or adapted melodies follow. Initials are employed only in the case of those who have provided harmonizations or adaptations for this hymnal; their names are given in the *Index of Composers and Arrangers.*

The *Pitch* of all tunes has been fixed as low as possible for mixed congregations. The normal melodic range is from middle C to the second D above. With one exception, the extreme range extends from B♭ below middle C to the second E above.

A distinctive notation has been used for different styles: half notes for the older chorales and more solemn melodies; quarter notes for the greater majority of tunes; eighth notes for Gregorian chant.

Expression marks and indications of *tempo* have been entirely omitted. Occasionally short pauses have been indicated by a comma (’); whereas a complete pause is designated by the sign (𝄐).

GREGORIAN CHANT

In rendering Gregorian chant, it must be remembered that Gregorian rhythm is free; that is, no fixed measure is maintained uniformly throughout; the melody moves in groups of two or three notes which alternate freely with each other.

The simple beat of Gregorian chant is normally represented by an eighth note in modern notation; it is indivisible. It can be doubled (♩) or tripled (♩.) or slightly lengthened. A slight prolongation (not a doubling) of a single note or the retarding of a group of notes is indicated by a horizontal line, an *episema,* over the note or group. The jagged symbol (𝆕) representing a *quilisma,* is placed over the middle note of an ascending group: the note before the quilisma is slightly lengthened, while the quilisma is given its full time value but sung lightly and delicately. In other instances, Gregorian notes are of equal duration and must be sung evenly and smoothly whether they occur singly or in groups.

The bar in Gregorian chant indicates melodic phrasing and the places where breath may be taken.

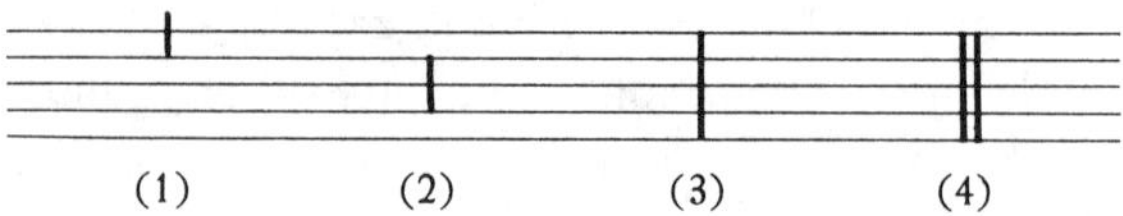

(1) (2) (3) (4)

The *quarter bar* (1) and the *half bar* (2) mark secondary pauses in which a quick breath may be taken from the value of the preceding note.

The *full bar* (3) marks off a melodic phrase and a pause of one note's value; a more deliberate breath should be taken. Where a longer pause seemed warranted, this has been indicated by a quarter-beat rest.

The *double-bar* (4) indicates the end of the chant or a section thereof. Where the congregation and choir chant alternately, no pause is made at the double bar.

It should be noted that, in the Gregorian accompaniment, frequently no indication has been given of the rest at the full bars and the double bars. A rest has been provided after such bars only when the next phrase begins with an upbeat. Elsewhere, the proper appreciation of such rests has been left to the choirmaster and organist.

The organist who accompanies the Gregorian chant should pay constant attention to the rhythm of the melodies and assist the singers in a supple rendering of the chant. The accompaniments should always be played in a *legato* style, and with just enough volume to support the voices.

* * *

In order to ensure a more effective use of this hymnal, several indexes have been provided. The *Metrical Index of Tunes*, for example, lists all the melodies which can be used for various meters. Thus, if a melody such as that for the May Crowning Hymn is found to be too difficult, other suitable tunes which can be substituted will be found grouped under the metrical heading *88.88.88*.

ACKNOWLEDGMENTS AND PERMISSIONS

The New Saint Basil Hymnal Committee extends its gratitude to the following for their gracious permission to include the copyright hymns listed below:

BURNS, OATES & WASHBOURNE, LTD., London, from *The Westminster Hymnal*, no. 4, 29, 94, 178, 179, 182.

CANTATE OMNES PUBLICATIONS, Buffalo, from *Cantate Omnes*, no. 144.

CARY & CO., London, from *Catholic Hymns*, no. 59.

E. C. SCHIRMER MUSIC COMPANY, Boston, no. 17, 51.

HOUGHTON MIFFLIN COMPANY, New York, from *The Chief Middle English Poets*, ed. Jessie L. Weston, 1914, no. 36.

MCLAUGHLIN & REILLY COMPANY, Boston, from *American Catholic Hymnal*, no. 72.

OXFORD UNIVERSITY PRESS, London, from *The English Hymnal*, no. 183, 184.

OXFORD UNIVERSITY PRESS, INC., New York, from *Poems of Gerard Manley Hopkins*, no. 89.

THE REVEREND THURSTON N. DAVIS, S. J., from *America*, no. 16.

THE RIGHT REVEREND ABBOT, the REVEREND ROGER SCHOENBECHLER, O.S.B., and THE LITURGICAL PRESS, St. John's Abbey, Collegeville, no. 29, 172; and from *Sponsa Regis*, no. 6, 65, 77, 191.

SISTER MARY GERTRUDE, C.S.J., no. 160; the REVEREND A. GREGORY MURRAY, O.S.B., no. 205; the REVEREND IRVIN UDULUTSCH, O.F.M. Cap., no. 40, 100, 122, 132, 136, 157.

MUSIC ACKNOWLEDGMENTS

Thanks are likewise due to the following for their kind permission to include the copyright tunes and arrangements listed below:

BOOSEY AND HAWKES, INC., New York, from *Arundel Hymns*: Roche Abbey, no. 154.

BURNS, OATES & WASHBOURNE, LTD., London, from *The Westminster Hymnal*: Corona, no. 75; Ecclesia, no. 200.

DESCLEE ET CIE, Tournai: the rhythmic signs and the Gregorian melodies taken from the editions of Solesmes.

OXFORD UNIVERSITY PRESS, INC., New York, from *Five Hymn Tunes*: St. Basil, no. 174.

THE FREDERICK HARRIS MUSIC COMPANY, LTD., Oakville, and DR. HEALEY WILLAN: Mass of Saint Teresa, no. 227, 228, 229, 230, 231.

THE RIGHT REVEREND ABBOT, Ramsgate Abbey: the settings of the Antiphon *Adoremus in aeternum*, no. 114.

THE RIGHT REVEREND JOHN E. RONAN, D.P., from *Jubilee Hymns*, no. 49, 132, 188.

SISTER MARY FLORIAN, S.S.J., no. 156; the RIGHT REVEREND ABBOT, Downside Abbey, no. 253.

For both the hymn and tune:

SISTER CECILIA MIRIAM, S.N.J.M., no. 169.

THE CATHOLIC EDUCATION PRESS, Washington, from *Hymnal, a Supplement to Music First & Second Year*, compiled by Justine Ward, no. 139.

SPECIAL ACKNOWLEDGMENTS

The Committee gratefully acknowledges a distinct debt to the following:

For original texts and translations, and for assistance in the work of textual revision:

Mrs. Stella Kelly; Sister Mary Francis, P.C.; the Reverend Basilian Fathers: Claude G. Arnold, Dennis C. Foy, T. James Hanrahan, W. James Howard, Charles W. Leland, Robert F. Neill, Ulysse E. Paré.

For the contribution of original melodies:

Messrs. Carroll T. Andrews, Arthur C. Becker, Richard K. Biggs, Thomas C. Kelly, John Lee, Quentin Maclean, William J. Marsh, Healey Willan; Sisters Mary Francis, P.C., Mary Theophane, O.S.F., the Reverend James E. Daley, C.S.B., Francis E. Monaghan, C.S.B., A. Gregory Murray, O.S.B.

For the arrangements and harmonizations of melodies:

Messrs. Carroll T. Andrews, George Coutts, David Fetler, Thomas C. Kelly, John Lee, William J. Marsh, Healey Willan; Sister Mary Florian, S.S.J.; the Reverend Francis J. Guentner, S.J., Cyril D. Udall, C.S.B.

The Committee is particularly indebted to the Reverend Jean-Hébert Desrocquettes, O.S.B., for the accompaniments of the Gregorian chant and for assistance in correcting the proofs thereof.

The generous co-operation of the following has likewise been of incalculable importance and is deeply appreciated:

The Very Reverend George B. Flahiff, Superior General, the Reverend Hubert P. Coughlin, J. Bernard Black, J. T. Roland Janisse, Francis E. Monaghan, Cyril D. Udall and many other Basilian Fathers and Scholastics who have offered aid and constant encouragement;

The Right Reverend Abbot of Our Lady of Gethsemani and the monks of his Abbey who have contributed admirable compositions and assisted in the correction of proofs, but who perforce remain anonymous;

The Reverend Mothers and Sisters of St. Joseph of London, Rochester and Toronto; Miss Elizabeth A. Currie for many valuable services;

Mr. Irvin C. Brogan, who has provided the Liturgical Directions for the guidance of choirmasters; Mr. John C. Menihan for his cover design and assistance in the preparation of the Hymnal;

Sister Marie Alma, S.C., the Reverend Francis J. Guentner, S.J., John C. Selner, S.S., Irvin Udulutsch, O.F.M. Cap., for the advice and criticism offered to the Committee as it commenced its work; Sister Mary Teresine, O.S.F., the Reverend Elmer Pfeil and Irvin Udulutsch, O.F.M. Cap., for their examination of the manuscripts and valuable suggestions; the Reverend John C. Selner, S.S., and Richard B. Curtin, and Messrs. Philip A. Bansbach, Frank Campbell-Watson and Joseph A. Murphy of the *White List Committee* of *The Society of Saint Gregory of America* for their examination and approbation of the contents of the Hymnal;

The Liturgical Press, Collegeville, Minnesota, for permission to quote from *Liturgy's Inner Beauty* by Abbot Ildefons Herwegen, O.S.B.

The Committee wishes also to thank all those who have submitted tunes or texts, and it regrets that it has been unable to use many of these.

PETER E. SHEEHAN, C.S.B., *Chairman*.
EDWARD C. CURRIE, *Editor*.
RALPH JUSKO
M. OWEN LEE, C.S.B.
THOMAS B. MAILLOUX, C.S.B.

CONTENTS

The Hymns

Service Music

Indexes

ON JORDAN'S BANK

Jordanis oras praevia.
CHARLES COFFIN, *d. 1749.*
Tr. JOHN CHANDLER, *d. 1876, alt.*

Adapted from a Chorale in 'Musikalisches Hand-Buch,'
Hamburg, 1690.

1. On Jor - dan's bank the Bap - tist's cry An -
2. Then cleansed be ev - 'ry heart from sin; Make
3. To heal the sick stretch out Thine hand, And
4. All praise, e - ter - nal Son, to Thee, Whose

1. noun - ces that the Lord is nigh; A - wake and hear - ken,
2. straight the way of God with - in; Oh, let us all our
3. bid the fal - len sin - ner stand; Shine forth, and let Thy
4. ad - vent sets Thy peo - ple free; Whom with the Fa - ther

1. for. He brings Glad ti - dings of the King of kings.
2. hearts pre - pare For Christ to come and en - ter there.
3. light re - store Earth's own true love - li - ness once more.
4. we a - dore And Ho - ly Ghost for - ev - er more.

ADVENT

RORATE CAELI

O Heavens, Send Your Rain

Isaias 45, 8.
Tr. M.O.L.

Mode .
(J.H.D.

Ro - rá - te cae - li dé - su - per,
O heav - ens, send your rain up - on us,
et nu - bes plu - ant ju - stum.
send down the Just One to Is - ra - el.
Fine
Ne i - ra - scá - ris Dó - mi - ne,
Do not be an - gry with us, Lord,
ne ul - tra me - mí - ne - ris in - i - qui - tá - tis:
re - mem - ber no lon - ger all our past trans - gres - sions:
ec - ce cí - vi - tas Sanc - ti fa - cta est de - sér - ta:
See, Your ci - ty of Ho - lies now has been de - ser - ted:

RORATE CAELI

Si - on de - sér - ta fa - cta est:
Si - on has been a - ban - doned:
Je - rú - sa - lem de - so - lá - ta est:
Je - ru - sa - lem has been made des - o - late:
do - mus san - cti - fi - ca - ti - ó - nis tu - ae
The house of Your kind and mer - ci - ful bles - sing
et gló - ri - ae tu - ae, u - bi
and of Your glo - ry, the place
lau - da - vé - runt te pa - tres no - stri.
where a - bun - dant praise rose from our fa - thers.
Repeat D. C.

3

ADVENT

CREATOR ALME SIDERUM

Anon., 7th Cent.
Mode
(J.H.D.
1. Cre - á - tor al - me sí - de - rum,
2. Qui daé - mo - nis ne fráu - di - bus
3. Com - mú - ne qui mun - di ne - fas
4. Vir - tus, ho - nor, laus, gló - ri - a
1. Ae - tér - na lux cre - dén - ti - um,
2. Per - í - ret or - bis ím - pe - tu
3. Ut ex - pi - á - res, ad cru - cem
4. Dé - o Pa - tri cum Fí - li - o,
1. Jé - su, Re - démp - tor ó - mni - um,
2. A - mó - ris a - ctus lán - gui - di
3. E Vír - gi - nis sa - crá - ri - o
4. San - cto si - mul Pa - rá - cli - to
1. In - tén - de vo - tis súp - pli - cum.
2. Mun - di me - dé - la fa - ctus es.
3. In - tá - cta pro - dis ví - cti - ma.
4. In sae - cu - ló - rum saé - cu - la. A - men.

DEAR MAKER OF THE STARRY SKIES

Creator alme siderum.
Anon., 7th. Cent
Tr. RONALD A. KNOX, d. 1957.
Old German Carol.
(E.C.C.)
1. Dear Ma - ker of the star - ry skies, Light
2. Thy love that pi - tied from on high A
3. So, at the e - ven - tide of earth, From
4. To God the Fa - ther, God the Son, And
1. nev - er lost by faith - ful eyes, Christ,
2. guil - ty race fore - doomed to die, Was
3. that bride - cham - ber of Thy birth Our
4. God the Spir - it, Three in One, Glo -
1. the Sal - va - tion sent to all, Be
2. fain that sen - tence to re - peal, Those
3. mor - tal flesh Thou didst as - sume, Born
4. ry and pow'r and maj - es - ty Through
1. near Thy ser - vants when they call.
2. fail - ing en - er - gies to heal.
3. of a spot - less Vir - gin's womb.
4. ev - er - las - ting a - ges be.

5

VENI, VENI, EMMANUEL

'Psalteriolum Cantionum Catholicarum', Cologne, 1710.

Melody adapted by T. HELMOR[E] *from a French Missal, 1854. Mode 1.* (J.H.D.)

1. Ve - ni, ve - ni, Em - má - nu - el; Cap - tí - vum sol - ve
2. Ve - ni, ve - ni, O Ó - ri - ens; So - lá - re nos ad -
3. Ve - ni, O Jes - se Vir - gu - la; Ex hos - tis tu - os
4. Ve - ni, ve - ni, A - dó - na - i, Qui pó - pu - lo in
1. Ís - ra - el Qui ge - mit in e - xí - li - o,
2. vé - ni - ens; No - ctis de - pél - le né - bu - las
3. ún - gu - la, De spe - cu tu - os tár - ta - ri
4. Si - na - i Le - gem de - di - sti vér - ti - ce
Refrain
1. Pri - vá - tus De - i fí - li - o.
2. Di - rás - que noctis té - ne - bras.
3. E - duc, et an - tro bá - ra - thri.
4. In ma - je - stá - te gló - ri - ae.
Gau - de! Gau - de!
Em - má - nu - el Na - scé - tur pro te Ís - ra - el.

O COME, O COME, EMMANUEL

'eni, veni, Emmanuel.
'salteriolum Cantionum Catholicarum',
'ologne, 1710. Tr. R.S.

Melody adapted by T. HELMORE
from a French Missal, 1854.
Mode 1. (J.H.D.)

1. O come, O come, Em - man - u - el, And ran - som cap - tive
2. O come, Thou Wis - dom, Son di - vine, Our weak-en'd wills to
3. O come, Thou Sprout of Jes - se's tree, Free us from Sa - tan's
4. O come, Thou King of all the earth, That we may share Thy
1. Is - ra - el, That lives in earth - ly ex - ile here,
2. Thee in - cline! And shed Thy light o'er life's dark way,
3. tyr - an - ny! From fires of hell Thy peo - ple save,
4. won - drous birth! Come, rule our heart and mind and will,
1. Un - til the Son of God ap - pear.
2. Lest, lured by sin, we go a - stray.
3. And give us vic - t'ry o'er the grave.
4. That we Thy pre - cepts may ful - fill.
Refrain
Re - joice! Re - joice!
O Is - ra - el, To thee shall come Em - ma - nu - el.

ADVENT

O COME, DIVINE MESSIAH

Venez, divin Messie.
ABBÉ PELLEGRIN, *d. 1745.*
Tr. SR. MARY OF ST. PHILIP.

16th Cent. Angevin Noë
(H.W.)

1. O come, Di - vine Mes - si - ah, The
2. O Thou whom na - tions sighed for, Whom
1. world in si - lence waits_ the day When
2. priest and pro - phet long_ fore - told, Wilt
1. hope shall sing its tri - umph, And
2. break the cap - tive fet - ters, Re -
1. sad - ness flee_ a - way.__
2. deem the long - lost fold.__
Refrain
Dear Sa - vior

O COME, DIVINE MESSIAH

haste! Come, come to earth. Dis - pel the
night and show Thy face, And bid us hail the dawn of
grace.___ O come, Di - vine Mes - si - ah, The
world in si - lence waits the day When hope shall sing its
tri - umph, And sad - ness flee___ a - way.___

8

CHRISTMAS

PUER NATUS IN BETHLEHEM

V. Babst's Gesangbuch.
Leipzig, 1545.

Mode
(J.H.D

1. Pu - er na - tus in Béth - le - hem, al - le - lú - ia:
2. Hic ja - cet in prae - sé - pi - o, al - le - lú - ia,
3. In hoc na - tá - li gaú - di - o, al - le - lú - ia,
4. Lau - dé - tur san - cta Trí - ni - tas, al - le - lú - ia;
1. Un - de gau - det Je - rú - sa - lem, al - le - lú - ia,
2. Qui re - gnat si - ne tér - mi - no, al - le - lú - ia,
3. Be - ne - di - cá - mus Dó - mi - no, al - le - lú - ia,
4. De - o di - cá - mus grá - ti - as, al - le - lú - ia,
Refrain
1. al - le - lú - ia.
2. al - le - lú - ia.
3. al - le - lú - ia.
4. al - le - lú - ia.
In cor - dis jú - bi - lo, Chri - stum
na - tum a - do - ré - mus Cum no - vo cán - ti - co.

9

RESONET IN LAUDIBUS

From 'Magnum nomen Domini Emmanuel'. Anon., 14th Cent.

14th Cent. German Melody. Mode 5. (J.H.D.)

1. Ré - so - net in laú - di - bus Cum ju - cún - dis
2. Si - on lau - da Dó - mi - num Sal - va - tó - rem
3. Na - tus est Em - má - nu - el, Quem prae - dí - xit
4. San - cta ti - bi Trí - ni - tas Os ó - mni - um
1. plaú - si - bus, Si - on cum fi - dé - li - bus.
2. ó - mni - um; Vir - go pa - rit Fí - li - um.
3. Gá - bri - el, Te - stis est E - ze - chi - el.
4. grá - ti - as Ré - son - et al - tís - si - mas.
Ap - pá - ru - it quem gé - nu - it Ma - rí - a.
Gau - dé - te, gau - dé - te, Chri - stus na - tus hó - di - e!
Gau - dé - te, gau - dé - te, ex Ma - rí - a Vír - gi - ne.

10

CHRISTMAS

ADESTE, FIDELES

Anon., 18th Cent.
Ascribed to JOHN F. WADE
d. 1786. (P.E.S.)
1. A - dé - ste, fi - dé - les, Lae - ti tri - um - phán - tes; Ve -
2. De - um de De - o, Lu - men de lú - mi - ne,
3. Can - tet nunc I - o! Cho - rus an - ge - ló - rum:
4. Er - go qui na - tus Di - e ho - di - ér - na,
1. ní - te, ve - ní - te in Béth - le - hem;
2. Ge - stant pu - él - lae ví - sce - ra;
3. Can - tet nunc au - la cae - lé - sti - um:
4. Je - su ti - bi sit gló - ri - a:
1. Na - tum vi - dé - te Re - gem an - ge - ló - rum:
2. De - um ve - rum, Gé - ni - tum, non fa - ctum:
3. Gló - ri - a, gló - ria, In ex - cél - sis De - o!
4. Pa - tris ae - tér - ni Ver - bum ca - ro fa - ctum!
Ve - ní - te a - do - ré - mus, Ve - ní - te a - do -
ré - mus, Ve - ní - te a - do - ré - mus Dó - mi - num.

O COME, ALL YE FAITHFUL

Adeste, fideles.
Anon., 18th Cent.
Tr. FREDERICK OAKELEY, *d. 1880.*

Ascribed to JOHN F. WADE, *d. 1786.*

1. O come, all ye faith - ful, Joy - ful and tri - um - phant, O
2. God of God, Light of Light,
3. Sing, choirs of an - gels, Sing in ex - ul - ta - tion,
4. Yea, Lord, we greet Thee, Born this hap - py morn - ing;
1. come ye, O come ye to Beth - le - hem;
2. Lo! He ab - hors not the Vir - gin's womb;
3. Sing, all ye cit - i - zens of heav'n a - bove:
4. Je - sus, to Thee be glo - ry giv'n;
1. Come and be - hold Him Born, the King of an - gels;
2. Ve - ry God, Be - got - ten, not cre - a - ted;
3. 'Glo - ry to God In the high - est':
4. Word of the Fa - ther, Now in flesh ap - pear - ing;
O come, let us a - dore Him, O come, let us a -
dore Him, O come, let us a - dore Him, Christ the Lord.

12

CHRISTMAS

ANGELS WE HAVE HEARD ON HIGH

Les anges dans nos campagnes.
Anon., French.
Tr. JAMES CHADWICK, *d. 1882.*

Traditional Languedoc Noël
(E.C.C.)

1. An-gels we have heard on high, Sweet-ly sing-ing o'er the plain;
2. Shepherds, why this ju - bi - lee? Why your joy - ous strain pro-long?
3. Come to Bethle'm, come and see Him, Whose birth the an - gels sing;
1. And the moun-tains in re - ply Ech - o back their joy - ous strain
2. Say what may the ti - dings be Which in - spire your heav'n - ly song.
3. Come, a - dore on bend - ed knee, Christ the Lord, the new - born King.
Gló - - - - - - - - - - - - - ri - a
in ex - cél - sis De - o!
Gló - - - - - - - - - - ri - a
in ex - cél - sis De - - o!

CHRISTMAS

13

BEHOLD A SIMPLE, TENDER BABE

BL. ROBERT SOUTHWELL, S.J., *d. 1595.* FRANCIS E. MONAGHAN, C.S.B.

1. Be - hold a sim - ple, ten - der Babe, In
2. The inns are full; no man will yield This
3. De - spise Him not for ly - ing there; First
4. Weigh not His crib, His wood - en dish, Nor
5. This sta - ble is a Prin - ce's court, This
6. The per - sons in that poor at - tire His
7. With joy ap - proach, O Chris - tian soul, Do
1. freez - ing win - ter night, In home - ly man - ger
2. lit - tle Pil - grim bed; But forced He is with
3. what He is in - quire: An or - ient pearl is
4. beasts that by Him feed; Weigh not His moth - er's
5. crib His chair of state, The beasts are par - cel
6. roy - al liv - 'ries wear; The Prince Him - self is
7. hom - age to thy King; And high - ly praise this
1. trem - bling lies: A - las! a pit - eous sight.
2. sim - ple beasts In crib to shroud His head.
3. of - ten found In depth of dir - ty mire.
4. poor at - tire, Nor Jo - seph's sim - ple weed.
5. of His pomp, The wood - en dish His plate.
6. come from heav'n. This pomp is priz - èd there.
7. hum - ble pomp, Which He from heav'n doth bring.

14

FROM STARRY HEAV'N DESCENDING

Tu scendi dalle stelle.
ST. ALFONSO DE LIGOURI, C.SS.R., *d. 1787.*
Tr. E.C.C.

Italian Carol Melody,
pub. Naples, 1755.
(E.C.C.)

1. From star - ry heav'n de - scend - ing, The King of worth un - told _ Was born in man-ger dwel - ling, A - mid the win - ter's cold. In - fant Sav - ior, Child Di - vine! Thy trem - bling, ba - by form I see. O bles - sed Lord of all! ___ How great the cost to Thee to show Thy love for me. _
2. For Thee, the world's cre - a - tor,—My God, so great, so good! — There was no warm-ing shel - ter, Nor wealth of robe, nor food. Dear - est Babe, how poor Thy state, To lie a - mong the sheep and kine. O Thou, my Cho - sen One, ___ What - ev - er love is mine, shall more and more be Thine.
3. Thou weep - est, Lord, full know - ing Of my in - grat - i - tude, _ When love a - lone Thou gav - est And ev - er sought my good. Ho - ly Babe, my heart's de - sire! I've lived too long a - way from Thee. I will no more Thee grieve; _ For now my aim shall be to love and hon - or Thee.

CHRISTMAS

IN DULCI JUBILO

15

Ascribed to BL. HENRY SUSO, O. P., *d. 1366.* *14th Cent. German Melody.*
Tr. ROBERT L. DE PEARSALL, *d. 1856.* (C. O'S.)

1. In dul - ci jú - bi - lo Let us our
2. O Je - su pár - vu - le, My heart is
3. O Pa - tris cá - ri - tas! O Na - ti
1. hom - age show; Our hearts' joy re - clin - eth
2. sore for Thee; Hear me, I be - seech Thee, O
3. lé - ni - tas! Deep - ly we were stain - èd Per
1. In prae - sé - pi - o, And like a bright star
2. Pu - er óp - ti - me; My prayer let it
3. no - stra crí - mi - na; But Thou for us hast
1. shin - eth Ma - tris in gré - mi - o;
2. reach Thee, O Prin - ceps gló - ri - ae;
3. gain - èd Cae - ló - rum gáu - di - a:
1. Al - pha es et O, Al - pha es et O.
2. Tra - he me post te, Tra - he me post te.
3. Oh, that we were there! Oh, that we were there!

CHRISTMAS

LET CHRISTIAN HEARTS REJOICE TODAY

Jesous Ahatonnia.
ST. JEAN DE BRÉBEUF, S. J., *d. 1649.*
Tr. FRANCIS X. HURLEY, S. J.

16th Cent. French Melody
(S.M.F.)

1. Let Chris - tian hearts re - joice to - day: our
2. The An - gels fill the star - lit sky; for
3. Three Chiefs to - geth - er made a pact when
4. The time has come for each of us to

1. Sav - ior, Christ, is born. To - day the reign of
2. you a - lone they sing. Ac - cept with all your
3. glo - ry filled the night. To fol - low where that
4. kneel be - fore his Lord. He came in an - swer

1. Sa - tan ends: his King - dom's o - ver -
2. heart their song; Oh, hear their mes - sage
3. glo - ry led and find the Source of
4 to our prayer, now let Him be a -

LET CHRISTIAN HEARTS REJOICE TODAY

1. thrown. So when his tempt - ing voice you hear Then
2. ring. The maid - en Ma - ry, sweet and mild, Brought
3. light, For God to them re - vealed His plan, They
4. dored. And as we kneel this ho - ly night For
1. quick - ly to the crib draw near:
2. forth the Spir - it Great, her Child;
3. has - tened towards the God - made - man,
4. ho - li - ness and Him we'll fight;
1. Our Sav - ior, Christ, is there, Je - sus is
2. Our Sav - ior, Christ, is born, Je - sus is
3. And Je - sus wel - comed them. Je - sus the
4. That pro - mise now we make, Make to our
1. there, Has - ten, then, to Beth - le - hem.
2. born. Has - ten, then, to Beth - le - hem.
3 Child Wel-comed Chiefs to Beth. - le - hem.
4. Chief, Je - sus Christ of Beth - le - hem.

LO, HOW A ROSE E'ER BLOOMING

Es ist ein' Ros' entsprungen. *Speier Gesangbuch, 1599.* *Tr.* THEODORE BAKER, *d. 1934.*

16th Cent. German Melody. *Harmony:* MICHAEL PRAETORIUS *d. 1621.*

1. Lo, how a Rose e'er bloom - ing From
2. I - sa - iah 'twas fore - told it, The
1. ten - der stem hath sprung! Of Jes - se's lin - eage
2. Rose I have in mind, With Ma - ry we be -
1. com - ing, As men of old have sung. It
2. hold it, The Vir - gin Moth - er kind. To
1. came, a flow - 'ret bright, A - mid the cold of
2. show God's love a - right, She bore to men a
1. win - ter, When half - spent was the night.
2. Sav - ior, When half - spent was the night.

O BETHLEHEM OF HOLY WORTH

EDWARD C. CURRIE.

Traditional Irish Melody. (C. O'S.)

1. O Beth - le - hem of ho - ly worth! O
2. No inn bade wel - come at its door To
3. No pomp of kings, nor prin - ces there, With
4. O Beth - le - hem, we pray the Babe, Once
1. hal - lowed town of Je - sus' birth! In thee a vir - gin
2. Ma - ry on that ho - ly night; But in a sta - ble
3. Jo - seph and the moth - er fair; But an - gel voi - ces
4. born with - in thy cheer - less cave, May grant the prom - ised
1. moth - er's Child Brought God from heav'n to earth.
2. Christ was born, With on - ly stars for light.
3. from on high, With glo - ry filled the air.
4. 'Peace on earth' To us He came to save.

19

CHRISTMAS

O COME, LITTLE CHILDREN

Ihr Kinderlein kommet.
CHRISTOPH VON SCHMID, *d. 1854.*
Tr. E.C.C.

JOHANN A. P. SCHULZ, *d. 1800.*
(E.C.C.)

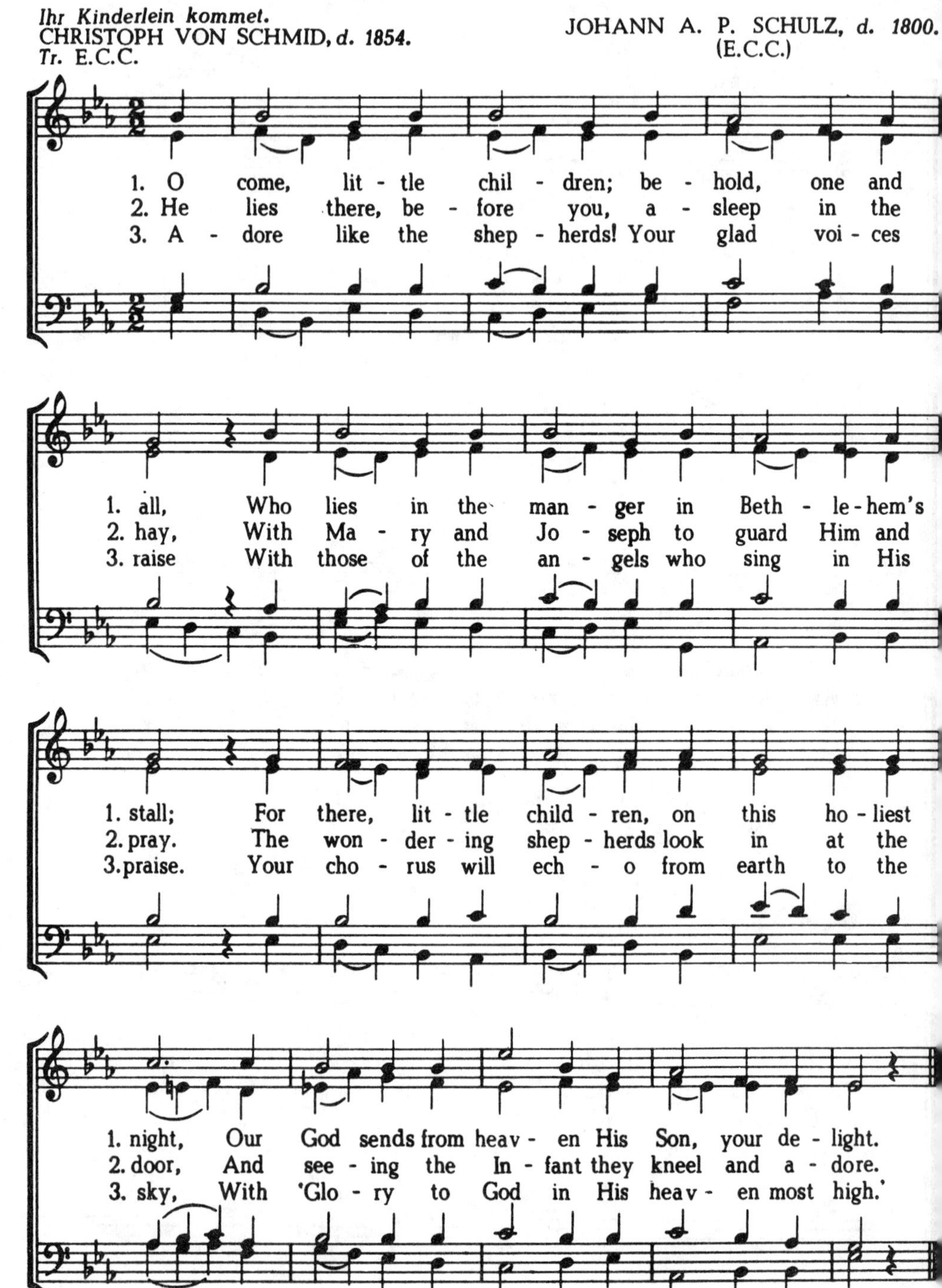

1. O come, lit - tle chil - dren; be - hold, one and
2. He lies there, be - fore you, a - sleep in the
3. A - dore like the shep - herds! Your glad voi - ces
1. all, Who lies in the man - ger in Beth - le - hem's
2. hay, With Ma - ry and Jo - seph to guard Him and
3. raise With those of the an - gels who sing in His
1. stall; For there, lit - tle child - ren, on this ho - liest
2. pray. The won - der - ing shep - herds look in at the
3. praise. Your cho - rus will ech - o from earth to the
1. night, Our God sends from heav - en His Son, your de - light.
2. door, And see - ing the In - fant they kneel and a - dore.
3. sky, With 'Glo - ry to God in His heav - en most high.'

SILENT NIGHT

Stille Nacht.
JOSEPH MOHR, *d. 1848.*
Tr. JOHN F. YOUNG, *c. 1860.*
FRANZ GRUBER, *d. 1863.*
(H.W.)
1. Si - lent night, ho - ly night! All is calm, all is bright, 'Round yon Vir - gin Moth - er and Child, Ho - ly In - fant so ten - der and mild: Sleep in heav - en - ly peace, Sleep in heav - en - ly peace!
2. Si - lent night, ho - ly night! Shep - herds quake at the sight! Glo - ries stream from heav - en a - far, Heav'n - ly hosts sing Al - le - lu - ia: Christ, the Sav - ior is born, Christ, the Sav - ior is born!
3. Si - lent night, ho - ly night! Son of God, love's pure light Ra - diant beams from Thy ho - ly face, With the dawn of re - deem - ing grace, Je - sus, Lord, at Thy birth, Je - sus, Lord, at Thy birth!

21

CHRISTMAS

SLEEP, HOLY BABE

EDWARD CASWALL, *d. 1878.*

Adapted from a Melody by
LOUISE REICHARDT, *1826.* (T.B.M.)

1. Sleep, ho - ly Babe, Up - on Thy Moth - er's
2. Sleep, ho - ly Babe, Thine an - gels watch a -
3. Sleep, ho - ly Babe, While I with Ma - ry
4. Sleep, ho - ly Babe, Now take Thy brief re -

1. breast; Great Lord of earth and sea and sky, How
2. round; All bend - ing low with fold - ed wings, Be -
3. gaze In joy up - on Thy face a - while, Up -
4. pose; Too quick - ly will Thy slum - bers break And

1. sweet it is to see Thee lie In such a place of rest.
2. fore th'In - car - nate King of kings In rev - 'rent awe pro - found.
3. on the lov - ing in - fant smile Which there di - vine - ly plays.
4. Thou to lengthen'd pains a - wake, That death a - lone shall close.

SLUMBER, OH SLUMBER, DEAR JESUS

Lulajże Jezuniu.
Traditional Polish Carol.
Tr. STELLA KELLY.

Polish Carol Melody.
(C.O'S.)

1. Slum - ber, oh slum - ber, dear Je - sus my treas - ure;
2. Soft - ly, oh soft - ly, all na - tions come creep - ing!
3. Si - lent, oh si - lent, there's sor - row be - fore us!
1. Slum - ber, oh slum - ber, true Love with - out meas - ure!
2. God's on - ly Son is here safe in my keep - ing:
3. Christ, by His Blood, will earn hap - pi - ness for us.
1. Shep - herds and wise men kneel down to a - dore Thee,
2. Je - sus is giv - en to thee as thy broth - er,
3. Then, in a King - dom won by our en - deav - or,
1. Hosts of bright an - gels sing glo - rious - ly o'er Thee.
2. So am I tru - ly for - ev - er thy moth - er.
3. Je - sus will reign with His loved ones for - ev - er.

23

CHRISTMAS

THE FIRST NOWELL

Old English Carol.

Traditional English Melody, pub. 1833.
Harmony: JOHN STAINER, *d. 1873.*

1. The first Now - ell the an - gel did say Was to
2. They look - ed up and saw a star Shin-ing
3. Then let us all with one ac - cord Sing
1. cer - tain poor shep-herds in fields as they lay; In
2. in the East be - yond them far; And
3. prais - es to our heav - en - ly Lord, Who
1. fields where they lay keep - ing their sheep On a
2. to the earth it gave great light, And
3. hath made heav'n and earth of nought, And
Refrain
1. cold win-ter's night that was so deep.
2. so it con - tin - ued both day and night. Now - ell, Now-
3. with His Blood man - kind hath bought.
ell, Now-ell, Now - ell, Born is the King of Is - ra - el.

THE CIRCUMCISION OF OUR LORD
(New Year's Day)

24

O BLESSED DAY, WHEN FIRST WAS POURED

Felix dies quam proprio.
SEBASTIEN BESNAULT, *d. 1724.*
Tr. JOHN CHANDLER, *d. 1876, alt.*
'Andernach Gesangbuch',
1608. (E.C.C.)
1. O bles - sed day, when first was poured The
2. While from His Moth - er's bos - om fed, His
3. Scarce come to earth, His Fa - ther's will With
4. Lord, cir - cum - cise our hearts, we pray, And
5. O Lord, the Vir - gin - born, to Thee E -
1. Blood of our re - deem - ing Lord! O hap - py day, when
2. pre - cious Blood He wills to shed; A fore-taste of His
3. prompt o - be-dience to ful - fil, A vic - tim e - ven
4. take what is not Thine a - way; Write Thine own Name up -
5. ter - nal praise and glo - ry be, Whom with the Fa - ther
1. Christ be - gan His sav - ing work for sin - ful man!
2. death He feels, An ear - nest of His love re - veals.
3. now see lie, The Lamb of God, pre - pared to die.
4. on our hearts, Thy Law with - in our in - ward parts.
5. we a - dore And Ho - ly Ghost for - ev - er - more.

EPIPHANY

BETHLEHEM, OF NOBLEST CITIES

O sola magnarum urbium.
AURELIUS PRUDENTIUS, *d. 413.*
Tr. EDWARD CASWALL, *d. 1878, alt.*

Ascribed to CHRISTIAN F. WITT
d. 1716. (P.E.S.)

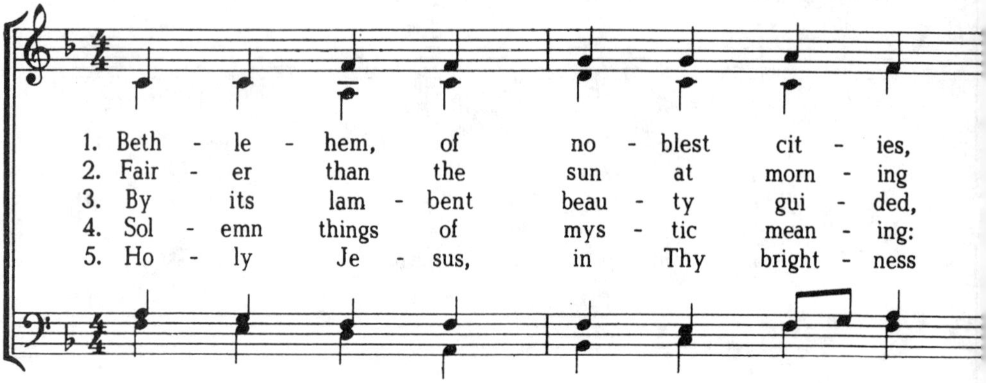

1. Beth - le - hem, of no - blest cit - ies,
2. Fair - er than the sun at morn - ing
3. By its lam - bent beau - ty gui - ded,
4. Sol - emn things of mys - tic mean - ing:
5. Ho - ly Je - sus, in Thy bright - ness

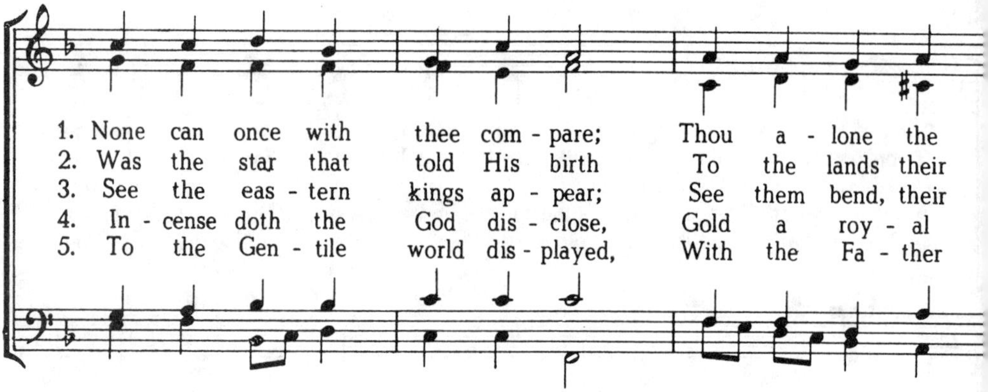

1. None can once with thee com - pare; Thou a - lone the
2. Was the star that told His birth To the lands their
3. See the eas - tern kings ap - pear; See them bend, their
4. In - cense doth the God dis - close, Gold a roy - al
5. To the Gen - tile world dis - played, With the Fa - ther

1. Lord from heav - en Didst for us In - car - nate bear.
2. God an - noun - cing, Hid be - neath a form of earth.
3. gifts to of - fer, Gifts of in - cense, gold and myrrh.
4. Child pro - claim - eth, Myrrh a fu - ture tomb fore - shows.
5. and the Spir - it, End - less praise to Thee be paid.

WHAT STAR IS THIS

Quae stella sole pulchrior.
CHARLES COFFIN, *d. 1749.*
Tr. M.O.L.

C. SCHMIDT.
(E.C.C.)

1. What star is this, so ra - di - ant, More love - ly than the
2. O Je - sus, glo - rious morn - ing star, We come be - fore Your
1. sun? It comes to tell the ris - ing of The
2. face And ask that, gui - ded by this sign, We
1. long a - wait - ed One; For Christ is come from
2. may be filled with grace; With hum - ble hearts we
1. Ja - cob's race, By pro - phets long fore - told, And
2. of - fer You, As did the kings of old, Our
1. kings from out the East a - dore With in - cense, myrrh and gold.
2. faith, our hope, our cha - ri - ty As in - cense, myrrh and gold.

AUDI, BENIGNE CONDITOR

ST. GREGORY THE GREAT, *d. 604.*

Mode 2. (J.H.D.)

1. Au - di, be - ní - gne Cón - di - tor,
2. Scru - tá - tor al - me cór - di - um,
3. Mul - tum qui - dem pec - cá - vi - mus,
4. Prae - sta be - á - ta Trí - ni - tas,
1. No - stras pre - ces cum flé - ti - bus,
2. In - fír - ma tu scis ví - ri - um:
3. Sed par - ce con - fi - tén - ti - bus:
4. Con - cé - de sim - plex Ú - ni - tas:
1. In hoc sa - cro je - jú - ni - o
2. Ad te re - vér - sis éx - hi - be
3. Ad nó - mi - nis lau - dem tu - i,
4. Ut fru - ctu - ó - sa sint tu - is
1. Fu - sas qua - dra - ge - ná - ri - o.
2. Re - mis - si - ó - nis grá - ti - am.
3. Con - fer me - dé - lam lán - gui - dis.
4. Je - ju - ni - ó - rum mú - ne - ra. A - men.

VEXILLA REGIS

VENANTIUS FORTUNATUS, *d. 609.*

Mode 1. (J.H.D.)

1. Ve - xil - la Re - gis pró - de - unt:
2. Quae vul - ne - rá - ta lán - ce - ae
3. O Crux a - ve, spes ú - ni - ca,
4. Te, fons sa - lú - tis Trí - ni - tas,
1. Ful - get Cru - cis my - sté - ri - um,
2. Mu - cró - ne di - ro, crí - mi - num
3.* Hoc Pas - si - ó - nis tém - po - re:
4. Col - laú - det o - mnis spí - ri - tus:
1. Qua vi - ta mor - tem pér - tu - lit,
2. Ut nos la - vá - ret sór - di - bus,
3. Pi - is ad - aú - ge grá - ti - am,
4. Qui - bus Cru - cis vi - ctó - ri - am
1. Et mor - te vi - tam pró - tu - lit.
2. Ma - ná - vit un - da et sán - gui - ne.
3. Re - is - que de - le crí - mi - na.
4. Lar - gí - ris, ad - de práe - mi - um.
A - men.

* During Paschal Time: *Paschále quae fers gáudium.*
Outside of Paschal Time: *In hac triúmphi glória.*

29

LENT

ATTENDE, DOMINE

Hear Our Entreaties, Lord

Anon., Tr. Anon.

Mode 5 (J.H.D.)

At - tén - de, Dó - mi - ne, et mi - se - ré - re,
Hear our en - treat - ies, Lord, and show Thy mer - cy;
qui - a pec - cá - vi - mus ti - bi.
for we are sin - ners be - fore___ Thee.
1. Ad te Rex sum - me,___ ó - mni - um Red - ém - ptor,
2. Ro - gá - mus, De - us,___ tu - am ma - je - stá - tem:
1. King high ex - alt - ed,___ all the world's Re - deem - er,
2. We, Thy e - ter - nal maj - es - ty en - treat - ing,
1. ó - cu - los no - stros sub - le - vá - mus flen - tes:
2. aú - ri - bus sa - cris gé - mi - tus ex - aú - di:
1. to Thee Thy chil - dren lift their eyes with weep - ing:
2. make lam - en - ta - tion in Thy ho - ly hear - ing:
1. ex - aú - di, Chri - ste, sup - pli - cán - tum pre - ces. *
2. crí - mi - na no - stra plá - ci - dus in - dúl - ge.
1. Christ, we im - plore Thee, hear our sup - pli - ca - tion. **
2. gra - cious - ly grant Thou to our sins in - dul - gence.

* Repeat: Attende.
** Repeat: Hear.

30

PARCE, DOMINE

Spare Your People, Lord

Joel 2, 17.
English adapted by C. W. L.

Mode 1.
(J. H. D.)

Par - ce, Dó - mi - ne, par - ce
Spare Your peo - ple, Lord, spare Your
pó - pu - lo tu - o:
peo - ple; see us here be - fore You:
Ne in ae - tér - num i -
Be not an - gry, Lord, with
ra - scá - ris no - bis.
Your peo - ple for - ev - er.

Repeat three times.

31

LENT

GLORIA, LAUS ET HONOR

ST. THEODULPH OF ORLÉANS, *d. 821.*

Mode 1
(J.H.D.

Gló - ri - a, laus et ho - nor, ti - bi sit,
Rex Chri - ste Red - ém - ptor: Cu - i pu - é -
ri - le de - cus prom - psit Ho - sán - na pi - um.
1. Ís - ra - el es tu Rex, Da - ví - dis
2. Plebs He - braé - a ti - bi cum pal - mis
3. Hi ti - bi pas - sú - ro sol - vé - bant
1. et in - cly - ta pro - les: Nó - mi - ne qui in
2. ób - vi - a ve - nit: Cum pre - ce, vo - to,
3. mú - ni - a lau - dis: Nos ti - bi re -
1. Dó - mi - ni, Rex be - ne - dí - cte, ve - nis.
2. hy - mnis, ád - su - mus ec - ce ti - bi.
3. gnán - ti pán - gi - mus ec - ce me - los.

Repeat: *Gloria*

ALL GLORY, LAUD AND HONOR

Gloria, laus et honor.
ST. THEODULPH OF ORLÉANS, *d. 821.*
Tr. J. MASON NEALE, *d. 1866, alt.*

MELCHIOR TESCHNER, *d. 1635.*

1. All glo - ry, laud and hon - or To Thee, Re-deem-er King,
2. The peo - ple of the He - brews With palms be - fore Thee went;
1. To Whom the lips of chil - dren Made sweet ho - san - nas ring.
2. Our praise and prayer and an - thems Be - fore Thee we pre - sent.
1. Thou art the King of Is - ra - el, Thou Da - vid's roy - al Son,
2. To Thee be - fore Thy Pas - sion They sang their hymns of praise;
1. Who in the Lord's name com - est, The King and bles - sed One.
2. To Thee now high ex - al - ted Our mel - o - dy we raise.

STABAT MATER DOLOROSA

Ascribed to
JACOPONE DA TODI, O.F.M., *d. 1306.*

'Maintzisch Gesangbuch', 1661
(J. H. D.)

1. Sta - bat Ma - ter do - lo - ró - sa Jux - ta cru - cem
2. Cu - jus á - ni - mam ge - mén - tem, Con - tri - stá - tam
3. O quam tri - stis et af - flí - cta Fu - it il - la
4. Quae mae - ré - bat, et do - lé - bat, Pi - a Ma - ter,
5. Quis est ho - mo qui non fle - ret, Ma - trem Chri - sti
6. Quis non pos - set con - tri - stá - ri, Chri - sti Ma - trem
7. Pro pec - cá - tis su - ae gen - tis, Vi - dit Je - sum
8. Vi - dit su - um dul - cem Na - tum Mo - ri - én - do
9. E - ja Ma - ter, fons a - mó - ris, Me sen - tí - re
10. Fac ut ár - de - at cor me - um In a - mán - do
11. San - cta Ma - ter, i - stud a - gas, Cru - ci - fí - xi
12. Tu - i Na - ti vul - ne - rá - ti, Tam di - gná - ti
13. Fac me te - cum pi - e fle - re, Cru - ci - fí - xo
14. Jux - ta cru - cem te - cum sta - re, Et me ti - bi
15. Vir - go vír - gi - num prae - clá - ra, Mi - hi jam non
16. Fac ut por - tem Chri - sti mor - tem, Pas - si - ó - nis
17. Fac me pla - gis vul - ne - rá - ri, Fac me Cru - ce in -
18. Flam - mis ne u - rar suc - cén - sus, Per te, Vir - go,
19. Chri - ste, cum sit hinc e - xí - re, Da per Ma - trem
20. Quan - do cor - pus mo - ri - é - tur, Fac ut á - ni -
1. la - cri - mó - sa, Dum pen - dé - bat Fí - li - us.
2. et do - lén - tem Per - trans - í - vit glá - di - us.
3. be - ne - dí - cta Ma - ter U - ni - gé - ni - ti!
4. dum vi - dé - bat Na - ti poe - nas ín - cly - ti.
5. si vi - dé - ret In tan - to sup - plí - ci - o?
6. con - tem - plá - ri Do - lén - tem cum Fí - li - o?
7. in tor - mén - tis, Et fla - gél - lis súb - di - tum.
8. de - so - lá - tum, Dum e - mí - sit spí - ri - tum.
9. vim do - ló - ris, Fac, ut te - cum lú - ge - am.
10. Chri - stum De - um, Ut si - bi com - plá - ce - am.
11. fi - ge pla - gas Cor - di me - o vá - li - de.
12. pro me pa - ti, Poe - nas me - cum dí - vi - de.
13. con - do - lé - re, Do - nec e - go ví - xe - ro.
14. so - ci - á - re In plan - ctu de - sí - de - ro.
15. sis a - má - ra: Fac me te - cum plán - ge - re.
16. fac con - sór - tem, Et pla - gas re - có - le - re.
17. e - bri - á - ri, Et cru - ó - re Fí - li - i.
18. sim de - fén - sus In di - e ju - dí - ci - i.
19. me ve - ní - re Ad pal - mam vic - tó - ri - ae.
20. mae do - né - tur Pa - ra - dí - si gló - ri - a. A - men.

AT THE CROSS HER STATION KEEPING

Stabat mater dolorosa.
Ascribed to JACOPONE DA TODI, O.F.M., *d. 1306.*
Tr. I. U. & M. O. L.

'Maintzisch Gesangbuch', 1661.
(P.E.S.)

1. At the cross her sta - tion keep - ing, Stood the mourn - ful
2. Through her heart, His sor - row shar - ing, All His bit - ter
3. Oh, what sad - ness and af - flic - tion Pressed that Child of
4. She who, bent in lam - en - ta - tion, Saw the bit - ter
5. Who un - moved could see her lan - guish, See those tears of
6. For her Child she saw de - ject - ed, For His peo - ple's
7. Mourn - ful Moth - er, let me bor - row Some of that most
8. That my heart, new fer - vor gain - ing, More de - vot - ed
9. Moth - er, share with me your sor - row; Let me of His
10. Since He wished to save me, dy - ing, Wound - ed in the
11. By the cross of my sal - va - tion, One with you in
12. Vir - gin, all the saints ex - ceed - ing, Be not of my
13. Be His wounds my con - so - la - tion. Be His Pas - sion
14. Christ, my Lord, in my last hour___ Grant that, through your
15. When my soul and bod - y sev - er, May I live with

1. Moth - er weep - ing, While her Je - sus hung a - bove.
2. an - guish bear - ing, Ran the sword of suf - f'ring love.
3. ben - e - dic - tion, Moth - er of the Ho - ly One.
4. des - o - la - tion Of her well be - lov - ed Son.
5. bit - ter an - guish Stream - ing down her ten - der cheek?
6. sins re - ject - ed, And with blood - y scour - ges rent.
7. bit - ter sor - row, Which for Je - sus you did feel:
8. love at - tain - ing, May to His pierced Heart ap - peal.
9. tor - ments bor - row; Print them on my sin - ful heart.
10. cru - ci - fy - ing, In His suff-'ring give me part.
11. rep - a - ra - tion, May He all my sins for - give.
12. prayer un - heed - ing; Let me share with you your grief.
13. my sal - va - tion. Be His dy - ing my be - lief.
14. Moth - er's pow - er, I may con - quer ev - 'ry sin.
15. You for - ev - er, To Your glo - ry ent - 'ring in. A - men.

35

LENT

BY THE BLOOD THAT FLOWED FROM THEE

CECILIA MARY CADDELL, *d. 1877.*

Adapted from a Melody by JOHN J. RICHARDSON, *d. 187*
(E.C.C.)

1. By the Blood that flowed from Thee In Thy bit - ter ag - o - ny; By the scourge so meek - ly_borne; By Thy pur - ple robe of scorn,
2. By the thorns that crowned Thy Head; By Thy scep - ter of a reed; By Thy foot - step faint and_slow, Weighed be - neath Thy cross of woe,
3. By the nails and point - ed spear; By Thy peo - ple's cru - el jeer; By Thy dy - ing prayer which rose, Beg - ging mer - cy for Thy foes,
4. By the dark - ness black as night, Blot - ting out the sun from sight; By the cry with which in_death, Thou didst yield Thy part - ing breath,
Refrain
Je - sus, Sav - ior, hear our cry; Thou wert suf - f'ring once as we; Hear the lov - ing lit - a - ny We Thy chil - dren sing to Thee.

LORD JESUS, WHEN I THINK OF THEE

ICHARD ROLLE OF HAMPOLE, *d. 1349.* A MONK OF GETHSEMANI.

1. Lord Je - sus, when I think of
2. Je - sus, true love I owe to
3. Je - sus, love made Thy tears to
4. Ma - ry, I pray, as thou art
1. Thee, And look up - on Thy cross a - right,
2. Thee Who on the cross didst show, that tide,
3. fall, 'Twas love that made Thy blood to flow,
4. free, A part of this thy grief I'll bear,
1. Thy bod - y stained with blood I see, Lord,
2. The crown of thorns, the sharp nails three, The
3. For love wast scourged and smit - ten all, For
4. That I may sor - row here with thee, And
1. pierce my heart with that sad sight!
2. cru - el spear that pierced Thy side.
3. love Thy life Thou didst fore - go.
4. bliss with thee here - af - ter share!

O COME AND MOURN WITH ME

FREDERICK W. FABER, *d. 1863.*

Adapted from a Slovc Melody. (P.E.S.)

1. O come and mourn with me a - while; See
2. Have we no tears to shed for Him, While
3. How fast His feet and hands are nailed; His
4. O love of God! O sin of man! In
1. Ma - ry calls us to her side; O
2. sol - diers scoff and Jews de - ride? Ah,
3. bles - sed tongue with thirst is tied; His
4. this dread act your strength is tried; And
1. come and let us mourn with her. Je -
2. look how pa - tient - ly He hangs. Je -
3. fail - ing eyes are blind with blood. Je -
4. vic - to - ry re - mains with love, For
1. sus, our Love, is cru - ci - fied.
2. sus, our Love, is cru - ci - fied.
3. sus, our Love, is cru - ci - fied.
4. He, our Love, is cru - ci - fied.

O SACRED HEAD SURROUNDED

O Haupt voll Blut und Wunden.
PAUL GERHARDT, *d. 1676.*
Tr. HENRY W. BAKER, *d. 1877.*

HANS LEO HASSLER, *d. 1612.*
Adapted & harmonized by
JOHANN S. BACH, *d. 1750.*

1. O Sa - cred Head sur - round - ed By crown of pierc-ing
2. I see Thy strength and vig - or All fad - ing in the
3. In this, Thy bit - ter pas - sion, Good Shep-herd, think of
1. thorn! O bleed - ing Head, so wound - ed, Re -
2. strife, And death with cru - el rig - or, Be -
3. me With Thy most sweet com - pas - sion, Un -
1. viled and put to scorn! Death's pal - lid hue comes
2. reav - ing Thee of life; O ag - o - ny and
3. wor - thy though I be: Be - neath Thy cross a -
1. o'er Thee, The glow of life de - cays, Yet an - gel hosts a -
2. dy - ing! O love to sin - ners free! Je - sus, all grace sup -
3. bid - ing For - ev - er would I rest, In Thy dear love con -
1. dore Thee, And trem - ble as they gaze.
2. ply - ing, O turn Thy face on me.
3. fid - ing, And with Thy pres - ence blest.

EASTER

VICTIMAE PASCHALI

Ascribed to WIPO, *d. c. 1048.*

Mode 1
(J.H.D.)

1. Vi - cti - mae Pa - schá - li lau - des
ím - mo - lent Chri - sti - á - ni.
2. A - gnus red - é -
3. Mors et vi - ta
2. mit o - ves: Chri - stus in - no - cens Pa - tri
3. du - él - lo con - fli - xé - re mi - rán - do:
2. re - con - cil - i - á - vit pec - ca - tó - res.
3. dux vi - tae mór - tu - us, re - gnat vi - vus.
4. Dic no - bis, Ma - rí - a, quid vi - dí - sti in vi - a?
6. An - gé - li - cos te - stes, su - dá - ri - um, et ve - stes.

VICTIMAE PASCHALI

5. Se - púl - crum Chri - sti vi - vén - tis,
7. Sur - ré - xit Chri - stus spes me - a:
5. et gló - ri - am vi - di re - sur - gén - tis:
7. prae - cé - det su - os in Ga - li - laé - am.
8. Sci - mus Chri - stum sur - re - xís - se
a mór - tu - is ve - re: tu no - bis, vi - ctor Rex,
mi - se - ré - re. A - men. Al - le - lú - ia.

40 CHRIST, THE LORD, IS RISEN TODAY

Victimae Paschali laudes.
Ascribed to WIPO, d.c. 1048.
Tr. JANE E. LEESON, d. 1882, & I. U.
Traditional Melody
(F.J.G.)
1. Christ, the Lord, is ris'n to - day;
2. Christ, the Vic - tim un - de - filed,
3. Christ, Who once for sin - ners bled,
1. Chris - tians, haste your vows to pay;
2. God and man has re - con - ciled,
3. Now the first - born from the dead,
1. Make your joy and prais - es known
2. When in fierce and blood - y strife
3. Throned in glo - rious maj - es - ty,
1. At the Pas - chal Vic - tim's throne.
2. Met to - geth - er Death and Life.
3. Reigns through all e - ter - ni - ty.

CHRIST, THE LORD, IS RISEN TODAY

1. For the sheep the Lamb has bled,
2. Chris - tians, on this hap - py day,
3. Hail, e - ter - nal Hope on high!
1. Sin - less in the sin - ner's stead;
2. Raise your hearts with joy and say:
3. Hail, Thou King of vic - to - ry!
1. Christ, the Lord, is ris'n on high;
2. Christ, the Lord, is ris'n on high;
3. Hail, Thou Prince of life a - dored!
1. Now He lives, no__ more to die!
2. Now He lives, no__ more to die!
3. Help us, save us,__ gra - cious Lord!

41 EASTER

O FILII ET FILIAE

JEAN TISSERAND, O.F.M., *d. 1494.*

Solesmes Version of the Traditional French Melody
(J.H.D.)

Al - le - lú - ia, al - le - lú - ia, al - le - lú - ia!
1. O fi - li - i et fi - li - ae, Rex cae - lé - stis,
2. Et Ma - rí - a Mag - da - lé - ne, Et Ja - có - bi
3. In al - bis se - dens, an - ge - lus Prae - dí - xit mu -
4. In hoc fe - sto san - ctís - si - mo Sit laus et ju -
5. De qui - bus nos hu - míl - li - mas, De - vó - tas at -
1. Rex gló - ri - ae Mor - te sur - ré - xit hó - di - e,
2. et Sa - ló - me Ve - né - runt cor - pus ún - ge - re,
3. li - é - ri - bus: In Ga - li - laé - a est Dó - mi - nus,
4. bi - lá - ti - o, Be - ne - di - cá - mus Dó - mi - no,
5. que dé - bi - tas De - o di - cá - mus grá - ti - as,
al - le - lú - ia! Al - le - lú - ia, al - le - lú - ia, al - le - lú - ia!

O SONS AND DAUGHTERS

O filii et filiae.
JEAN TISSERAND, O. F. M., *d. 1494.*
Tr. J. MASON NEALE, *d. 1866.*

Adapted, with Alleluia, by
W. H. MONK, *d. 1889, from*
GIOVANNI DA PALESTRINA, *d. 1594.*

Al - le - lú - ia! Al - le - lú - ia! Al - le - lú - ia!
1. O sons and daugh - ters, let us sing!
2. That East - er morn, at break of day,
3. An an - gel clad in white they see,
4. On this most ho - ly day of days,
5. And we with Ho - ly Church u - nite,
1. The King of heav'n, the glo - rious King, O'er death to -
2. The faith - ful wom - en went their way To seek the
3. Who sat, and spoke un - to the three, "Your Lord doth
4. To God your hearts and voi - ces raise, In laud and
5. As ev - er - more is just and right, In glo - ry
1. day rose tri - umph - ing.
2. tomb where Je - sus lay.
3. go to Gal - i - lee."
4. ju - bi - lee and praise.
5. to the King of light.
Al - le - lú - ia!

43

EASTER
HAEC DIES

Ps. 117, 24, 1. HEALEY WILLAN

Haec di - es quam fe - cit Dó - mi - nus: ex - sul -
té - mus, et lae - té - mur in e - a.
Con - fi - té - mi - ni Dó - mi - no, quó - ni - am
bo - nus: quo - ni - am in saé - cu - lum
mi - se - ri - cór - di - a e - jus. Al - le -
lú - ia, al - le - lú - ia.

JESUS CHRIST IS RISEN TODAY

'Lyra Davidica', 1708, and Tate & Brady's 'Supplement', c.1816.

Altered from a Melody in 'Lyra Davidica', 1708.

1. Je - sus Christ is ris'n to - day,
2. Hymns of praise then let us sing,
3. But the pains which He en - dured,
4. Sing we to our God a - bove,
Al - - le - lú - ia!
1. Our tri - um - phant ho - ly day,
2. Un - to Christ, our heav'n-ly King,
3. Our sal - va - tion have se - cured,
4. Praise, e - ter - nal as His love,
Al - - le - lú - ia!
1. Who did once up - on the cross,
2. Who en - dured the cross and grave,
3. Now a - bove the sky He's King,
4. Praise Him, all ye heav'n-ly host,
Al - - le - lú - ia!
1. Suf - fer to re - deem our loss.
2. Sin - ners to re - deem and save.
3. Where the an - gels ev - er sing.
4. Fa - ther, Son and Ho - ly Ghost.
Al - - le - lú - ia!

THIS JOYFUL EASTERTIDE

Stanza 1 & Refrain: Anon.
Stanzas 2 & 3: M. OWEN LEE, C.S.B.

Amsterdam Psalter, 1685
(F.J.G.)

1. This joy - ful East - er - tide, A - way with sin and sor - - - row! For Christ, the Cru - ci - fied, Has sprung to life this mor - - - row.
2. As Vic - tor in the strife And know - ing no sur - ren - - - der, He comes to bring us life: A ris - en life of splen - - - dor.
3. In Ad - am all men died; Then Je - sus came to save us. For He was cru - ci - fied And, dy - ing, new life gave us.

THIS JOYFUL EASTERTIDE

Refrain
If Christ, Who once was slain, Had nev - er
burst His pris - on, Our faith had been in
vain; But now is Christ a - ris - en, a -
ris - en, a - ris - en, a - ris - - - en.

46

EASTER

THE SUN IN SPLENDOR ROSE

EDWARD C. CURRIE.

Traditional Melody of the Isle of Arran. (E.C.C.)

1. The sun in splen - dor rose On
2. A - ris - en from the dead, Our
3. Then let all men give praise, With
4. Let earth and air and sky With
1. that first East - er morn, When Christ tri - um - phant
2. Sav - ior won for all Re - demp - tion, when for
3. songs of joy and love, To God Who, by our
4. al - le - lu - ias ring! U - nite with an - gel
1. o'er death's woes, Brought man - kind hope re - born.
2. us He bled, A - ton - ing A - dam's fall.
3. Sav - ior's grace, Re - o - pened heav'n a - bove.
4. hosts on high, In praise of Christ, the King.

REGINA CAELI, LAETARE*

Simple Tone, Mode 6.
(J.H.D.)
Anon., 14th Cent.
Re - gí - na cae - li, * lae - tá - re, Al - le - lú - ia:
Qui - a quem me - ru - í - sti por - tá - re, Al - le - lú - ia:
Re - sur - ré - xit si - cut di - xit, Al - le - lú - ia:
O - ra pro no - bis De - um, Al - le - lú - ia.

* From Easter Sunday until None of Saturday after the Feast of Pentecost.

48

REGINA CAELI, JUBILA

Anon., 17th Cent.

MICHAEL PRAETORIUS, *d. 1621.*
(T.C.K.)

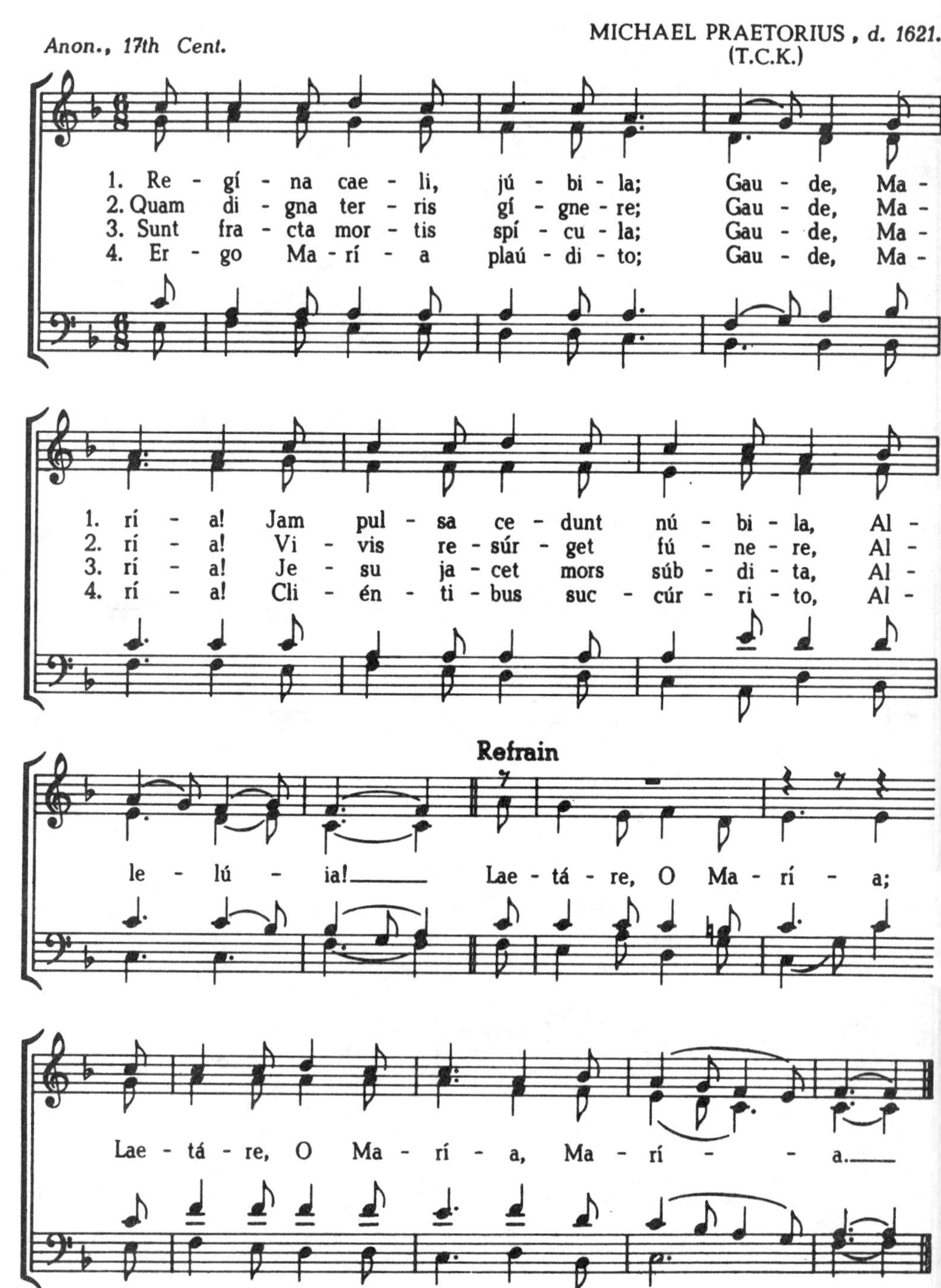
1. Re - gí - na cae - li, jú - bi - la; Gau - de, Ma -
2. Quam di - gna ter - ris gí - gne - re; Gau - de, Ma -
3. Sunt fra - cta mor - tis spí - cu - la; Gau - de, Ma -
4. Er - go Ma - rí - a plaú - di - to; Gau - de, Ma -
1. rí - a! Jam pul - sa ce - dunt nú - bi - la, Al -
2. rí - a! Vi - vis re - súr - get fú - ne - re, Al -
3. rí - a! Je - su ja - cet mors súb - di - ta, Al -
4. rí - a! Cli - én - ti - bus suc - cúr - ri - to, Al -
Refrain
le - lú - ia! Lae - tá - re, O Ma - rí - a;
Lae - tá - re, O Ma - rí - a, Ma - rí - - a.

49

BE JOYFUL, MARY, HEAVENLY QUEEN

Regina caeli, jubila.
Anon., 17th Cent.
Tr. Anon.

Leisentritt's Gesangbuch, 1584.
Harmony: JOHN E. RONAN.

1. Be joy - ful, Ma - ry, heav'n - ly Queen;
2. Whom thou didst bear by heav - en's grace;
3. The Lord has ris - en from the dead;
4. O pray to God, thou Vir - gin fair;
1. Be joy - ful, Ma - ry: Now let thine eyes with glad - ness beam,
2. Be joy - ful, Ma - ry: Didst all our guilt and sin ef - face,
3. Be joy - ful, Ma - ry: He rose with might as He had said,
4. Be joy - ful, Ma - ry: That He our souls to heav - en bear,
1. Al - le - lú - ia. Re - joice, re - joice, O Ma - ry.
2. Al - le - lú - ia. Re - joice, re - joice, O Ma - ry.
3. Al - le - lú - ia. Re - joice, re - joice, O Ma - ry.
4. Al - le - lú - ia. Re - joice, re - joice, O Ma - ry.

TELL US NOW, O DEATH

T. JAMES HANRAHAN, C.S.B.

Melody from 'Geistliche Kirchengesäng', Cologne, 1623. (E.C.C.)

1. Tell us now, O Death, where is thy sting? Al - le - lú - ia! Ev - er - more you serve our ris - en King, Al - le - lú - ia! Both sin and death He o - ver -
2. Ma - ry came her bur - ied Lord to seek, Al - le - lú - ia! Joy - ful - ly she heard the an - gel speak, Al - le - lú - ia! "Why seek the liv - ing with the
3. Come and see the place where He was laid, Al - le - lú - ia! Come, and let your hearts be un - a - fraid, Al - le - lú - ia! Re - mem - ber that He told you

TELL US NOW, O DEATH

1. came, Al - le - lú - ia! And
2. dead?" Al - le - lú - ia! "For
3. then, Al - le - lú - ia! That
1. won from God the high - est name,
2. Christ is ris - en as He said,"
3. He must die and rise a - gain,
Refrain
1. Al - le - lú - ia!
2. Al - le - lú - ia! Al - le - lú - ia,
3. Al - le - lú - ia!
al - le - lú - ia, al - le - lú - ia!

PRAISE WE OUR GOD

Gelobt sei Gott.
MICHAEL WEISSE, *d. 1534.*
Tr. KATHERINE K. DAVIS.

MELCHIOR VULPIUS, *d. 1616.*
(C.T.A.)

1. Praise we our God upon His throne;
2. Death and the grave He leaves below;
3. Lord, on Thy throne beyond the skies,
1. Praise we His sole begotten Son
2. Solace He brings for all our woe;
3. Since from the grave Thou didst arise,
1. Who for mankind such deeds hath done.
2. Darkness and sin He doth o'erthrow.
3. Lead us, at last, to Paradise!
Al - le - lú - ia, al - le - lú - ia, al - le - lú - ia!

TU, CHRISTE, NOSTRUM GAUDIUM

O Christ, Thou Art Our Joy Alone

Anon., c. 5th Cent. *Grenoble Church Melody.*
Tr. J. MASON NEALE, *d. 1866, alt.* (E.C.C.)

1. Tu, Chri - ste, no - strum gaú - di - um, Ma - nens o -
2. Hinc te pre - cán - tes quaé - su - mus, I - gnó - sce
3. Tu e - sto no - strum gaú - di - um, Qui es fu -
1. O Christ, Thou art our joy a - lone, Ex - al - ted
2. We sup - pliants, there - fore, ask of Thee To par - don
3. Be Thou our joy, and Thou our guard, As Thou wilt
1. lým - po praé - di - tum, Mun - di re - gis qui
2. cul - pis ó - mni - bus, Et cor - da sur - sum
3. tú - rus praé - mi - um; Sit no - stra in te
1. on Thy glo - rious throne: To Thee all pow'r in
2. our in - i - qui - ty: And lift up ev - 'ry
3. be our great re - ward: So shall the light that
1. fá - bri - cam, Mun - dá - na vin - cens gaú - di - a.
2. súb - le - va Ad te su - pér - na grá - ti - a.
3. gló - ri - a Per cun - cta sem - per saé - cu - la.
1. earth and heav'n As vic - tor o'er the world is giv'n.
2. Chris - tian heart By grace to find Thee where Thou art.
3. springs from Thee Be ours through all e - ter - ni - ty.

O THOU ETERNAL KING MOST HIGH
Aeterne Rex altissime.
Anon., 5th Cent.
Tr. EDWARD CASWALL, d. 1878.
Traditional Melody.
(T.B.M.)
1. O Thou e - ter - nal King most high, Who didst the world re - deem, And conqu-'ring death and hell, re - ceive A dig - ni - ty su - preme, Thou to Thy heav'n - ly throne this day Didst in Thy might as - cend, Thence- forth to reign in sov-'reign power, And glo - ry with - out end.
2. There seat - ed in Thy ma - jes - ty, To Thee sub - mis - sive bow The spa - cious earth, the high - est heav'n, The depths of hell be - low; There, wait - ing for Thy faith - ful souls, Be Thou to us, O Lord, Our peer - less joy while here we stay, In heav'n our great re - ward.

AGAIN THE SLOWLY CIRCLING YEAR

Beata nobis gaudia.
Ascribed to ST. HILARY, d. 368.
Tr. EDWARD CASWALL, d. 1878.
Adapted from a Melody by
JOHN J. RICHARDSON, d. 1879.
(E.C.C.)
1. A - gain the slow - ly circ - ling year Brings round the bles - sed
2. Thou Who in a - ges past didst pour Thy gra - ces from a -
1. hour, When on the Church the Com - fort - er Came
2. bove, Thy grace in us, where lost, re - store And
1. down in grace and pow'r. God of all grace, to
2. kin - dle peace and love. All glo - ry to the
1. Thee we pray, To Thee a - dor - ing bend; In -
2. Fa - ther be, And praise un - to the Son, Glo -
1. to our hearts this sa - cred day Thy Spir - it's ful - ness send.
2 ry, O Ho - ly Ghost, to Thee, While end - less a - ges run.

VENI, SANCTE SPIRITUS

Ascribed to POPE INNOCENT III, *d. 1216.*

13th Cent.
Mode 1. (J.H.D.)

1. Ve - ni, San - cte Spí - ri - tus, Et e - mít - te caé - li - tus
2. Ve - ni, pa - ter paú - pe - rum, Ve - ni, da - tor mú - ne - rum,
1. Lu - cis tu - ae rá - di - um.
2. Ve - ni, lu - men cór - di - um.
3. Con - so - lá - tor ó - pti - me,
4. In la - bó - re ré - qui - es,
3. Dul - cis ho - spes á - ni - mae, Dul - ce re - fri - gé - ri - um.
4. In ae - stu tem - pé - ri - es, In fle - tu so - lá - ti - um.
5. O lux be - a - tís - si - ma, Re - ple cor - dis ín - ti - ma
6. Si - ne tu - o nú - mi - ne Ni - hil est in hó - mi - ne,

VENI, SANCTE SPIRITUS

5. Tu - ó - rum fi - dé - li - um. 7. La - va quod_ est sór - di - dum,
6. Ni - hil est in - nó - xi - um. 8 Fle - cte quod_ est rí - gi - dum,
7. Ri - ga quod_ est á - ri - dum, Sa - na quod est saú - ci - um.
8. Fo - ve quod_ est frí - gi - dum, Re - ge quod est dé - vi - um.
9. Da tu - is fi - dé - li - bus, In te con - fi - dén - ti - bus,
10. Da vir - tú - tis mé - ri - tum, Da sa - lú - tis é - xi - tum,
9. Sa - crum se - pte - ná - ri - um.
10. Da per - én - ne gaú - di - um. A - men._ Al - le - lú - ia.

HOLY SPIRIT, LORD OF LIGHT

Veni, Sancte Spiritus.
Ascribed to POPE INNOCENT III, *d. 1216.*
Tr. EDWARD CASWALL, *d. 1878.*

SAMUEL WEBBE THE ELDER, *d. 1816.*

1. Ho - ly Spir - it, Lord of Light, From the clear ce -
2. Thou, of all con - sol - ers best, Thou, the soul's de -
3. Light im - mor - tal, Light di - vine, Vis - it Thou these
4. Heal our wounds, our strength re - new; On our dry - ness
5. Thou, on us who ev - er - more Thee con - fess and

1. les - tial height, Thy pure beam - ing ra - diance give.
2. light - ful guest, Dost re - fresh - ing peace be - stow.
3. hearts of Thine, And our in - most be - ing fill.
4. pour Thy dew; Wash the stains of guilt a - way.
5. Thee a - dore, With Thy sev'n - fold gifts de - scend.

1. Come, Thou Fa - ther_ of the poor, Come with treas - ures
2. Thou in toil art_ com - fort sweet; Plea - sant cool - ness
3. If Thou take Thy_ grace a - way, Noth - ing pure in
4. Bend the stub - born_ heart and will; Melt the fro - zen,
5. Give us com - fort_ when we die; Give us life with

1. which en - dure; Come, Thou Light of all that live.
2. in the heat; So - lace in the midst of woe.
3. man will stay; All his good is turned to ill.
4. warm the chill; Guide the steps that go a - stray.
5. Thee on high; Give us joys that nev - er end.

O GOD, ALMIGHTY FATHER

Gott Vater! sei gepriesen.
Anon. Tr. E.C.C.

Mainz Gesangbuch, 1833.
(H.W.)

1. O God, Al - might - y Fa - ther, Thou Maj - es - ty di - vine, All glo - ry, laud and hon - or E - ter - nal - ly be Thine.
2. To - geth - er with the Fa - ther We praise His ho - ly Son, Through Je - sus, Word In - car - nate, Was our Re - demp - tion won.
3. And God the Ho - ly Spi - rit Who dwells with - in the soul, — With truth and com - fort guide us To heav'n's e - ter - nal goal.
Refrain
O most ho - ly Trin - i - ty, Three in One and One in Three; God of Love, God of Might, God e - ter - nal, be a - dored.

58

O THOU IMMORTAL HOLY LIGHT

Aeterna Lux, Divinitas.
'Corolla Hymnorum', Cologne, 1806.
Tr. EDWARD CASWALL, *d. 1878, alt.*

THOMAS TALLIS, *d. 1585.*

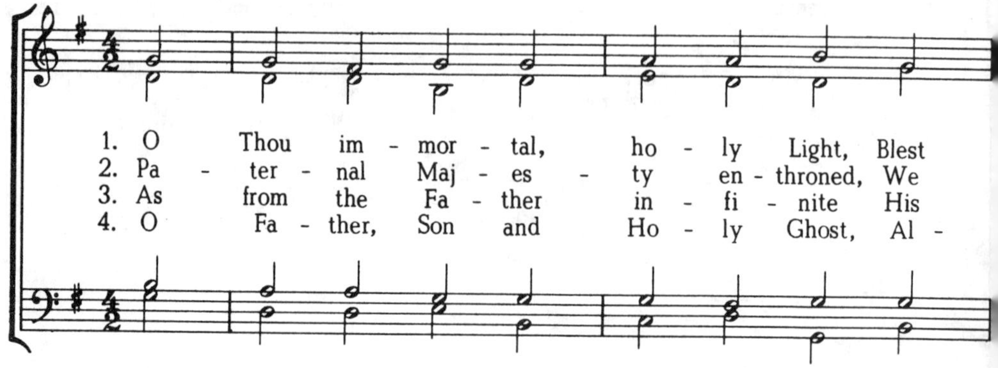

1. O Thou im - mor - tal, ho - ly Light, Blest
2. Pa - ter - nal Maj - es - ty en - throned, We
3. As from the Fa - ther in - fi - nite His
4. O Fa - ther, Son and Ho - ly Ghost, Al -

1. Trin - i - ty in u - ni - ty, For - ev - er in - fi -
2. Thee con - fess with Christ Thy Son; Thee, Ho - ly Ghost, e -
3. Son and Word e - ter - nal came, So too from Both the
4. might - y God of heav'n and earth, All mor - tals and the

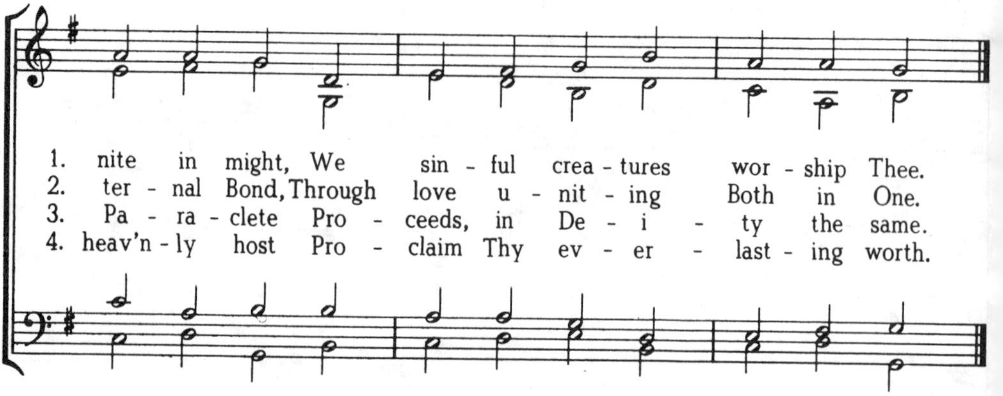

1. nite in might, We sin - ful crea - tures wor - ship Thee.
2. ter - nal Bond, Through love u - nit - ing Both in One.
3. Pa - ra - clete Pro - ceeds, in De - i - ty the same.
4. heav'n - ly host Pro - claim Thy ev - er - last - ing worth.

CHRIST THE LORD IS MY TRUE SHEPHERD

After Ps. 22:
Dominus regit me.
RICHARD R. TERRY, *d. 1938.*

EDWARD C. CURRIE.

1. Christ the Lord is my true Shep - herd: He doth rule me, He doth guide; Noth - ing can I lack if near Him Con - stant I a - bide.
2. Where the ver - dant pas - ture spring - eth, Where the liv - ing wa - ters flow, There His ten - der love hath set me On this earth be - low.
3. Though I walk through death's dark val - ley, Yet no e - vil shall I fear; Pow'rs of dark - ness have no ter - rors: Christ, my Lord, is near.
4. So through - out life's toil - some jour - ney Shall His mer - cy fol - low me, Till at length in ra - diant glo - ry I my Lord shall see.

60

PRAYER OF SAINT FRANCIS

O Signore, fa' di me un istrumento.
Ascribed to ST. FRANCIS OF ASSISI, *d. 1226.*
English adapted by M.O.L.

A MONK OF GETHSEMANI.

Make me, O Lord, an in - stru-ment of Thy_ peace.
Fine
Where there is hat - red, let me sow love; Where there is e - vil, good;
Where there is doubt - ing, faith; Where there is sor - row, hope;
Where there is dark - ness, light; Where there is sad - ness, joy!
D. C.

SAINT PATRICK'S BREASTPLATE

Ascribed to ST. PATRICK, d. 466.
Tr. CECIL F. ALEXANDER, d. 1895.
Adapted from an Ancient Irish Melody.
(T.C.K.)
1. Christ be with me, Christ with - in me,
2. Christ be - neath me, Christ a - bove me,
1. Christ be - hind me, Christ be - fore me,
2. Christ in qui - et, Christ in dan - ger,
1. Christ be - side me, Christ to win me,
2. Christ in hearts of all that love me,
1. Christ to com - fort and re - store me.
2. Christ in mouth of friend and stran - ger.

PRAISE TO THE LORD

Lobe den Herren.
JOACHIM NEANDER, *d. 1680.*
Tr. CATHERINE WINKWORTH, *d. 1878, alt.*

Stralsund Gesangbuch, 1665

1. Praise to the Lord, the Al - might-y, the King of cre - a - tion!
2. Praise to the Lord, let us of - fer our gifts at His al - tar;
3. Praise to the Lord, oh, let all that is in us a - dore Him!

1. O my soul, praise Him, for He is your health and sal - va - tion.
2. Let not our sins and trans-gres-sions now cause us to fal - ter.
3. All that has life and breath, come now in prais - es be - fore Him.

1. All you who hear, now to His al - tar draw near,
2. Christ, the High Priest, bids us all join in His feast,
3. Let the A - men sound from His peo - ple a - gain,

1. Join in pro - found ad - o - ra - tion.
2. Vic - tims with Him on the al - tar.
3. Now as we wor - ship be - fore Him.

TO THE NAME THAT BRINGS SALVATION

Gloriosi Salvatoris.
Late 15th Cent.
Tr. J. MASON NEALE, *d. 1866,* & R.F.N.

JOHANN CHRISTOPH BACH,
d. 1795.

1. To the Name that brings sal - va - tion Let the na - tions
2. He through ev - 'ry gen - er - a - tion Rules in end - less
3. Lord, we pray for up - right ru - lers: Guard them sure - ly

1. bow the head; Let them kneel in ad - o - ra - tion
2. maj - es - ty; May the kings of ev - 'ry na - tion
3. in their need From the van - i - ty of pow - er

1. When this Name of names is said; Let them pray for
2. Now fore - swear their en - mi - ty, And with hum - ble
3. And the emp - ti - ness of greed; Let them see the

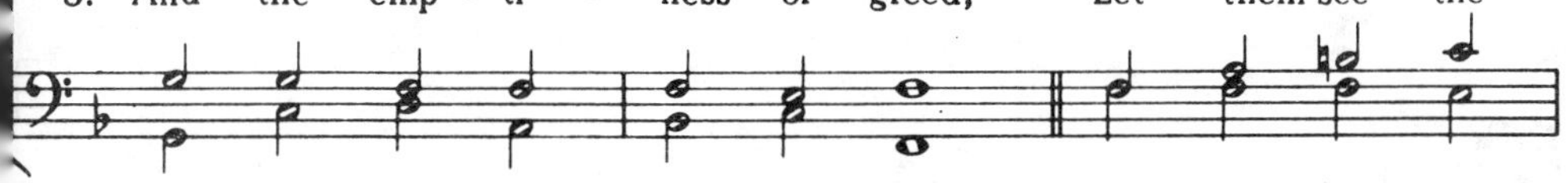

1. res - to - ra - tion Of all things in Christ the Head.
2. ven - er - a - tion In the love of God a - gree.
3. truth of low - ness, And on jus - tice let them feed.

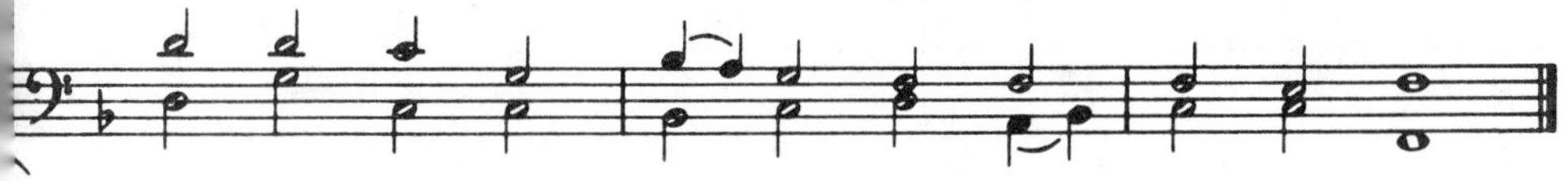

64

THE HOLY NAME

JESU, DULCIS MEMORIA

Ascribed to
ST. BERNARD OF CLAIRVAUX, *d. 1153.*

Mode I
(J.H.D.)

1. Je - su, dul - cis me - mó - ri - a, Dans ve - ra
2. Nil cá - ni - tur su - á - vi - us, Nil au - dí -
3. Je - su, spes pae - ni - tén - ti - bus, Quam pi - us
4. Nec lin - gua va - let dí - ce - re, Nec lít - te -
5. Sis Je - su no - strum gaú - di - um, Qui es fu -
1. cor - dis gaú - di - a: Sed su - per mel et ó - mni - a,
2. tur ju - cún - di - us, Nil co - gi - tá - tur dúl - ci - us,
3. es pe - tén - ti - bus! Quam bo - nus te quae - rén - ti - bus!
4. ra ex - prí - me - re: Ex - pér - tus po - test cré - de - re,
5. tú - rus praé - mi - um: Sit no - stra in te gló - ri - a,
1. E - jus dul - cis prae - sén - ti - a.
2. Quam Je - sus De - i Fí - li - us.
3. Sed quid in - ve - ni - én - ti - bus?
4. Quid sit Je - sum di - lí - ge - re.
5. Per cun - cta sem - per saé - cu - la. A - men.

65
JESUS, HOW GOOD THE THOUGHT OF THEE

Jesu, dulcis memoria.
Ascribed to ST. BERNARD OF CLAIRVAUX,
d. 1153. Tr. R.S.

Adapted from a Melody in
'Tochter Sion', Cologne, 1741.
(W.J.M.)

1. Jesus, how good the thought of Thee — Our
hearts are filled with pure delight! Yet Thine own Presence
richer far Than any earthly joy or sight.

2. No song is more melodious, No
sound more pleasing to the ear, No thought is ever
more sublime Than Jesus' Name each day to hear.

3. O Jesus, Thou the sinner's hope, The
rich reward of humble plea, The joy of all who
seek for Thee, While words fail those who rest in Thee.

4. No tongue can say nor word describe, But
only those whose faith is strong, Whose soul is one in
grace with Thee, Know how Thy love for us doth long.

5. O Jesus, be our joy on earth, And
grant that we may dwell with Thee, To share Thy glory
evermore And be with Thee eternally.

COR, ARCA LEGEM CONTINENS

Anon., 18th Cent. *Adapted from a Slovak Melod*
(E.C.C.)

1. Cor, ar - ca le - gem cón - ti - nens
2. Cor, san - ctu - á - ri - um no - vi
3. Hoc sub a - mó - ris sým - bo - lo
4. Je - su, ti - bi sit gló - ri - a,
1. Non ser - vi - tú - tis vé - te - ris,
2 In - te - me - rá - tum foé - de - ris,
3. Pas - sus cru - én - ta et mý - sti - ca,
4. Qui Cor - de fun - dis grá - ti - am,
1. Sed grá - ti - ae, sed vé - ni - ae,
2. Tem - plum ve - tú - sto sán - cti - us,
3. U - trúm - que sa - cri - fí - ci - um
4. Cum Pa - tre et al - mo Spí - ri - tu
1. Sed et mi - se - ri - cór - di - ae.
2. Ve - lúm - que scis - so u - tí - li - us.
3. Chri - stus Sa - cér - dos ób - tu - lit.
4. In sem - pi - tér - na saé - cu - la.

67

COR JESU SACRATISSIMUM

Most Sacred Heart of Jesus

Litany of the Sacred Heart.
English adapted by C.G.A.

Mode 1.
(J.H.D.)

Cor Je - su sa - cra - tís - si - mum,
Most Sa - cred Heart of Je - - - sus,
Mi - se - ré - re no - bis.
Have mer - cy on us.
Fine
Cor Je - su sa - cra - tís - si - mum,
Most Sa - cred Heart of Christ our Lord,
Mi - se - ré - re no - bis.
Show Your mer - cy to sin - ners.
D.C.

68

COR DULCE, COR AMABILE

German Melody, 1669
Anon.
(J.L.)
1. Cor dul - ce, Cor a - má - bi - le,
2. Cor Je - su mel - le dúl - ci - us,
3. Tu por - tus or - bi naú - fra - go,
1. A - mó - re no - stri saú - ci - um,
2. Cor so - le pu - ro pú - ri - us,
3. Se - cú - ra pars fi - dé - li - bus,
1. A - mó - re no - stri lán - gui - dum,
2. Ver - bi De - i sa - crá - ri - um,
3. Re - is a - sý - lum mén - ti - bus,
1. Fac sis mi - hi pla - cá - bi - le.
2. O - pum De - i com - pén - di - um.
3. Pi - is re - cés - sus cór - di - bus.

HEART OF OUR LORD

Cor dulce, Cor amabile.
Anon., English adapted by M.O.L.

Adapted from a Slovak Melody
by MIKULAS SCHNEIDER-TRNAVSKY.
(C. O'S.)

1. Heart of our Lord, O lov - ing Heart,
2. O Je - sus, meek and pure of heart,
3. Heart of the might - y Son of God,
1. For our of - fen - ses bruised and torn,
2. Make Thou our hearts like un - to Thine.
3. See how our world is torn with strife;
1. Wound - ed, o - bey - ing un - to death,
2. There did the Word of God re - side,
3. All of our hope is placed in Thee:
1. Cov - ered with sin - ners' bit - ter scorn.
2. There did His works re - splend - ent shine.
3. Grant us to see e - ter - nal life.

ALL YOU WHO SEEK A COMFORT SURE

Quicumque certum quaeritis.
Anon., 18th Cent.
Tr. EDWARD CASWALL, *d. 1878, alt.*

JOHN LE

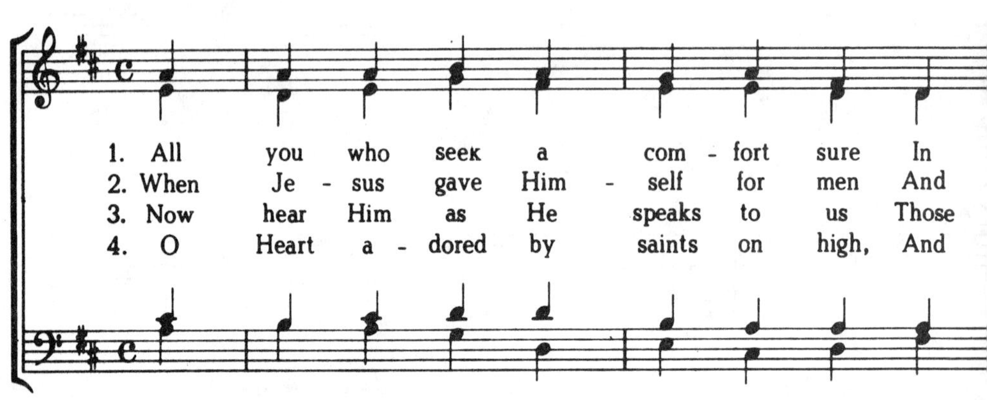
1. All you who seek a com - fort sure In
2. When Je - sus gave Him - self for men And
3. Now hear Him as He speaks to us Those
4. O Heart a - dored by saints on high, And

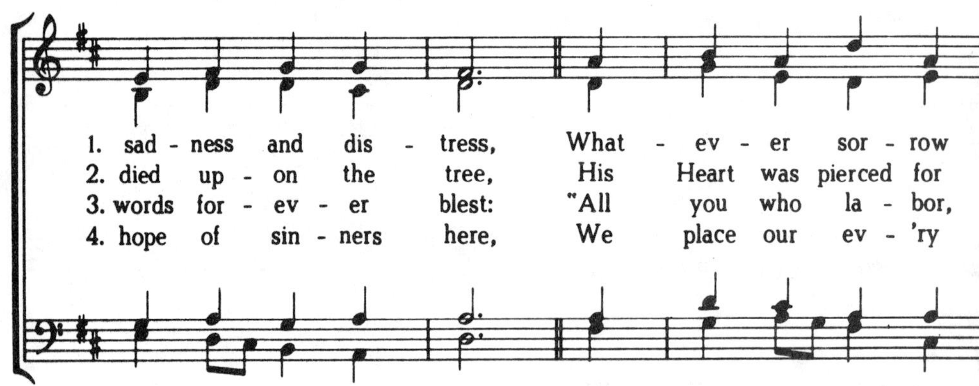
1. sad - ness and dis - tress, What - ev - er sor - row
2. died up - on the tree, His Heart was pierced for
3. words for - ev - er blest: "All you who la - bor,
4. hope of sin - ners here, We place our ev - 'ry

1. bur - dens you, What - ev - er griefs op - press:
2. love of us: He died to set us free.
3. come to Me, And I will give you rest."
4. trust in You And lift to You our prayer.

O SACRED HEART OF CHRIST AFLAME

Traditional, alt.

From a Chorale by
JOHANN CRÜGER, *d. 1662.* (E.C.C.)

1. O Sa - cred Heart of Christ a flame With
2. O wound - ed Heart of Christ, my Lord, O
1. burn - ing love for me, Oh, make my heart like
2. throne of grief and pain, Where - on through all e -
1. un - to Thine, That I may ho - ly be.
2. ter - ni - ty Thy love and mer - cy reign.
Refrain
Dear Heart of Je - sus, hear! O Heart of love di - vine!
Give ear un - to my prayer, And keep me ev - er Thine.

O SACRED HEART OF JESUS, HEAR

ISABEL WILLIAMS, *d. 1911, alt.*
Stanza 3: CLAUDE G. ARNOLD, C.S.B.

Abbreviated from a Melody b
LOUIS BOURGEOIS, *d.c. 156*

1. O Sa - cred Heart, O Heart of Je - sus, hear!
2. Pierced by the lance on Cal - v'ry's cru - el tree,
3. O Sa - cred Heart, which shows such love for men,
1. O Sa - cred Heart a - flame with love di - vine!
2. A sav - ing flood of price - less gra - ces poured,
3. O Sa - cred Heart, so lit - tle loved in turn,
1. Take Thou my heart, draw me each day more near;
2. From His dear Heart, Whose Blood was shed for me;
3. Take Thou my heart and make it Thine a - gain:
1. Take Thou my heart and let it rest in Thine.
2. The Sa - cred Heart of my e - ter - nal Lord.
3. May it with love of Thee for - ev - er burn.

73

GLORY BE TO JESUS

Viva! viva! Gesu.
Anon. 18th Cent.
Tr. EDWARD CASWALL, *d. 1878, alt.*

FRIEDRICH FILITZ, *d. 1876.*

1. Glo - ry be to Je - sus,
2. Grace and life e - ter - nal
3. Blest through end - less a - ges
4. Sing with joy, ye na - tions;
1. Who in bit - ter pains Poured for us the
2. In His Blood we find; Blest be His com -
3. Be the pre - cious streams; Je - sus, by His
4. All your voi - ces raise: Je - sus' Blood has
1. life - blood From His sa - cred veins.
2. pas - sion, In - fin - ite - ly kind.
3. mer - cy, All the world re - deems.
4. saved us, Kneel and give Him praise.

HAIL, JESUS, HAIL

Viva! viva! Gesù.
Anon., 18th Cent.
Tr. FREDERICK W. FABER, *d. 1863, alt.*

'Song 18'. ORLANDO GIBBONS, *d. 1625*
Median Parts: DAVID FETLER.

1. Hail, Je - sus, hail, Who for my sake Sweet Blood from
2. To end - less a - ges let us praise The Pre - cious
3. O sweet - est Blood, that can im - plore Par - don of
4. Ah, there is joy a - mid the saints, And hell's de -

1. Ma - ry's veins did take And shed it all for me;
2. Blood, whose price could raise The world from wrath and sin;
3. God, and heav'n re - store, The heav'n which sin had lost;
4. spair - ing cour - age faints When this sweet song we raise:

1. Oh, bles - sed be my Sav - ior's Blood, My life, my
2. Whose streams our in - ward thirst ap - pease And heal the
3. While A - bel's blood for ven-geance pleads, The Blood of
4. Oh, loud - er then, and loud - er still, Earth with one

1. light, my on - ly good, To all e - ter - ni - ty.
2. sin - ner's worst dis - ease, If he but bathe there - in.
3. Christ still in - ter - cedes For those who trust there - in.
4. might - y cho - rus fill, The Pre - cious Blood to praise.

75

CROWN HIM WITH MANY CROWNS

MATTHEW BRIDGES, *d. 1894.*
RICHARD R. TERRY, *d. 1938.*
1. Crown Him with man - y crowns, The Lamb up - on His
2. Crown Him the Lord of life, Who tri-umphed o'er the
3. Crown Him the Lord of heav'n, En - throned in worlds a -
1. throne; Hark, how the heav'n - ly an - them drowns All
2. grave, And rose vic - to - rious in the strife For
3. bove; Crown Him the King, to Whom is giv'n The
1. mu - sic but its own; A - wake, my soul, and
2. those He came to save; His glo - ries now we
3. won - drous name of love; Crown Him with man - y
1. sing Of Him Who died for thee, And hail Him as thy
2. sing Who died, and rose on high, Who died, e - ter - nal
3. crowns, As thrones be - fore Him fall, Crown Him, ye kings, with
1. match - less King Through all e - ter - ni - ty.
2. life to bring, And lives that death may die.
3. man - y crowns, For He is King of all.

CHRIST THE KING
CHRISTUS VINCIT

Acclamations of the 8th Cent.

Ambrosian Chant, Vatican Version. (J.H.D.

Choir (the People repeat)
Chri-stus vin-cit! Chri-stus re-gnat! Chri-stus ím-pe-rat!
Choir (the People repeat)
Ex-aú-di, Chri-ste.
Choir
Ec-clé-si-ae san-ctae De-i sa-lus per-pé-tu-a.
Choir
Red-ém-ptor mun-di,
People
Tu il-lam ád-ju-va!
Choir
1. San-cta Ma-rí-a,
2. San-cte Jo-seph,
3. San-cte Mí-cha-el,
People
Tu il-lam ád-ju-va!
Tu il-lam ád-ju-va!
Tu il-lam ád-ju-va! *

* **All repeat:** Christus vincit! Christus regnat! Christus ímperat

CHRISTUS VINCIT

Choir (the People repeat)
Choir
Ex - aú - di, Chri - ste.
[Pi - o] sum - mo Pon - tí - fi - ci
et u - ni - ver - sá - li Pa - pae, sa - lus et vi - ta!
Choir
People
Sal - vá - tor mun - di,
Tu il - lum ád - ju - va!
Choir
People
Choir
1. San - cte Pe - tre,
2. San - cte Pa'u - le,
Tu il - lum ád - ju - va!
Tu il - lum ád - ju - va!
Rex re - gum!
People
Choir
People
Rex no - ster!
Spes no - stra!
Gló - ri - a no - stra,

CHRISTUS VINCIT

Choir
People
Mi - se - ri - cór - di - a no - stra! Au - xí - li - um no - strum!
Choir
People
For - ti - tú - do no - stra, Ar - ma no - stra in - vi - ctís - si - ma!
Choir
Mu - rus no - ster in - ex - pu - gná - bi - lis!
People
De - fén - si - o et ex - al - tá - ti - o no - stra!
Choir & People
Choir
Lux, Vi - a, et Vi - ta no - stra!* Ip - si so - li im - pé - ri - um,
* All repeat: Christus vincit, etc.

CHRISTUS VINCIT

laus et ju - bi - lá - ti - o, per in - fi - ní - ta
People
Choir
saé - cu - la sae - cu - ló - rum. A - men. Tém - po - ra bo - na vé - ni - ant!
People
Choir
Pax Chri - sti vé - ni - at Red - ém - ptis Sán - gui - ne Chri - sti:
People
Choir
Choir & People
Fe - lí - ci - ter! Fe - lí - ci - ter! Fe - lí - ci - ter!
Choir
Choir & People
Re - gnum Chri - sti vé - ni - at! De - o grá - ti - as! A - men.

TRIUMPHANTLY DOTH CHRIST UNFURL

Vexilla Christus inclyta.
Hymn at Lauds, 1925.
Tr. R. S.

RICHARD KEYS BIGG

1. Tri - um - phant - ly doth Christ un - furl His
2. He con - quers king - doms not by wars, Nor
3. O lov - ing King, Thy light we seek, To
4. To Thee be glo - ry, Je - sus King, Who
1. ban - ners far and wide! Ye na - tions, come, give
2. bru - tal force, nor fear; But raised on high up -
3. shine by night and day! And may the world, blessed
4. rul - est all with might, For - ev - er with the
1. praise, ap - plaud The King Who for us died!
2. on the Cross, He draws His sub - jects near.
3. with Thy peace, A - dore Thee and o - bey!
4. Fa - ther, God, And Spir - it, Lord of Light!

O SALUTARIS HOSTIA

Verbum supernum prodiens, nec Patris. *Mode 1.*
ST. THOMAS AQUINAS, O. P., *d. 1274.* (J.H.D.)

1. O sa - lu - tá - ris Hó - sti - a,
2. U - ni tri - nó - que Dó - mi - no
1. Quae cae - li pan - dis ó - sti - um,
2. Sit sem - pi - tér - na gló - ri - a,
1. Bel - la pre - munt ho - stí - li - a,
2. Qui vi - tam si - ne tér - mi - no
1. Da ro - bur, fer au - xí - li - um.
2. No - bis do - net in pá - tri - a. A - men.

79

THE BLESSED SACRAMENT

O SALUTARIS HOSTIA

Verbum supernum prodiens, nec Patris.
ST. THOMAS AQUINAS, O. P., *d. 1274.*

Mode 7
(J.H.D.

1. O sa - lu - tá - ris Hó - sti - a,
2. U - ni___ tri - nó - que Dó - mi - no

1. Quae cae - li pan - dis ó - sti - um,
2. Sit sem - pi - tér - na gló - ri - a,

1. Bel - la pre - munt ho - stí - li - a,___
2. Qui vi - tam si - ne tér - mi - no___

1. Da ro - bur, fer au - xí - li - um.
2. No - bis___ do - net in pá - tri - a. A - men.__

THE BLESSED SACRAMENT

O SALUTARIS HOSTIA

Verbum supernum prodiens, nec Patris.
ST. THOMAS AQUINAS, O. P., *d. 1274.*

Mode 8.
(J.H.D.)

1. O sa - - lu - tá - ris Hó - sti - a,
2. U - ni tri - nó - que Dó - mi - no

1. Quae cae - li pan - dis ó - sti - um,
2. Sit sem - pi - tér - na gló - ri - a,

1. Bel - la pre - munt ho - stí - li - a,
2. Qui vi - tam si - ne tér - mi - no

1. Da ro - bur, fer au - xí - li - um.
2. No - bis do - net in pá - tri - a. A - men.

81

THE BLESSED SACRAMENT
O SALUTARIS HOSTIA

Verbum supernum prodiens, nec Patris.
ST. THOMAS AQUINAS, O. P., *d. 1274.*
LOUIS BOURGEOIS, *d. c.* 1561
(P.E.S.)
1. O sa - lu - tá - ris Hó - sti - a,
2. U - ni tri - nó - que Dó - mi - no
1. Quae cae - li pan - dis ó - sti - um,
2. Sit sem - pi - tér - na gló - ri - a,
1. Bel - la pre - munt ho - stí - li - a,
2. Qui vi - tam si - ne tér - mi - no
1. Da ro - bur, fer au - xí - li - um.
2. No - bis do - net in pá - tri - a. A - men.

THE BLESSED SACRAMENT

O SALUTARIS HOSTIA

Verbum supernum prodiens, nec Patris.
ST. THOMAS AQUINAS, O. P., *d. 1274.*

ABBÉ DUGUET, *d. c. 1767.*

1. O sa - lu - tá - ris Hó - sti - a,
2. U - ni tri - nó - que Dó - mi - no

1. Quae cae - li pan - dis ó - sti - um,
2. Sit sem - pi - tér - na gló - ri - a,

1. Bel - la pre - munt ho - stí - li - a,
2. Qui vi - tam si - ne tér - mi - no

1. Da ro - bur, fer au - xí - li - um.
2. No - bis do - net in pá - tri - a. A - men.

O SALUTARIS HOSTIA

Verbum supernum prodiens, nec Patris.
ST. THOMAS AQUINAS, O. P., *d. 1274.*

SAMUEL WEBBE THE ELDER, *d. 1816*
(E.C.C.)

1. O sa - lu - tá - ris Hó - sti - a,
2. U - ni tri - nó - que Dó - mi - no

1. Quae cae - li pan - dis ó - sti - um,
2. Sit sem - pi - tér - na gló - ri - a,

1. Bel - la pre - munt ho - stí - li - a,
2. Qui vi - tam si - ne tér - mi - no

1. Da ro - bur, fer au - xí - li - um.
2. No - bis do - net in pá - tri - a. A - men.

O SALUTARIS HOSTIA

Verbum supernum prodiens, nec Patris.
ST. THOMAS AQUINAS, O. P., *d. 1274.*

A. WERNER.
(E.C.C.)

1. O sa - lu - tá - ris Hó - sti - a,
2. U - ni tri - nó - que Dó - mi - no
1. Quae cae - li pan - dis ó - sti - um,
2. Sit sem - pi - tér - na gló - ri - a,
1. Bel - la pre - munt ho - stí - li - a,
2. Qui vi - tam si - ne tér - mi - no
1. Da ro - bur, fer au - xí - li - um.
2. No - bis do - net in pá - tri - a. A - men.

85

THE BLESSED SACRAMENT

AVE VERUM CORPUS

Ascribed to
POPE INNOCENT VI, *d. 1362.*

Mode 6.
(J.H.D.)

A - ve ve - rum Cor - pus na - tum
de Ma - rí - a Vír - gi - ne:
Ve - re pas - sum, im - mo - lá - tum
in cru - ce pro hó - mi - ne:
Cu - jus la - tus per - fo - rá - tum

AVE VERUM CORPUS

flu - xit a - qua et sán - gui - ne:
E - sto no - bis prae - gu - stá - tum
mor - tis in ex - á - mi - ne.
O Je - su dul - cis! O Je - su pi - e!
O Je - su, fi - li Ma - rí - ae.

ECCE PANIS ANGELORUM

Lauda Sion. Mode 7.
ST. THOMAS AQUINAS, O. P., *d. 1274.* (J.H.D.)

1. Ec - ce pa - nis an - ge - ló - rum,
2. In fi - gú - ris prae - si - gná - tur,

1. Fa - ctus ci - bus vi - a - tó - rum:
2. Cum Í - sa - ac im - mo - lá - tur,

1. Ve - re pa - nis fi - li - ó - rum,
2. A - gnus Pa - schae de - pu - tá - tur,

1. Non mit - tén - dus_____ cá - ni - bus.
2. Da - tur man - na_____ pá - tri - bus.

ECCE PANIS ANGELORUM

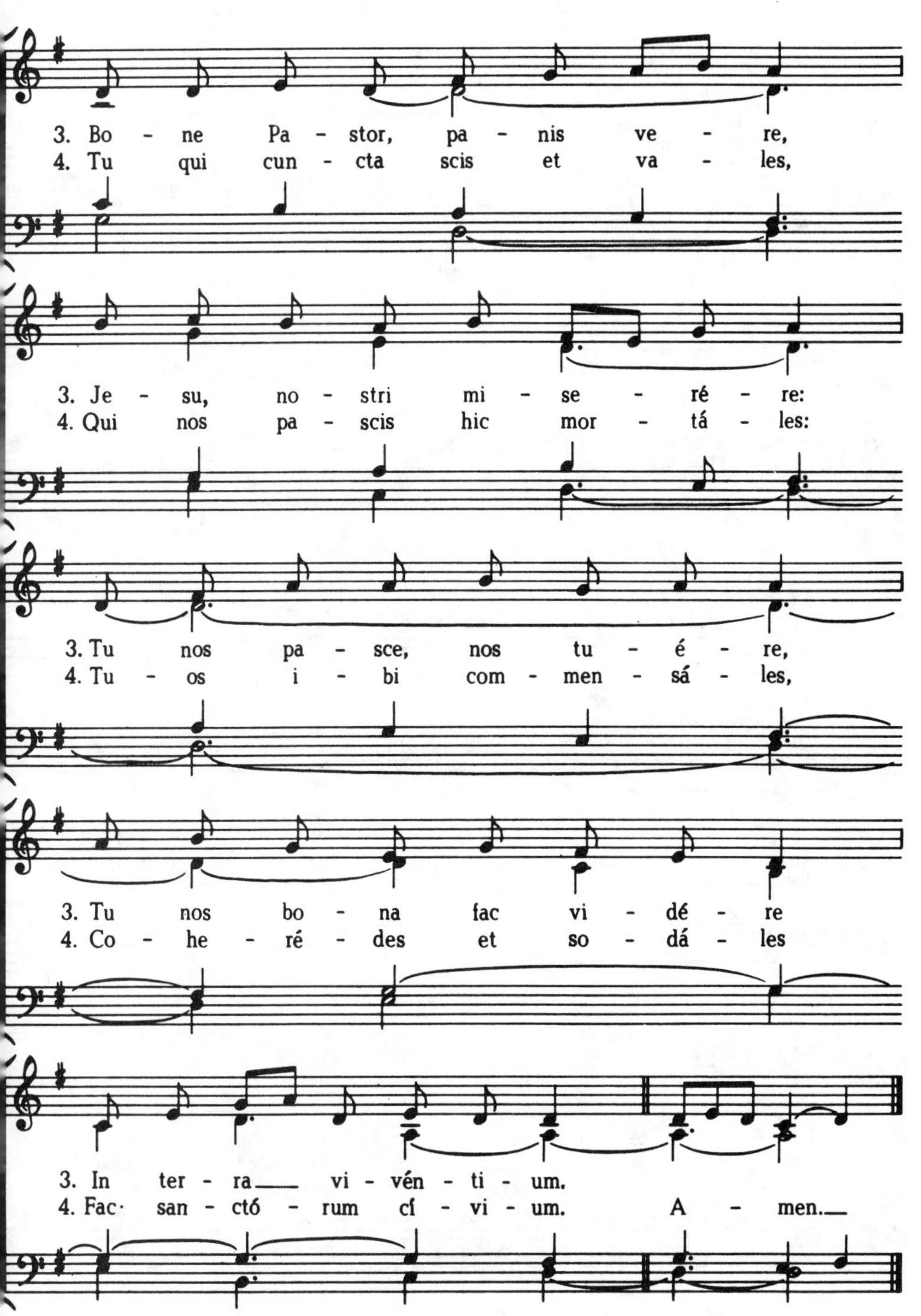
3. Bo - ne Pa - stor, pa - nis ve - re,
4. Tu qui cun - cta scis et va - les,
3. Je - su, no - stri mi - se - ré - re:
4. Qui nos pa - scis hic mor - tá - les:
3. Tu nos pa - sce, nos tu - é - re,
4. Tu - os i - bi com - men - sá - les,
3. Tu nos bo - na fac vi - dé - re
4. Co - he - ré - des et so - dá - les
3. In ter - ra___ vi - vén - ti - um.
4. Fac san - ctó - rum cí - vi - um.
A - men.__

UBI CARITAS ET AMOR

Mandatum of Holy Thursday.

Mode 6 (J.H.D.)

U - bi cá - ri - tas et a - mor,
De - us i - bi est.
1. Con - gre - gá - vit nos in u - num Chri - sti a - mor.
2. Si - mul er - go cum in u - num con - gre - gá - mur,
3. Si - mul quo - que cum be - á - tis vi - de - á - mus
1. Ex - sul - té - mus et in ip - so
2. Ne nos men - te di - vi - dá - mur
3. Glo - ri - án - ter vul - tum tu - um,

UBI CARITAS ET AMOR

1. ju - cun - dé - mur. Ti - me - á - mus
2. ca - ve - á - mus. Ces - sent júr - gi -
3. Chri - ste De - us: Gaú - di - um quod
1. et a - mé - mus De - um vi - vum,
2. a ma - lí - gna, ces - sent li - tes,
3. est im - mén - sum, at - que pro - bum,
1. Et ex cor - de di - li - gá - mus
2. Et in mé - di - o no - stri sit
3. Saé - cu - la per in - fi - ní - ta
1. nos sin - cé - ro.
2. Chri - stus De - us.
3. sae - cu - ló - rum. A - men.
Repeat: *Ubi caritas.*

ADORO TE DEVOTE

Ascribed to ST. THOMAS AQUINAS, O. P., *d. 1274.*

Mode 5
(J.H.D.)

1. A - dó - ro te de - vó - te, la - tens Dé - i - tas,
2. Vi - sus, ta - ctus, gu - stus in te fál - li - tur,
3. In cru - ce la - té - bat so - la Dé - i - tas,
4. Pla - gas, si - cut Tho - mas, non in - tú - e - or:
5. O me - mo - ri - á - le mor - tis Dó - mi - ni,
6. Pi - e pel - li - cá - ne Je - su Dó - mi - ne,
7. Je - su, quem ve - lá - tum nunc a - spí - ci - o,

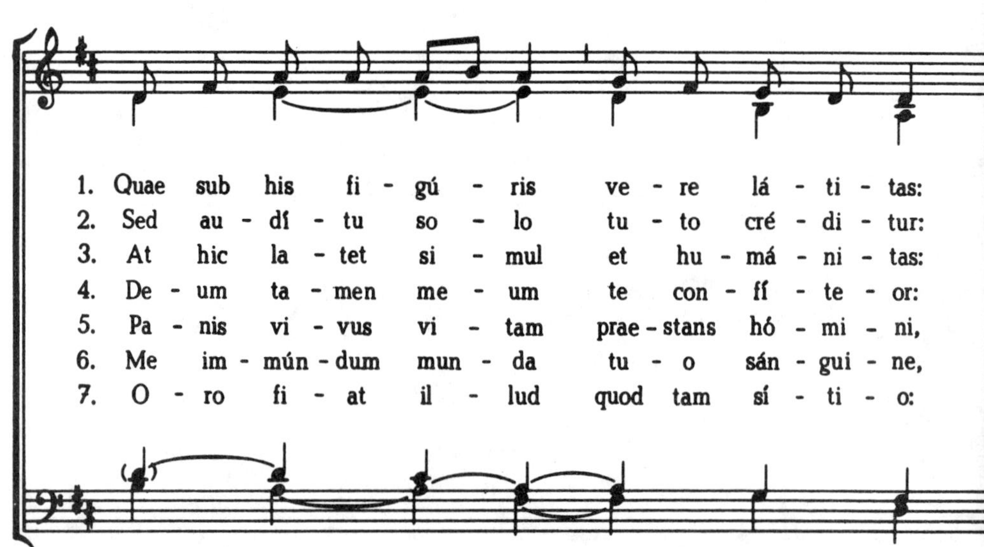
1. Quae sub his fi - gú - ris ve - re lá - ti - tas:
2. Sed au - dí - tu so - lo tu - to cré - di - tur:
3. At hic la - tet si - mul et hu - má - ni - tas:
4. De - um ta - men me - um te con - fí - te - or:
5. Pa - nis vi - vus vi - tam prae - stans hó - mi - ni,
6. Me im - mún - dum mun - da tu - o sán - gui - ne,
7. O - ro fi - at il - lud quod tam sí - ti - o:

ADORO TE DEVOTE

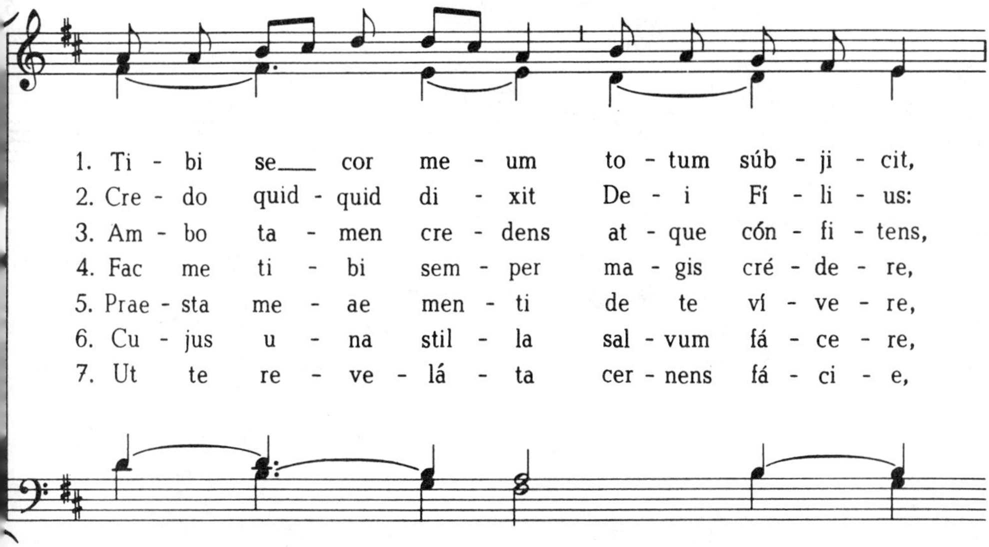

1. Ti - bi se___ cor me - um to - tum súb - ji - cit,
2. Cre - do quid - quid di - xit De - i Fí - li - us:
3. Am - bo ta - men cre - dens at - que cón - fi - tens,
4. Fac me ti - bi sem - per ma - gis cré - de - re,
5. Prae - sta me - ae men - ti de te ví - ve - re,
6. Cu - jus u - na stil - la sal - vum fá - ce - re,
7. Ut te re - ve - lá - ta cer - nens fá - ci - e,

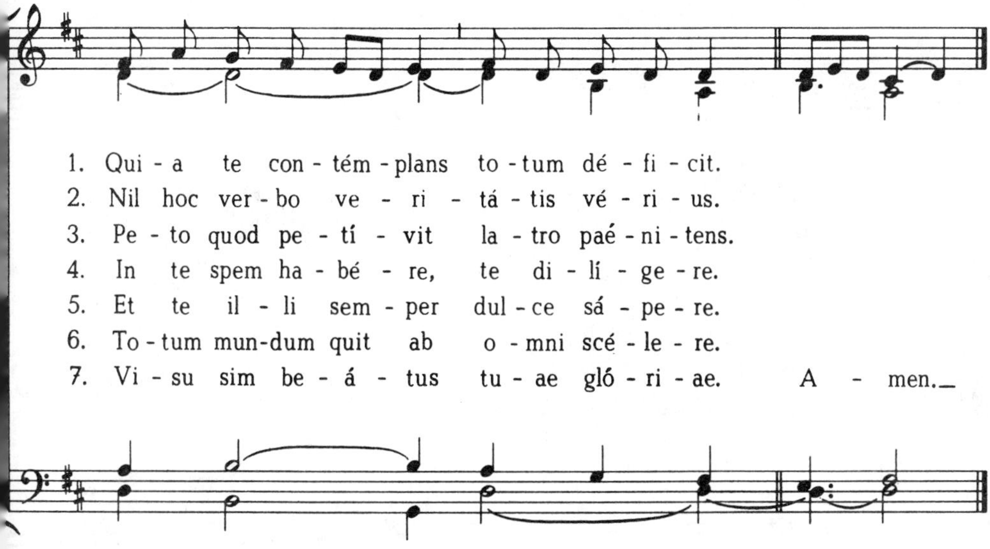

1. Qui - a te con - tém - plans to - tum dé - fi - cit.
2. Nil hoc ver - bo ve - ri - tá - tis vé - ri - us.
3. Pe - to quod pe - tí - vit la - tro paé - ni - tens.
4. In te spem ha - bé - re, te di - lí - ge - re.
5. Et te il - li sem - per dul - ce sá - pe - re.
6. To - tum mun-dum quit ab o - mni scé - le - re.
7. Vi - su sim be - á - tus tu - ae gló - ri - ae. A - men.__

GODHEAD HERE IN HIDING

Adoro te devote.
Ascribed to ST. THOMAS AQUINAS, O. P., *d. 1274.*
Tr. GERARD M. HOPKINS, S. J., *d. 1889.*

16th Cent. French Carol Melody
(P.E.S.)

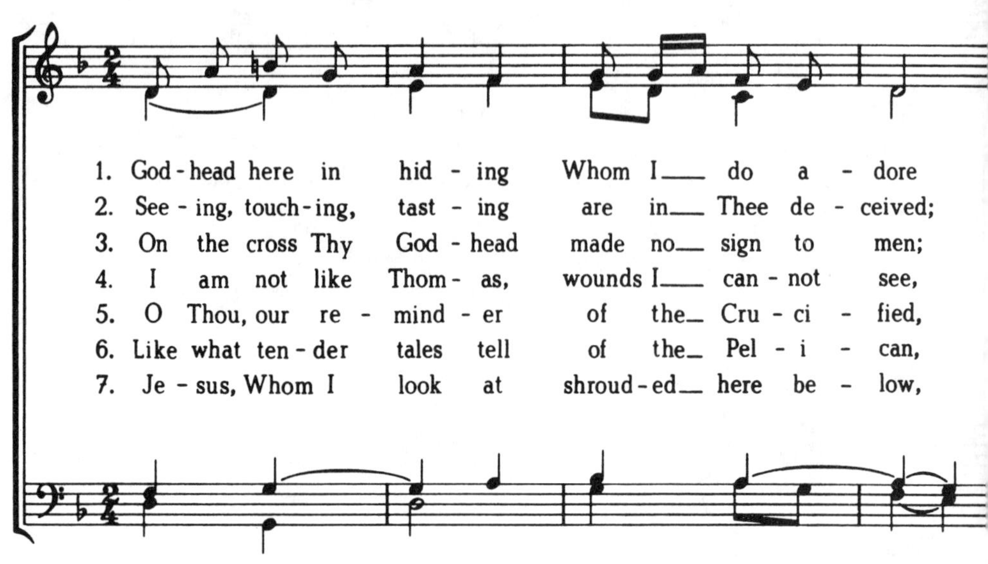
1. God-head here in hid-ing Whom I do a-dore
2. See-ing, touch-ing, tast-ing are in Thee de-ceived;
3. On the cross Thy God-head made no sign to men;
4. I am not like Thom-as, wounds I can-not see,
5. O Thou, our re-mind-er of the Cru-ci-fied,
6. Like what ten-der tales tell of the Pel-i-can,
7. Je-sus, Whom I look at shroud-ed here be-low,

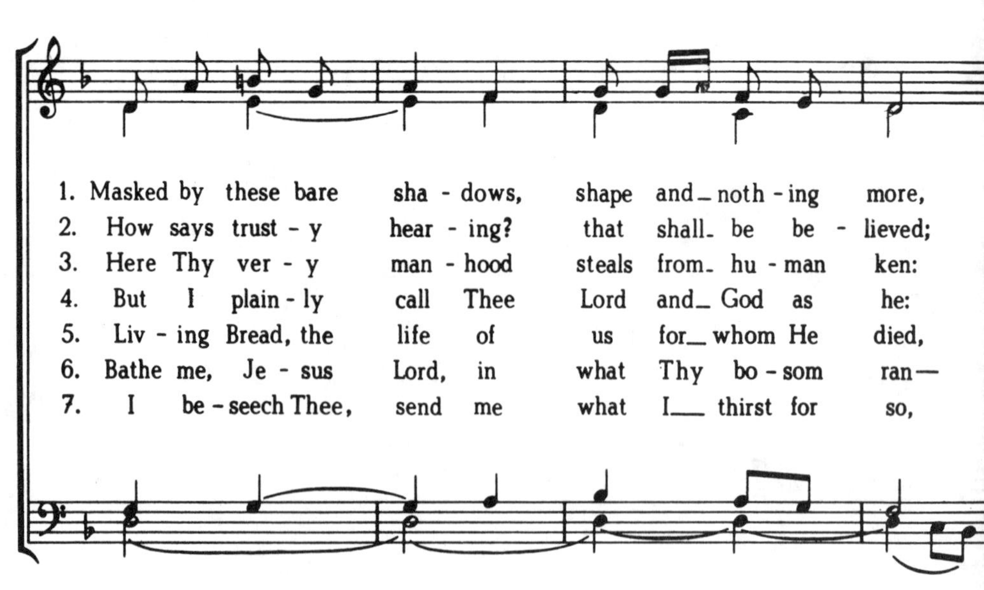
1. Masked by these bare sha-dows, shape and noth-ing more,
2. How says trust-y hear-ing? that shall be be-lieved;
3. Here Thy ver-y man-hood steals from hu-man ken:
4. But I plain-ly call Thee Lord and God as he:
5. Liv-ing Bread, the life of us for whom He died,
6. Bathe me, Je-sus Lord, in what Thy bo-som ran—
7. I be-seech Thee, send me what I thirst for so,

GODHEAD HERE IN HIDING

1. See, Lord, at Thy ser - vice low lies here a heart
2. What God's Son has told me, take for truth I do;
3. Both are my con - fes - sion, both are my be - lief,
4. This faith each day deep - er be my hold - ing of,
5. Lend this life to me, then; feed and feast my mind,
6. Blood that but one drop of has the pow'r to win
7. Some day to gaze on Thee face to face in light
1. Lost, all lost in won - der at the God Thou art.
2. Truth Him - self speaks tru - ly or there's noth-ing true.
3. And I pray the prayer of the dy - ing thief.
4. Dai - ly make me hard - er hope and dear - er love.
5. There be Thou the sweet - ness man was meant to find.
6. All the world for - give - ness of its world of sin.
7. And be blest for - ev - er with Thy glo - ry's sight.

90

O ESCA VIATORUM

'Maintzisch Gesangbuch', 1661.
JOHANN M. HAYDN, d. 1806
(T.C.K.)
1. O— e - sca vi - a - tó - rum, O pa - nis an - ge - ló - rum, O man - na caé - li - tum! E - su - ri - én - tes— ci - ba, Dul - cé - di - ne non— pri - va Cor - da quae - rén - ti - um, Cor - da quae - rén - ti - um.
2. O— lym - pha, fons a - mó - ris, Qui pu - ro Sal - va - tó - ris E cor - de pró - flu - is! Te si - ti - én - tes— po - ta, Haec so - la no - stra— vo - ta, His u - na súf - fi - cis, His u - na súf - fi - cis.
3. O— Je - su, tu - um vul - tum Quem có - li - mus oc - cúl - tum Sub pa - nis spé - ci - e, Fac, ut re - mó - to— ve - lo, A - pér - ta nos in— cae - lo Cer - ná - mus á - ci - e, Cer - ná - mus á - ci - e.

O FOOD OF EXILES LOWLY

O esca viatorum.
'Maintzisch Gesangbuch', 1661.
Tr. M.O.L.

Ascribed to HEINRICH ISAAK, *d. c. 1531.*
Slightly altered from the version of
JOHANN S. BACH, *d. 1750.* (E.C.C.)

1. O Food of ex - iles low - ly, O Bread of
2. O cleans - ing Wa - ter, stream - ing From Je - sus'
3. O Lord, we kneel be - fore You And fer - vent -
1. an - gels ho - ly, O Man - na from on high!
2. side, re - deem - ing All men of A - dam's race!
3. ly a - dore You, All hid be - neath this bread.
1. We hun - ger for Your bles - sing, All good in
2. O lim - pid Foun - tain flow - ing, Our ev - 'ry
3. But make to us this prom - ise: To see You
1. You pos - sess - ing, Oh, hear our heart's out - cry.
2. want be - stow - ing, Come, fill our souls with grace.
3. in Your ful - ness, The Bo - dy's mys - tic Head.

PANIS ANGELICUS

O Bread of Angels

Sacris solemniis.
ST. THOMAS AQUINAS, O. P., *d. 1274.*
Tr. C.G.A.

LOUIS LAMBILLOTTE, S. J., *d. 1855*
(J.L.)

1. Pa - nis an - gé - li-cus fit — pa - nis hó - mi -num,
2. Te, tri - na Dé - i-tas, ú - na - que pó - sci -mus,

1. O Bread of an - gels made Bread of men be - low!
2. O God-head Three in One, we — one to - ge - ther pray

1. Dat pa - nis caé - li - cus fi - gú - ris tér - mi - num:
2. Sic nos tu ví - si - ta si - cut te có - li - mus:

1. All gifts of an - cient times this Bread will now — be - stow.
2. That as we come to You, You too will come and stay,

1. O res mi - rá - bi - lis! man - dú - cat Dó - mi -num
2. Per tu - as sé - mi -tas duc nos quo tén - di -mus

1. O won - der un - sur-passed! Poor, hum - ble peo - ple all
2. And by Your ho - ly ways lead us un - to the day

1. Pau - per, ser - vus et hú - mi - lis.
2. Ad lu - cem quam in - há - bi - tas.

1. Eat the Flesh of the Lord, — their God.
2. Where You dwell in e - ter - nal light.

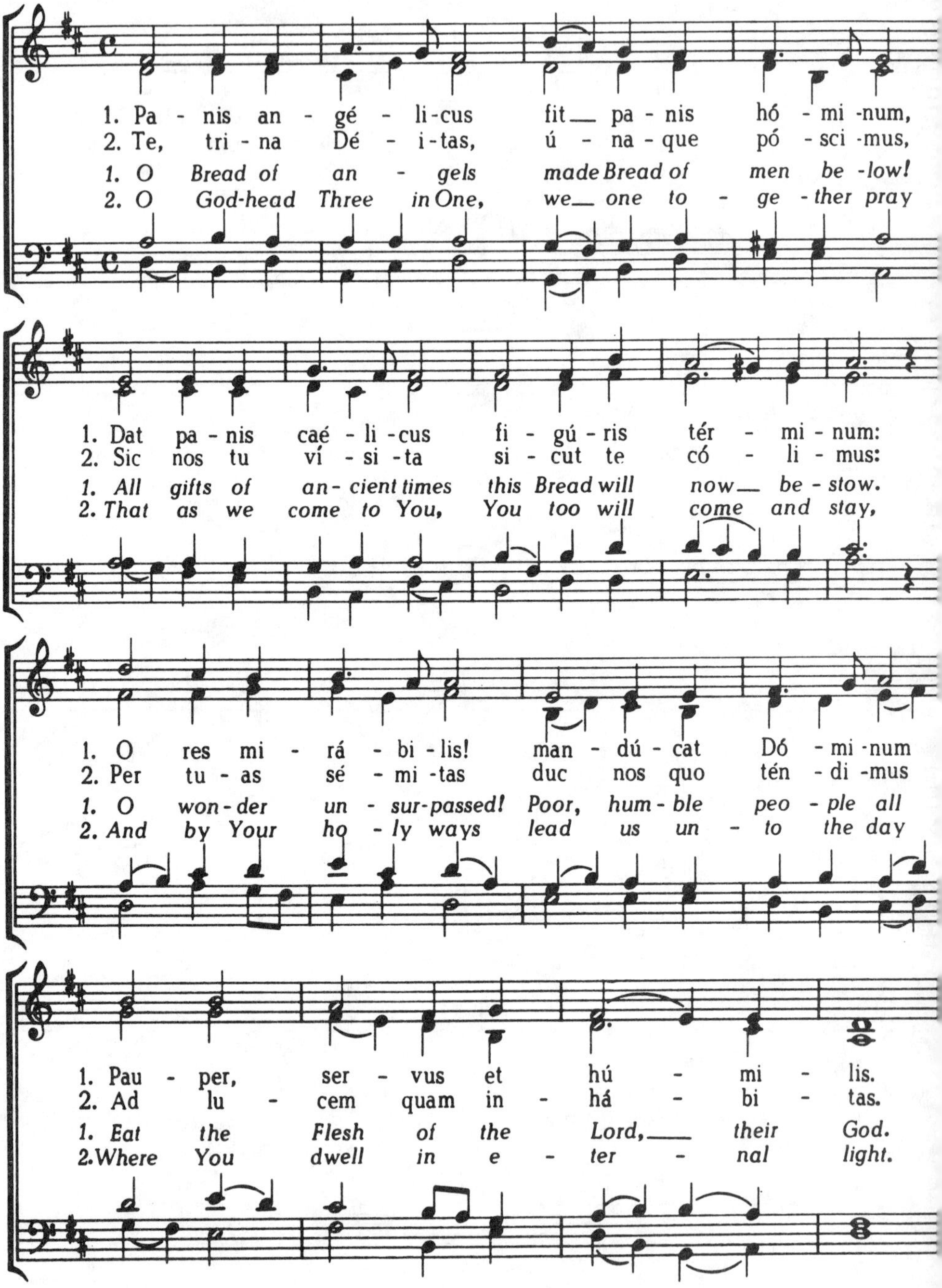

CHRIST THE WORD TO EARTH DESCENDED

Verbum supernum prodiens, nec Patris.
ST. THOMAS AQUINAS, O. P., *d. 1274.*
Tr. D. C. F.
Adapted from a Chorale, 'Ringe recht', in 'Erbaulicher musikalischer Christenschatz', 1745. (C.O'S.)
1. Christ the Word to earth des - cen - ded, Yet re -
2. While the false dis - ci - ple wai - ted To be -
3. Un - der two - fold spe - cies giv - en, Flesh as
4. Might - y Vic - tim, earth's sal - va - tion, Heav - en's
5. To Thee, God - head, three - fold es - sence, Be un -
1. mained in heav - en still; When His earth - ly jour - ney
2. tray his Mas - ter's life, Christ for men, tho' by men
3. bread and blood as wine, He be - came a pledge of
4. gates un - fold - ing wide, See, we cry in des - o -
5. end - ing praise and love; Make us wor - thy of Thy
1. en - ded He ful - filled the Fa - ther's will.
2. ha - ted, Gave in love the bread of life.
3. heav - en: Man par - took of Life Di - vine.
4. la - tion: Be our strength, be at our side.
5. pre - sence In our heav'n - ly home a - bove.

HAIL, TRUE VICTIM, LIFE AND LIGHT

Ave vivens Hostia.
JOHN PECKHAM, *d. 1294.*
Tr. RONALD A. KNOX, *d. 1957.*

Leisentritt's Gesangbuch, 1584
(E.C.C.)

1. Hail, true Vic-tim, life and light Un - to sin - ners lend - ing—
2. Je - sus tru - ly in this place God and man re - sid - eth;—
3. Plead, true Vic-tim, in our stead To the Fa - ther cry - ing,—
1. Ev -'ry old - er form and rite Hath in Thee its end - ing—
2. Him no shad - ow doth re - place, Him no rent di - vi - deth,—
3. Thou, Thy chil-dren's dai - ly bread, Dai - ly health sup - ply - ing;—
1. Spot - less in the Fa - ther's sight Ev - er - more as - cend - ing,
2. Ver - y flesh, al - though His face, Glo - ri - fied, He hid - eth;
3. Ban - quet for the ex - ile spread, Grant us life un - dy - ing:
1. Ho - ly Church in bit - ter fight Ev - er - more be - friend - ing.
2. Gar-nered in this lit - tle space All of Christ a - bid - eth.
3. May our love from Thine be fed, Self and sense de - ny - ing!

IN THIS SACRAMENT, LORD JESUS

JOHN J. FURNISS, C. SS. R., *d. 1865, alt.* WILLIAM J. MARSH.

1. In this Sa - cra - ment, Lord Je - sus, We re -
2. Yes, Lord Je - sus, we be - lieve it, And Your
3. Come, Lord Je - sus, in Your mer - cy, Give Your
4. Be our pledge of fu - ture glo - ry, Mem - o -
5. 'Eat this Bread,' You have com - mand - ed, 'If you

1. ceive Your Flesh and Blood, With Your Soul and God - head
2. pres - ence we a - dore; And with all our hearts we
3. Flesh and Blood to me; Come to me, my God and
4. ry of Pas - sion spent; Fill our hearts with grace a -
5. wish to live in Me; Liv - ing thus you shall not

1. al - so, As our own most pre - cious food.
2. love You; May we love You more and more.
3. Sav - ior; Let me live e - ter - nal - ly.
4. bun - dant In this ho - ly Sa - cra - ment.
5. per - ish, But shall live e - ter - nal - ly.'

JESUS, GENTLEST SAVIOR

FREDERICK W. FABER, d. 1863, alt.
Adapted from a Melody ascribed t
JOHN STAINER, d. 1873. (E.C.C
1. Je - sus, gent - lest Sav - ior,
2. Na - ture can - not hold You,
3. Out be - yond the shin - ing
4. Yet the hearts of chil - dren
1. God of might and pow'r, You, Your - self, are
2. Heav'n can - not em - brace All Your time - less
3. Of the far - thest star, You are ev - er
4. Hold what worlds can - not: You, the God of
1. dwell - ing In us at this hour.
2. glo - ry, All Your end - less grace.
3. reach - ing In - fin - ite - ly far.
4. won - ders, Share our hum - ble lot.

JESUS, MY LORD, MY GOD, MY ALL

FREDERICK W. FABER, *d. 1863.*

Anon. Adapted by JOHANN S. BACH, *d. 1750.*

1. Je - sus, my Lord, my God, my all! How can I
2. Had I but Ma - ry's sin - less heart With which to
3. Thy Bod - y, Soul and God - head, all! O mys - ter -
4. Sound, then, His prais - es high - er still, And come, ye
1. love Thee as I ought? And how re - vere this
2. love Thee, dear - est King, Oh, with what ev - er
3. y of love di - vine! I can - not com - pass
4. an - gels, to our aid; For this is God, the
1. won - drous gift, So far sur - pass - ing hope or thought?
2. fer - vent praise Thy good - ness, Je - sus, would I sing!
3. all I have, For all Thou hast and art is mine!
4. ver - y God Who hath both men and an - gels made!
Refrain
Sweet Sa - cra - ment, we Thee a - dore!
Oh, make us love Thee more and more.

JESUS, THOU ART COMING

A SISTER OF NOTRE DAME.

Freely adapted from a Melody by FRANZ SCHUBERT, *d. 1828.* (P.E.S

1. Je - sus, Thou art com - ing, Ho - ly as Thou art,
2. Who am I, my Je - sus, That Thou com'st to me?
3. Dear - est Lord, I love Thee, With my whole, whole heart,
1. Thou, the God who made me, To my sin - ful heart.
2. I have sinned a - gainst Thee, Of - ten griev - ous - ly;
3. Not for what Thou giv - est, But for what Thou art.
1. Je - sus, I be - lieve it, On Thy on - ly word;
2. I am ver - y sor - ry I have caused Thee pain,
3. Come, oh come, my Sav - ior, Come to me and stay,
1. Kneel - ing, I a - dore Thee As my King and Lord.
2. I will nev - er, nev - er Wound Thy Heart a - gain.
3. For I want Thee, Je - sus, More than I can say.

O KING OF NATIONS

W. JAMES HOWARD, C. S. B. QUENTIN MACLEAN.

1. O King of na - tions, splen - dor, hon - or,
2. O Sa - cra - men - tal Son of God per -
3. E - ter - nal King, we come to You and
1. maj - es - ty di - vine! Our strength, our hope, our
2. ceived by faith a - lone, You gave Your - self, You
3. ad - o - ra - tion give; With faith we come be -
1. con - so - la - tion rest in this one sign.
2. died for men, and yet You live un - known.
3. fore Your pre - sence, and by faith we live.
Refrain
Streng-then our poor faith, Lord, And let our hope in - crease;
Grant that we may love_ You, And in You find our peace.

O LORD, I AM NOT WORTHY

Stanzas 1 & 4: Anon.
Stanzas 2 & 3: FR. IRVIN, O. F. M. CAP.

Traditional Melody.
(T.C.K.)

1. O___ Lord, I am not wor - thy That___
2. Oh,_ come, all you who la - bor In___
3. O___ Je - sus, we a - dore Thee, Our___
4. O___ Sa - cra - ment most ho - ly, O___
1. Thou should'st come to me, But___ speak the words of
2. sor - row and in pain, Come, eat This Bread from
3. Vic - tim and our Priest, Whose pre - cious Blood and
4. Sa - cra - ment di - vine! All___ praise and all thanks -
1. com - fort, My spir - it healed shall be.
2. hea - ven; Thy peace and strength re - gain.
3. Bo - dy Be - come our sa - cred Feast.
4. giv - ing Be ev - 'ry mo - ment Thine.

SANCTIFY ME WHOLLY

Anima Christi.
Anon., 14th Cent.
Tr. THOMAS BALL, *d. 1916.*

WILLIAM PITTS, *d. 1903.*
(E.C.C.)

1. Sanc - ti - fy me whol - ly, Soul of_Christ a - dored;
2. Pas - sion of my Sav - ior, be my strength in need;
3. At death's fi - nal hour___ call me_to Thy face;

1. Be my sure sal - va - tion, Bod - y of the Lord;
2. Good and gra - cious Je - sus, to_my prayer give heed.
3. Bid me stand be - side_ Thee in_the heav'n - ly place:

1. Fill my yearn - ing spir - it, O Thou Blood un - priced:
2. In Thy wounds most pre - cious, let me re - fuge find:
3. There with saints and an - gels I shall sing to Thee

1. Wash me, Sa - cred Wa - ter from the_side of Christ.
2. All the en - vious pow - er of the_foe - man bind.
3. Through the count - less a - ges of e - ter - ni - ty.

SING, MY TONGUE, THE MYSTERY HOLY

Pange lingua.
ST. THOMAS AQUINAS, O. P., *d. 1274.* A MONK OF GETHSEMANI
Tr. M. O. L.

1. Sing, my tongue, the mys-t'ry ho - ly Of the Bo - dy of my
2. On the night be-fore His pas - sion, His A - pos - tles by His
3. The In - car - nate Word now chan - ges Bread to flesh at His com -
4. Praise to the Al-might - y Fa - ther; Hon - or, glo - ry to the
1. Lord, And His Pre - cious Blood, the ran - som Which u -
2. side, He ful - filled the law com - plete - ly With the
3. mand, And the wine be - comes His life - blood. Sen - ses
4. Son; A - dor - a - tion to the Spir - it, Who with
1. pon the earth was poured. Fruit of Ma - ry's womb all
2. food He pur - i - fied; Then He gave Him - self un -
3. fail to un - der - stand; But the heart that is in
4. Them is ev - er one, And pro - cedes from both for -
1. ho - ly, May He ev - er be a - dored.
2. to them, Bread His hands had sanc - ti - fied.
3. ear - nest Can by faith its doubt with - stand.
4. ev - er, As e - ter - nal a - ges run.
A - men.

SOUL OF MY SAVIOR

Anima Christi.
Anon., 14th Cent.
Tr. 'St. George's Hymn Book', 1882.

WILLIAM J. MAHER, S. J., *d. 1877.*
(C.D.U.)

1. Soul of my Sav - ior, sanc - ti - fy my breast;
2. Strength and pro - tec - tion may Thy Pas - sion be;
3. Save me from e - vil, make me Thine a - lone;
1. Bod - y of Christ, be Thou my sav - ing guest;
2. O bles - sed Je - sus, hear and an - swer me;
3. In my last mo - ments take me for Thine own;
1. Blood of my Sav - ior, bathe me in Thy tide;
2. Deep in Thy wounds, Lord, hide and shel - ter me;
3. Call me and bid me has - ten to Thy side,
1. Wash me, ye wa - ters, flow - ing from His side.
2. So___ shall I nev - er, nev - er part from Thee.
3. That_ I may see Thee praised and glo - ri - fied.

WHAT HAPPINESS CAN EQUAL MINE

FREDERICK W. FABER, *d. 1863, alt.*

JOHANN H. SCHEIN, *d. 1630.* (J.L.)

1. What hap - pi - ness can e - qual mine? I've
2. He_ comes to make my heart His own, His
3. How_ full of love for men is He Who
4. A_ dai - ly food He of - fers men To
1. found the ob - ject of my love; My Lord and God, my
2. Flesh be-comes my dai - ly bread; And now I live for
3. gives His ver - y Flesh to eat! The God who died for
4. keep and nour - ish them in grace; My Sav - ior, keep me
1. King di - vine Has come to me_ from heav'n a - bove.
2. Him a - lone, For with His life_ my soul is fed.
3. love of me, By giv - ing makes His love com - plete.
4 now, and when I come to see_ You face to face.

BENEDICTION OF THE BLESSED SACRAMENT

(Simple-Solemn-Pontifical)

TANTUM ERGO immediately followed by the VERSICLE and RESPONSE:

V. *Panem de caelo praestitísti eis (Allelúia).**

R. *Omne delectaméntum in se habéntem (Allelúia).**

Then the ORATION, sung by the priest, with the choir's AMEN.

The above are the only musical requirements for Benediction. It is customary to precede these with the *O salutaris Hostia* or some other hymn in honor of the Blessed Sacrament, either in Latin or in English. Hymns in honor of Our Lady or of the Saints, as well as hymns of the season may also be used.

If the *Te Deum* is sung, it must precede the *Tantum ergo,* and it must be sung in its entirety and in Latin.

Between the oration and the blessing with the Blessed Sacrament, nothing may be sung. During the actual blessing nothing is sung, but the organ may be played softly. Present day custom has the blessing in silence, except for the altar bell.

The service is frequently concluded with the antiphon *Adoremus in aeternum* and Psalm 116, *Laudate Dominum,* or with *Holy God, we praise Thy Name.* An English or Latin hymn of the season may replace these if desired. (Also see pages 130—131 for additional antiphons to be substituted for the *Adoremus in aeternum.)*

* The *Alleluias* are added only in Paschal Time and on the Feast of Corpus Christi.

PANGE LINGUA

ST. THOMAS AQUINAS, O. P., *d. 1274.*

Mode 3.
(J.H.D.)

1. Pan - ge lin - gua glo - ri - ó - si Cór - po - ris
2. No - bis da - tus, no - bis na - tus, Ex in - tá -
3. In su - pré - mae no - cte cae - nae, Re - cúm - bens
4. Ver - bum ca - ro, pa - nem ve - rum, Ver - bo car -
5. TAN - TUM ER - GO SA - CRA - MÉN - TUM Ve - ne - ré -
6. GE - NI - TÓ - RI GE - NI - TÓ - QUE Laus et ju -
1. my - sté - ri - um, San - gui - nis - que pre - ti - ó - si,
2. cta Vír - gi - ne, Et in mun - do con - ver - sá - tus,
3. cum frá - tri - bus, Ob - ser - vá - ta le - ge ple - ne,
4. nem éf - fi - cit: Fit - que san - guis Chri - sti me - rum,
5. mur cér - nu - i: Et an - tí - quum do - cu - mén - tum
6. bi - lá - ti - o, Sa - lus, ho - nor, vir - tus quo - que,
1. Quem in mun - di pré - ti - um Fru - ctus ven - tris
2. Spar - so ver - bi sé - mi - ne, Su - i mo - ras
3. Ci - bis in le - gá - li - bus, Ci - bum tur - bae
4. Et si sen - sus dé - fi - cit, Ad fir - mán - dum
5. No - vo ce - dat rí - tu - i: Prae - stet fi - des
6. Sit et be - ne - dí - cti - o: Pro - ce - dén - ti
1. ge - ne - ró - si Rex ef - fú - dit gén - ti - um.
2. in - co - lá - tus, Mi - ro clau - sit ór - di - ne.
3. du - o - dé - nae, Se dat su - is má - ni - bus.
4. cor sin - cé - rum, So - la fi - des súf - fi - cit.
5. sup - ple - mén - tum Sén - su - um de - fé - ctu - i.
6. ab u - tró - que Com - par sit lau - dá - ti - o. A - men.

TANTUM ERGO SACRAMENTUM

Pange lingua. *Mode 1.*
ST. THOMAS AQUINAS, O. P., *d. 1274.* (J.H.D.)

1. Tan - tum er - go Sa - cra - mén - tum Ve - ne -
2. Ge - ni - tó - ri Ge - ni - tó - que Laus et
1. ré - mur cér - nu - i: Et an - tí - quum
2. ju - bi - lá - ti - o, Sa - lus, ho - nor,
1. do - cu - mén - tum No - vo ce - dat rí - tu - i:
2. vir - tus quo - que, Sit et be - ne - dí - cti - o:
1. Prae - stet fi - des sup - ple - mén - tum
2. Pro - ce - dén - ti ab u - tró - que
1. Sén - su - um de - fé - ctu - i.
2. Com - par sit lau - dá - ti - o. A - men.

108

BENEDICTION OF THE BLESSED SACRAMENT

TANTUM ERGO SACRAMENTUM

Pange lingua.
ST. THOMAS AQUINAS, O. P., *d. 1274.*

Mode 5
(J.H.D.)

1. Tan - tum er - go___ Sa - cra - mén - tum Ve - ne - ré - mur cér - nu - i: Et an - tí - quum do - cu - mén - tum No - vo ce - dat rí - tu - i: Prae - stet fi - des___ sup - ple - mén - tum Sén - su - um___ de - fé - ctu - i.
2. Ge - ni - tó - ri___ Ge - ni - tó - que Laus et ju - bi - lá - ti - o, Sa - lus, ho - nor, vir - tus quo - que, Sit et be - ne - dí - cti - o: Pro - ce - dén - ti___ ab u - tró - que Com - par sit___ lau - dá - ti - o. A - men.___

TANTUM ERGO SACRAMENTUM

Pange lingua.
ST. THOMAS AQUINAS, O. P., d. 1274.
Mode 5, Mozarabic.
(J.H.D.)
1. Tan - tum er - go Sa - cra - mén - tum Ve - ne -
2. Ge - ni - tó - ri Ge - ni - tó - que Laus et
1. ré - mur cér - nu - i: Et an - tí - quum
2. ju - bi - lá - ti - o, Sa - lus, ho - nor,
1. do - cu - mén - tum No - vo ce - dat rí - tu - i:
2. vir - tus quo - que, Sit et be - ne - dí - cti - o:
1. Prae - stet fi - des sup - ple - mén - tum
2. Pro - ce - dén - ti ab u - tró - que
1. Sén - su - um de - fé - ctu - i.
2. Com - par sit lau - dá - ti - o. A - men.

TANTUM ERGO SACRAMENTUM

Pange lingua.
ST. THOMAS AQUINAS, O. P., *d. 1274.*

CASPAR ETT, *d. 1847, in*
Cantica Sacra', Munich, 1840.

1. Tan - tum er - go Sa - cra - mén - tum Ve - ne -
2. Ge - ni - tó - ri Ge - ni - tó - que Laus et
1. ré - mur cér - nu - i: Et an - tí - quum
2. ju - bi - lá - ti - o, Sa - lus, ho - nor,
1. do - cu - mén - tum No - vo ce - dat rí - tu - i:
2. vir - tus quo - que, Sit et be - ne - dí - cti - o:
1. Prae - stet fi - des sup - ple - mén - tum
2. Pro - ce - dén - ti ab u - tró - que
1. Sén - su - um de - fé - ctu - i.
2. Com - par sit lau - dá - ti - o. A - men.

111

TANTUM ERGO SACRAMENTUM

Pange lingua.
ST. THOMAS AQUINAS, O. P., *d. 1274.*

FRIEDRICH FILITZ, *d. 1876, in 'Vierstimmiges Choralbuch', Berlin, 1847.* (E.C.C.)

1. Tan - tum er - go Sa - cra - mén - tum Ve - ne -
2. Ge - ni - tó - ri Ge - ni - tó - que Laus et
1. ré - mur cér - nu - i: Et an - ti - quum
2. ju - bi - lá - ti - o, Sa - lus, ho - nor,
1. do - cu - mén - tum No - vo ce - dat rí - tu - i;
2. vir - tus quo - que, Sit et be - ne - dí - cti - o:
1. Prae - stet fi - des sup - ple - mén - tum
2. Pro - ce - dén - ti ab u - tró - que
1. Sén - su - um de - fé - ctu - i.
2. Com - par sit lau - dá - ti - o. A - men.

112

TANTUM ERGO SACRAMENTUM

Pange lingua.

ST. THOMAS AQUINAS, O. P., *d. 1274.* E. LEONARD RUSH, C. S. B.

1. Tan - tum er - go Sa - cra - mén - tum Ve - ne -
2. Ge - ni - tó - ri Ge - ni - tó - que Laus et
1. ré - mur cér - nu - i: Et an - tí - quum
2. ju - bi - lá - ti - o, Sa - lus, ho - nor,
1. do - cu - mén - tum No - vo ce - dat rí - tu - i:
2. vir - tus quo - que, Sit et be - ne - dí - cti - o:
1. Prae - stet fi - des sup - ple - mén - tum
2. Pro - ce - dén - ti ab u - tró - que
1. Sén - su - um de - fé - ctu - i.
2. Com - par sit lau - dá - ti - o. A - men.

TANTUM ERGO SACRAMENTUM

Pange lingua.
ST. THOMAS AQUINAS, O. P., d. 1274.
SAMUEL WEBBE THE ELDER, d. 1816.
(E.C.C.)
1. Tan - tum er - go Sa - cra - mén - tum Ve - ne -
2. Ge - ni - tó - ri Ge - ni - tó - que Laus et
1. ré - mur cér - nu - i: Et an - tí - quum
2. ju - bi - lá - ti - o, Sa - lus, ho - nor,
1. do - cu - mén - tum No - vo ce - dat rí - tu - i:
2. vir - tus quo - que, Sit et be - ne - dí - cti - o:
1. Prae - stet fi - des sup - ple - mén - tum
2. Pro - ce - dén - ti ab u - tró - que
1. Sén - su - um de - fé - ctu - i.
2. Com - par sit lau - dá - ti - o. A - men.

ANTIPHONS FOR PSALM 116.

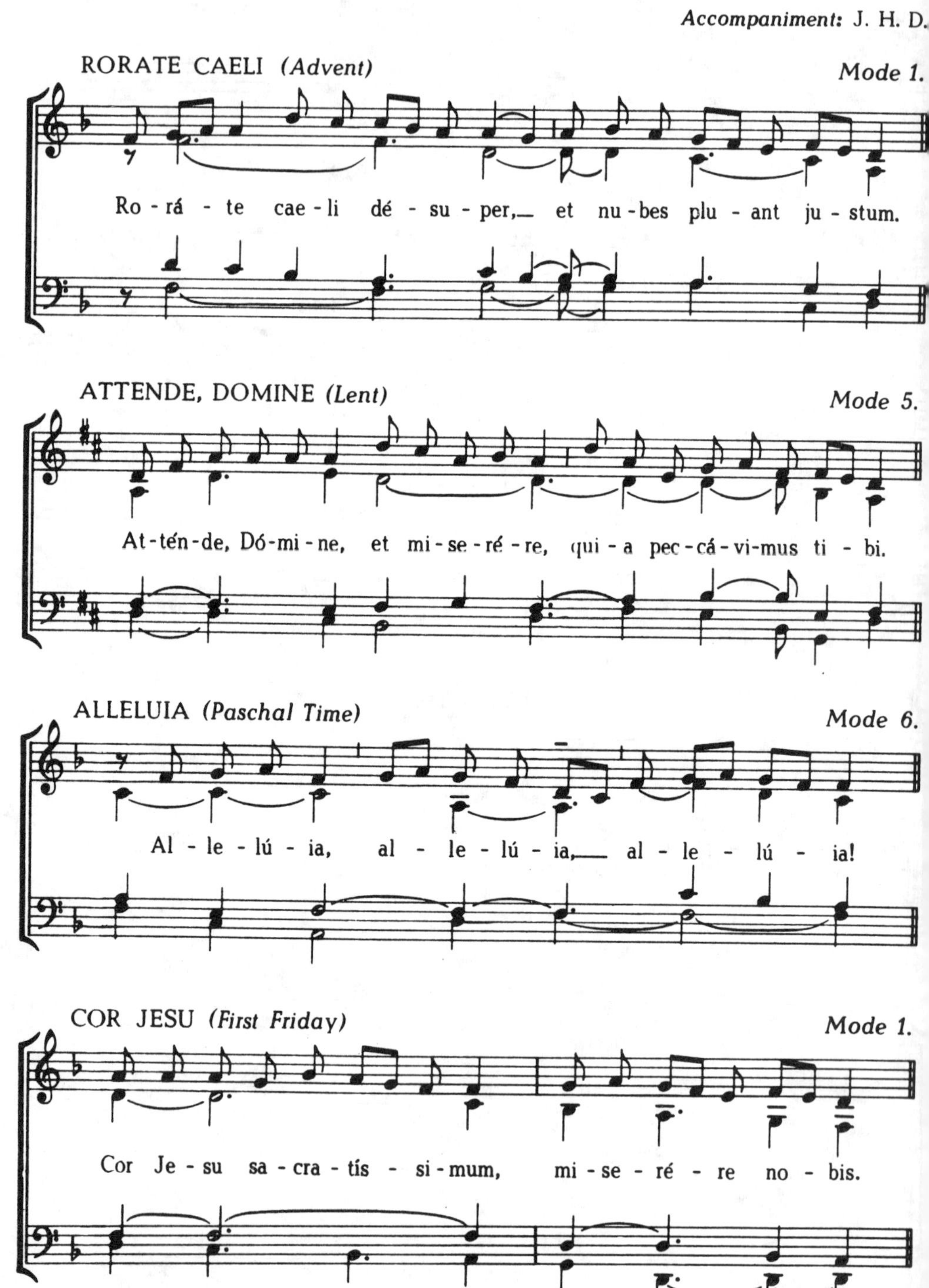

Accompaniment: J. H. D.
RORATE CAELI (Advent)
Mode 1.
Ro - rá - te cae - li dé - su - per, et nu - bes plu - ant ju - stum.
ATTENDE, DOMINE (Lent)
Mode 5.
At - tén - de, Dó - mi - ne, et mi - se - ré - re, qui - a pec - cá - vi - mus ti - bi.
ALLELUIA (Paschal Time)
Mode 6.
Al - le - lú - ia, al - le - lú - ia, al - le - lú - ia!
COR JESU (First Friday)
Mode 1.
Cor Je - su sa - cra - tís - si - mum, mi - se - ré - re no - bis.

ANTIPHONS FOR PSALM 116.

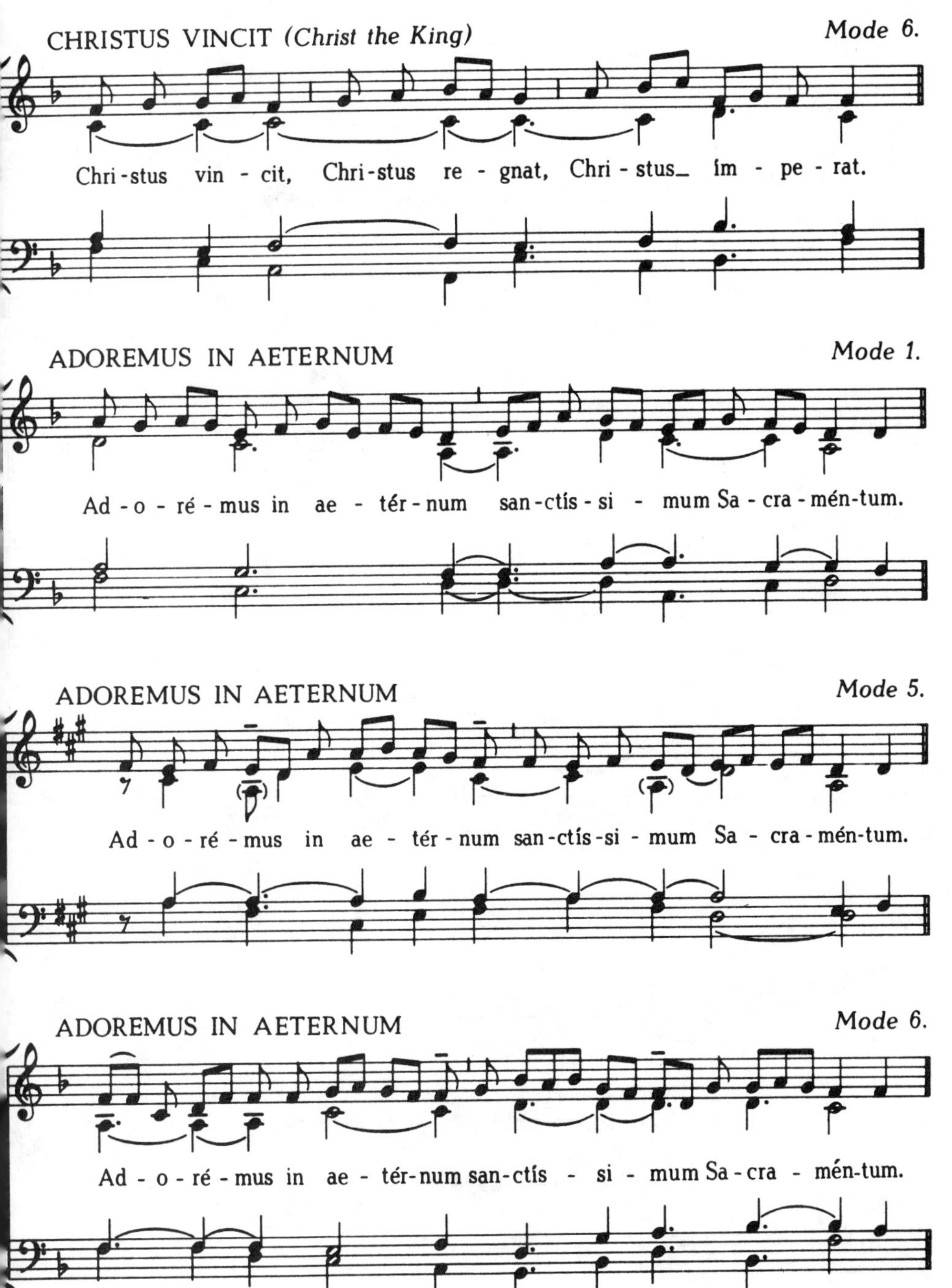
CHRISTUS VINCIT (Christ the King)
Mode 6.
Chri-stus vin - cit, Chri-stus re - gnat, Chri - stus_ ím - pe - rat.
ADOREMUS IN AETERNUM
Mode 1.
Ad - o - ré - mus in ae - tér - num san-ctís - si - mum Sa - cra - mén-tum.
ADOREMUS IN AETERNUM
Mode 5.
Ad - o - ré - mus in ae - tér - num san-ctís-si - mum Sa - cra - mén-tum.
ADOREMUS IN AETERNUM
Mode 6.
Ad - o - ré - mus in ae - tér-num san-ctís - si - mum Sa - cra - mén-tum.

PSALM 116: LAUDATE DOMINUM

Accompaniment: J. H. D
115
Mode 1
1. Lau - dá - te Dóminum o - mnes gen - tes: *
2. Quóniam confirmáta est super nos miseri-cór - di - a e - jus: *
3. Glória Pa - tri et Fí - li - o, *
4. Sicut erat in princípio, et nunc et sem - per, *
1. laudáte eum o - mnes pó - pu - li.
2. et véritas Dómini manet in ae - tér - num.
3. et Spirí - - - - - - - - - tu - i San - cto.
4. et in saécula saecu - - - - - - ló - rum. A - men.
Repeat Antiphon.
116
Mode 5.
1. Lau - dá - te Dóminum o-mnes gen - tes: *
2. Quóniam confirmáta est super nos misericórdi-a e - jus: *
3. Glória Patri et Fí - li - o, *
4. Sicut erat in princípio, et nunc et sem - per, *

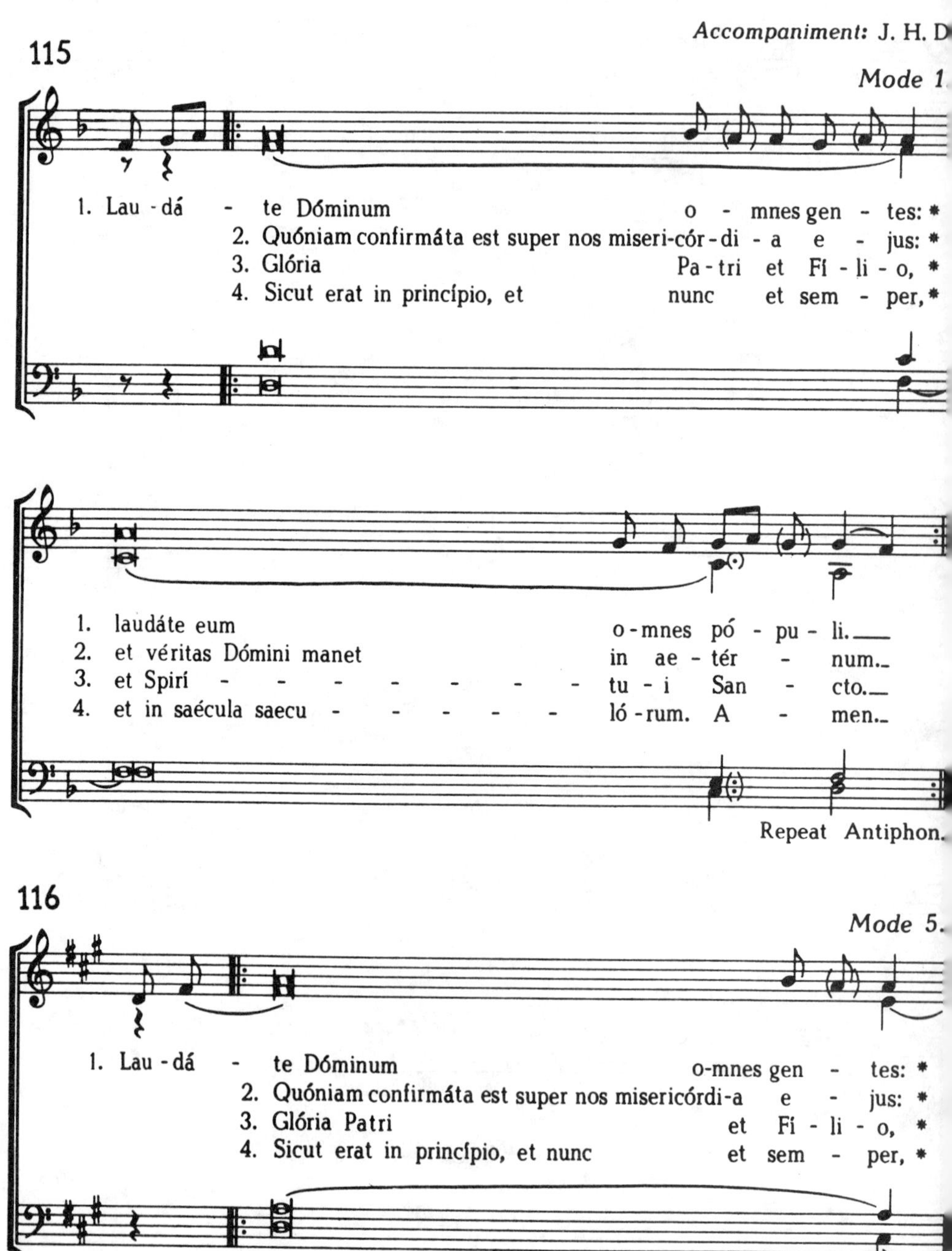

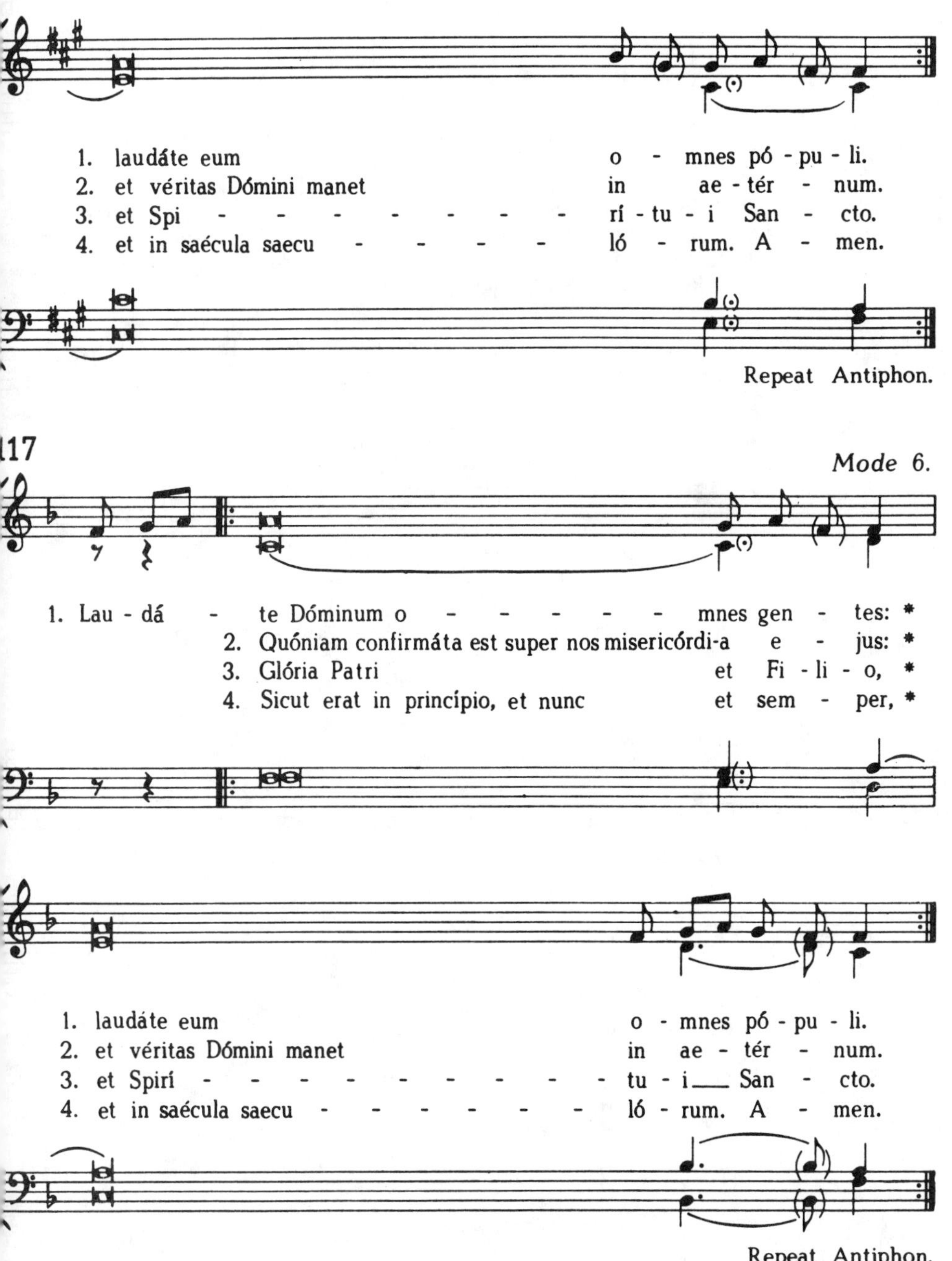
1. laudáte eum o - mnes pó - pu - li.
2. et véritas Dómini manet in ae - tér - num.
3. et Spi - - - - - - - - rí - tu - i San - cto.
4. et in saécula saecu - - - - ló - rum. A - men.
Repeat Antiphon.
117
Mode 6.
1. Lau - dá - te Dóminum o - - - - - - mnes gen - tes: *
2. Quóniam confirmáta est super nos misericórdi-a e - jus: *
3. Glória Patri et Fi - li - o, *
4. Sicut erat in princípio, et nunc et sem - per, *
1. laudáte eum o - mnes pó - pu - li.
2. et véritas Dómini manet in ae - tér - num.
3. et Spirí - - - - - - - - - - tu - i San - cto.
4. et in saécula saecu - - - - - - - ló - rum. A - men.
Repeat Antiphon.

VENI, CREATOR SPIRITUS

Ascribed to
RABANUS MAURUS, d. 856.
Mode 8
(J.H.D
1. Ve - ni, Cre - á - tor Spí - ri - tus, Men - tes tu - ó - rum
2. Qui di - cé - ris Pa - rá - cli - tus, Al - tís - si - mi do -
3. Tu se - pti - fór - mis mú - ne - re, Dígi - tus pa - tér - nae
4. Ac - cén - de lu - men sén - si - bus, In - fún - de a-mó - rem
5. Ho - stem re - pél - las lón - gi - us, Pa - cém - que do - nes
6. Per te sci - á - mus da Pa - trem, No - scá - mus at - que
7. De - o Pa - tri sit gló - ri - a, Et Fí - li - o, qui a
1. ví - si - ta: Im - ple su - pér - na grá - ti - a
2. num De - i, Fons vi - vus, i - gnis, cá - ri - tas,
3. déx - te - rae, Tu ri - te pro - mís - sum Pa - tris,
4. cór - di - bus, In - fír - ma no - stri cór - po - ris
5. pró - ti - nus: Du - ctó - re sic te praé - vi - o
6. Fí - li - um, Te que u - tri - ús - que Spí - ri - tum
7. mór - tu - is Sur - ré - xit, ac Pa - rá - cli - to,
1. Quae tu cre - á - sti pé - cto - ra.
2. Et spi - ri - tá - lis ún - cti - o.
3. Ser - mó - ne di - tans gút - tu - ra.
4. Vir - tú - te fir - mans pér - pe - ti.
5. Vi - té - mus o - mne nó - xi - um.
6. Cre - dá - mus o - mni tém - po - re.
7. In sae - cu - ló - rum saé - cu - la. A - men.

119

COME, HOLY GHOST, CREATOR BLEST

Veni, Creator Spiritus.
Ascribed to RABANUS MAURUS, *d. 856.*
Tr. EDWARD CASWALL, *d. 1878, alt.*

LOUIS LAMBILLOTTE, S. J., *d. 1855.*
(T.B.M.)

1. Come, Ho - ly Ghost, Cre - a - tor blest, And in our
2. O Com - fort - er, to Thee we cry, Thou heav'n-ly
3. O Ho - ly Ghost, through Thee a - lone Know we the
4. Praise we the Fa - ther and the Son, And the blest

1. hearts take up Thy rest; Come with Thy grace
2. Gift of God most high; Thou fount of life
3. Fa - ther and the Son; Be this our nev -
4. Spir - it with Them one; And may the Son

1. and heav'n-ly aid To fill the hearts which Thou hast
2. and fire of love, And sweet a - noint - ing from a -
3. er chang-ing creed: That Thou dost from Them both pro -
4. on us be - stow The gifts that from the Spir - it

1. made, To fill the hearts which Thou hast made.
2. bove, And sweet a - noint - ing from a - bove.
3. ceed, That Thou dost from Them both pro - ceed.
4. flow, The gifts that from the Spir - it flow.

COME, HOLY GHOST, WHO EVER ONE

Nunc Sancte nobis Spiritus.
Ascribed to ST. AMBROSE, *d. 397.*
Tr. after JOHN H. NEWMAN, *d. 1890.*

ORLANDO GIBBONS, *d. 162*

1. Come, Ho - ly Ghost, Who ev - er one
2. In will and deed, by heart and tongue,
3. Al - might - y Fa - ther, hear our cry

1. Art with the Fa - ther and the Son;
2. With all our pow'rs Thy praise be sung;
3. Through Je - sus Christ, our Lord most high,

1. Come, Ho - ly Ghost, our souls pos - sess
2. And love light up our mor - tal frame,
3. Who with the Ho - ly Ghost and Thee

1. With Thy full flood of ho - li - ness.
2. Till oth - ers catch the liv - ing flame.
3. Doth live and reign e - ter - nal - ly.

O BREATHE ON ME, THOU BREATH OF GOD

EDWIN HATCH, *d. 1889.*
Ancient Irish Melody.
(E.C.C.)
1. O — breathe on me, Thou Breath of
2. O — breathe on me, Thou Breath of
3. O — breathe on me, Thou Breath of
4. O — breathe on me, Thou Breath of
1. God, Fill — me with life a - new, —
2. God, Un - til my heart is — pure, —
3. God, Till — I am whol - ly — Thine, —
4. God, So shall I nev - er — die, —
1. — That I may love what Thou dost
2. — Un - til with Thee I have one
3. — Un - til this earth - ly part of
4. — But live with Thee the per - fect
1. love, And do what Thou wouldst do. —
2. will To do and to en - dure. —
3. me Glows with Thy fire di - vine. —
4. life Of Thine e - ter - ni - ty. —

SING THE HOLY FAMILY'S PRAISES

EDMUND VAUGHAN, C. SS. R., *d. 1908*,
& FR. IRVIN, O. F. M. CAP.

Melody from 'Andächtige und auserlesene Gesänge', Würzburg, 1705. (T.B.M

1. Sing the Ho - ly Fam - 'ly's prais - es:
2. Ma - ry, you a - lone were cho - sen
3. Jo - seph, you were called the fa - ther
1. Ma - ry, moth - er of her Lord;
2. to be moth - er of your Lord;
3. of your Mak - er and your Lord;
1. Jo - seph, cho - sen to pro - tect her;
2. You were guide un - to the foot - steps
3. You were sent to save your Sav - ior
1. Je - sus, sub - ject to their word.
2. of the In - fant, Christ a - dored.
3. from the cru - el Her - od's sword.

SING THE HOLY FAMILY'S PRAISES

1. Je - sus, Ma - ry, Jo - seph, help us,
2. Dear - est Moth - er, make us hum - ble,
3. Grant that we may call you fa - ther;
1. that our homes on earth may be
2. for your Son will take His rest
3. show to us a fa - ther's love:
1. One in love and deep af - fec - tion
2. In the poor and hum - ble dwel - ling
3. Lead us safe from ev - 'ry dan - ger
1. with the Ho - ly Fam - i - ly.
2. of a hum - ble sin - ner's breast.
3. till we meet in heav'n a - bove.

AVE MARIA

Luke 1, 28, 42.
Sancta Maria: c. 13th Cent.
Mode
(J.H.D.
A - ve Ma - rí - a, * grá - ti - a ple - na,
Dó - mi - nus te - cum, be - ne - dí - cta tu
in mu - li - é - ri - bus, et be - ne - dí - ctus fru - ctus
ven - tris tu - i, Je - sus. San - cta Ma - rí - a,
Ma - ter De - i, o - ra pro no - bis pec - ca - tó - ri - bus,
nunc et in ho - ra mor - tis no - strae. A - men.

124

OUR LADY

O GLORIOSA VIRGINUM

Ascribed to
VENANTIUS FORTUNATUS, *d. 609.*
Mode 2.
(J.H.D.)
1. O Glo - ri - ó - sa vír - gi - num,
2. Quod He - va tri - stis áb - stu - lit,
3. Tu re - gis al - ti já - nu - a,
4. Je - su, ti - bi sit gló - ri - a,
1. Su - blí - mis in - ter sí - de - ra,
2. Tu red - dis al - mo gér - mi - ne:
3. Et au - la lu - cis fúl - gi - da:
4. Qui na - tus es de Vír - gi - ne,
1. Qui te cre - á - vit, pár - vu - lum
2. In - trent ut a - stra flé - bi - les,
3. Vi - tam da - tam per Vír - gi - nem,
4. Cum Pa - tre et al - mo Spí - ri - tu
1. La - ctén - te nu - tris ú - be - re.
2. Cae - li re - clú - dis cár - di - nes.
3. Gen - tes red - ém - ptae, pláu - di - te.
4. In sem - pi - tér - na saé - cu - la.

SALVE, MATER

Ancient Carmelite Hymn.

Mode 5
(J.H.D.)

Sal - ve, Ma - ter mi - se - ri - cór - di - ae,
Ma - ter De - i et Ma - ter vé - ni - ae,
Ma - ter spe - i et Ma - ter grá - ti - ae,
Ma - ter ple - na sanctae lae - tí - ti - ae, O Ma - rí - a!

SALVE, MATER

1. Sal - ve, de - cus hu - má - ni gé - ne - ris,
2. Sal - ve, fe - lix Vir - go pu - ér - pe - ra:
1. Sal - ve, Vir - go dí - gni - or cé - te - ris,
2. Nam qui se - det in Pa - tris déx - te - ra,
1. Quae vír - gi - nes o - mnes trans - gré - de - ris,
2. Cae - lum re - gens, ter - ram et áe - the - ra,
1. Et ál - ti - us se - des in sú - pe - ris, O Ma - rí - a!
2. In - tra tu - a se clau - sit ví - sce - ra, O Ma - rí - a!

Repeat: *Salve, Mater.*

126

OUR LADY

O SANCTISSIMA

O Most Holy One

Anon.
Tr. C.W.L.

Sicilian Melody, pub. 1794
(H.W.)

1. O san - ctís - si - ma, O pi - ís - si - ma, Dul - cis Vir - go, Ma - rí - a!
2. Vir - go, ré - spi - ce, Ma - ter, á - spi - ce, Au - di nos, O Ma - rí - a!
1. O most ho - ly one, O most low - ly one, Lov - ing Vir - gin, Ma - ri - a!
2. Vir - gin ev - er fair, Moth - er, hear our prayer, Look up - on us, Ma - ri - a!
1. Ma - ter a - má - ta, In - te - me - rá - ta,
2. Tu me - di - ci - nam Por - tas di - ví - nam,
1. Moth - er, Maid of fair - est love, La - dy, Queen of all a - bove,
2. Bring to us your treas - ure, Grace be - yond all mea - sure;
O - ra, o - ra pro no - bis!

127

AVE, MARIS STELLA

Mode 1.
(J.H.D.)
Anon., 9th Cent.
1. A - ve, ma - ris stel - la, De - i
2. Su - mens il - lud A - ve Ga - bri -
3. Sol - ve vin - cla re - is, Pro - fer
4. Mon - stra te es - se ma - trem: Su - mat
5. Sit laus De - o Pa - tri, Sum - mo
1. Ma - ter al - ma, At - que sem - per Vir - go,
2. é - lis o - re, Fun - da nos in pa - ce,
3. lu - men cae - cis: Ma - la no - stra pel - le,
4. per te pre - ces, Qui pro no - bis na - tus
5. Chri - sto de - cus, Spi - rí - tu - i San - cto,
1. Fe - lix cae - li por - ta.
2. Mu - tans He - vae no - men.
3. Bo - na cun - cta po - sce.
4. Tu - lit es - se tu - us.
5. Tri - bus ho - nor u - nus. A - men.

128

OUR LADY

AVE, MARIS STELLA

First appeared in
Anon., 9th Cent.
Est's 'Whole Booke of Psalmes
1592. (E.C.C.)
1. A - ve, ma - ris stel - la, De - i
2. Su - mens il - lud A - ve Ga - bri -
3. Sol - ve vin - cla re - is, Pro - fer
4. Mon - stra te_es - se ma - trem: Su - mat
5. Sit laus De - o Pa - tri, Sum - mo
1. Ma - ter al - ma, At - que sem - per Vir - go,
2. é - lis o - re, Fun - da nos in pa - ce,
3. lu - men cae - cis: Ma - la no - stra pel - le,
4. per te pre - ces, Qui pro no - bis na - tus
5. Chri - sto de - cus, Spi - rí - tu - i San - cto,
1. Fe - lix cae - li por - ta.
2. Mu - tans He - vae no - men.
3. Bo - na cun - cta po - sce.
4. Tu - lit es - se tu - us.
5. Tri - bus ho - nor u - nus. A - men.

OCEAN STAR, WE GREET YOU

Ave, maris stella.
Anon., 9th Cent.
Tr. M. O. L.

CASPAR ETT, *d. 1847, in 'Cantica Sacra', Munich, 1840.*

1. O - cean star, we greet you: Maid of fame im - mor - tal, God's be - lov - èd Moth - er, Heav - en's joy - ous por - tal.
2. E - ven as the an - gel Used the name of E - va, Chang - ing it to A - ve,— Greet us, make us peace - ful.
3. Break our chains for - ev - er; Ban - ish ev - 'ry sad - ness; Be our light to guide us; Be our ev - 'ry glad - ness.
4. Be our in - ter - cess - or; Show your - self a moth - er: Je - sus came to save us Through you and no oth - er.
5. Praise to God the Fa - ther, To the Son for - ev - er, And the Ho - ly Spir - it, Three in One to - geth - er.

MAGNIFICAT ANIMA MEA

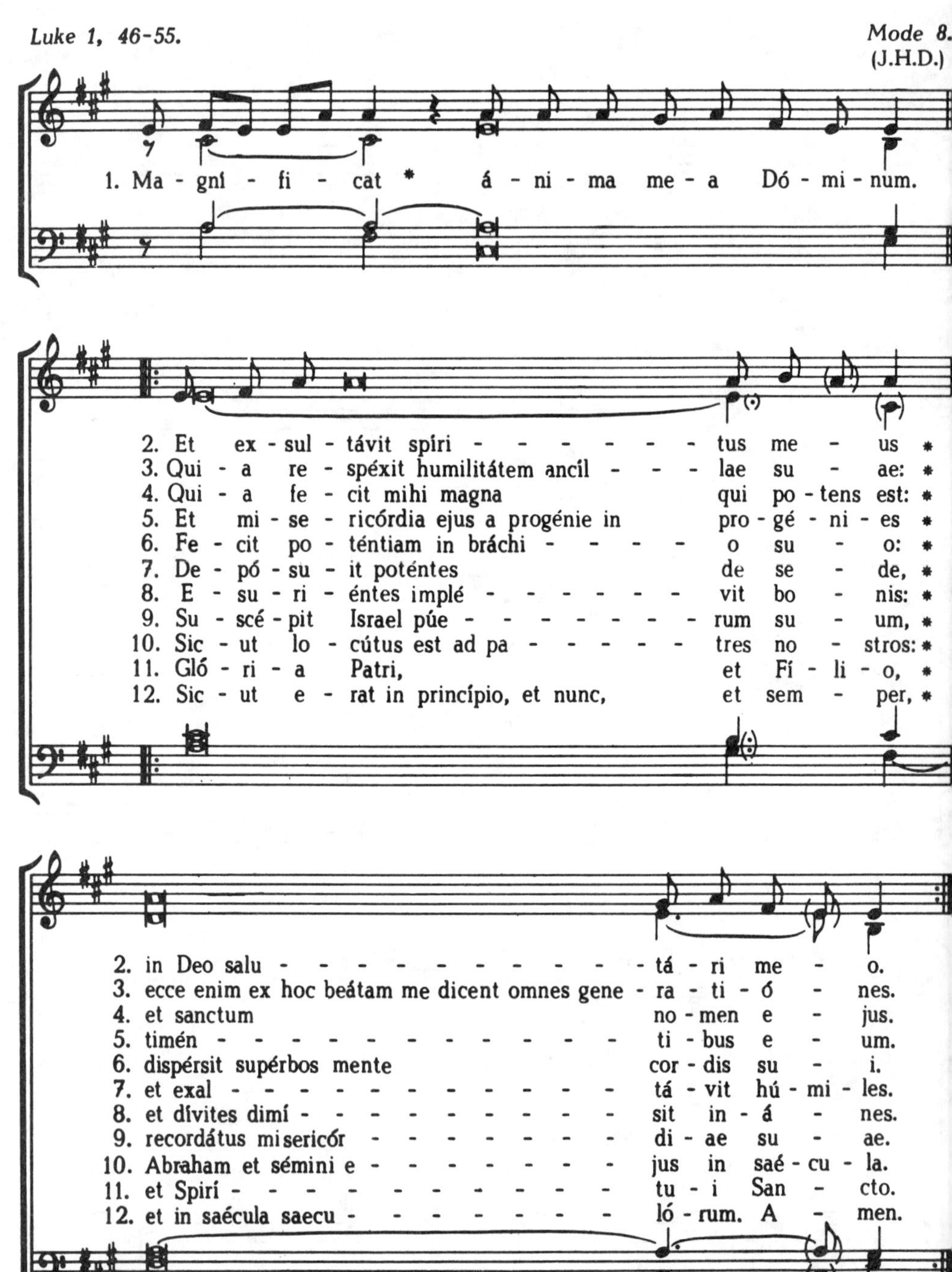
Luke 1, 46-55.
Mode 8.
(J.H.D.)
1. Ma - gní - fi - cat * á - ni - ma me - a Dó - mi - num.
2. Et ex - sul - távit spíri - - - - - - - - tus me - us *
3. Qui - a re - spéxit humilitátem ancíl - - - lae su - ae: *
4. Qui - a fe - cit mihi magna qui po - tens est: *
5. Et mi - se - ricórdia ejus a progénie in pro - gé - ni - es *
6. Fe - cit po - téntiam in bráchi - - - - - o su - o: *
7. De - pó - su - it poténtes de se - de, *
8. E - su - ri - éntes implé - - - - - - - vit bo - nis: *
9. Su - scé - pit Israel púe - - - - - - - - rum su - um, *
10. Sic - ut lo - cútus est ad pa - - - - - tres no - stros: *
11. Gló - ri - a Patri, et Fí - li - o, *
12. Sic - ut e - rat in princípio, et nunc, et sem - per, *
2. in Deo salu - - - - - - - - - - - - - tá - ri me - o.
3. ecce enim ex hoc beátam me dicent omnes gene - ra - ti - ó - nes.
4. et sanctum no - men e - jus.
5. timén - - - - - - - - - - - - - - ti - bus e - um.
6. dispérsit supérbos mente cor - dis su - i.
7. et exal - - - - - - - - - - - - - tá - vit hú - mi - les.
8. et dívites dimí - - - - - - - - - - - sit in - á - nes.
9. recordátus misericór - - - - - - - - - di - ae su - ae.
10. Abraham et sémini e - - - - - - - - - jus in saé - cu - la.
11. et Spirí - - - - - - - - - - - - - tu - i San - cto.
12. et in saécula saecu - - - - - - - - - ló - rum. A - men.

MY SOUL MAGNIFIES THE LORD

Magnificat anima mea.
Luke 1, 46-55.
Confraternity Tr., 1950.

Mode 8.
(J.H.D.)

1. My soul mag-ni-fies the Lord, * and my spir-it re-joic-es in God my Sav-ior;

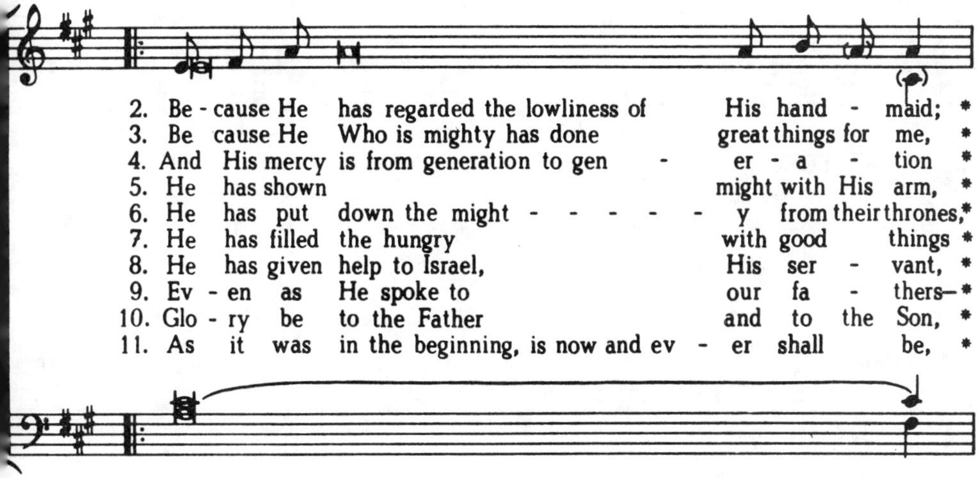

2. Be-cause He has regarded the lowliness of His hand - maid; *
3. Be cause He Who is mighty has done great things for me, *
4. And His mercy is from generation to gen - er - a - tion *
5. He has shown might with His arm, *
6. He has put down the might - - - - - - y from their thrones,*
7. He has filled the hungry with good things *
8. He has given help to Israel, His ser - vant, *
9. Ev - en as He spoke to our fa - thers— *
10. Glo - ry be to the Father and to the Son, *
11. As it was in the beginning, is now and ev - er shall be, *

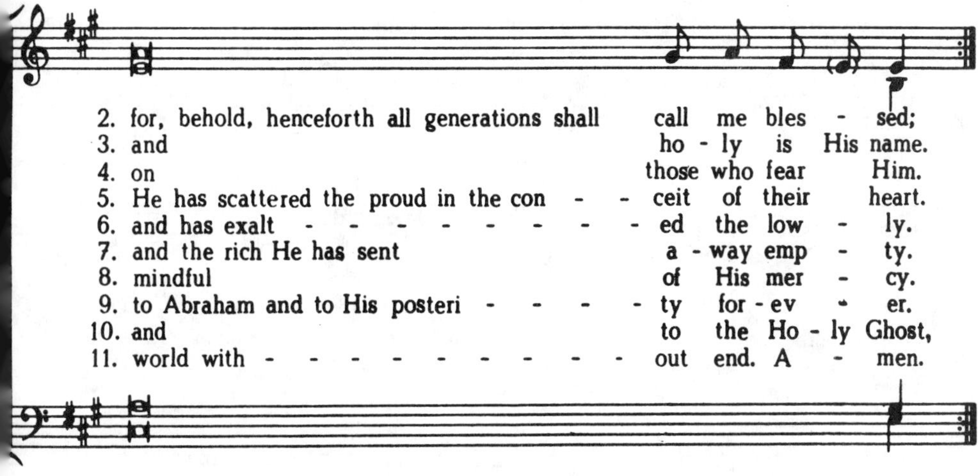

2. for, behold, henceforth all generations shall call me bles - sed;
3. and ho - ly is His name.
4. on those who fear Him.
5. He has scattered the proud in the con - - - ceit of their heart.
6. and has exalt - - - - - - - - - - - ed the low - ly.
7. and the rich He has sent a - way emp - ty.
8. mindful of His mer - cy.
9. to Abraham and to His posteri - - - - - ty for - ev - er.
10. and to the Ho - ly Ghost,
11. world with - - - - - - - - - - - - - out end. A - men.

DAILY, DAILY SING TO MARY

Omni die dic Mariae.
BERNARD OF CLUNY, *d.c. 1150.*
Tr. HENRY BITTLESTON, *d. 1886, &* I. U.

Trier Gesangbuch, 1695.
Harmony: JOHN E. RONAN

1. Dai - ly, dai - ly sing to Ma - ry, Sing, my soul, her prais - es due:
2. She is might - y in her plead - ing, Ten - der in her lov - ing care;
3. All our gra - ces flow through Ma - ry; All then join her praise to sing:

1. All her feasts, her ac - tions hon - or With the heart's de - vo - tion true.
2. Ev - er watch - ful, un - der - stand - ing, All our sor - rows she will share.
3. Fair - est work of all cre - a - tion, Moth - er of cre - a - tion's King.

1. Lost in wond-'ring con - tem - pla - tion, Be her maj - es - ty con - fessed:
2. Ad - vo - cate and lov - ing moth - er, Me - di - a - trix of all grace:
3. Sing in songs of peace un - end - ing, Call up - on her lov - ing - ly:

1. Call her Moth - er, call her Vir - gin, Hap - py Moth - er, Vir - gin blest.
2. Heav - en's bless - ings she dis - pens - es On our sin - ful hu - man race.
3. Seat of wis - dom, Gate of heav - en, Morn - ing star up - on the sea.

HAIL, QUEEN OF HEAVEN, THE OCEAN STAR

After 'Salve, Regina'.
JOHN LINGARD, *d. 1851.*

After a Traditional English Melody.
(H.W.)

1. Hail, Queen of heav'n, the o - cean star, Guide of the
2. O gen - tle, chaste, and spot - less Maid, We sin - ners
3. And while to Him Who reigns a - bove In God - head
1. wan-d'rer here be - low; Thrown on_life's surge, we claim thy care:
2. make our prayers through thee; Re - mind thy Son that He_ has paid
3. one, in Per - sons three, The Source of life, of grace, of love,
1. Save us from per - il and from woe. Moth-er of Christ, O
2. The price of our_ in - i - qui - ty. Vir - gin most pure, O
3. Hom-age we pay_ on bend - ed knee: Do thou, bright Queen, O
1. Star of the sea, Pray for the wan-der-er, pray for me.
2. Star of the sea, Pray for the sin - ner, pray for me.
3. Star of the sea, Pray for thy chil - dren, pray for me.

HOLY QUEEN, WE COME BEFORE THEE

Pulchra tota sine nota.
BERNARD OF CLUNY, *d.c. 1150.*
Tr. EDWARD CASWALL, *d. 1878, alt.*

GEORGE HERBERT, *d. 1906.*
(H.W.)

1. Ho - ly Queen, we come be-fore thee, Queen of pur - i - ty di - vine,
2. Teach thy chil - dren, ho - ly Moth-er, How to con - quer ev - 'ry sin,
3. Oh, by that Al - might - y Mak - er Whom thy-self a vir - gin bore,
1. Make us love thee, we im-plore thee, Make us tru - ly to be thine.
2. How to love and help each oth - er, How e - ter - nal life to win —
3. Oh, by that su - preme Cre - a - tor Whom you praise for - ev - er - more,
1. Thou by faith the gates un-fold - ing Of the king-dom in the skies
2. Thou to whom a Child was giv - en Great - er than the sons of men,
3. By the hope thy name in-spires,_ By our doom re - versed through thee,
1. Hast to us, by faith be-hold - ing, Shown the land of Par - a - dise.
2. Com - ing down from high - est heav - en To cre - ate the world a - gain.
3. Help us, Queen of an - gel choirs,_ To a blest e - ter - ni - ty.

O MOTHER BLEST

Sei pura, sei pia.
ST. ALFONSO DE LIGOURI, C. SS. R., *d. 1787.*
Tr. EDMUND VAUGHAN, C.SS.R., *d. 1908, alt.*

Adapted from a Melody in 'The Roman Hymnal', 1884.
(P.E.S.)

1. O Moth-er blest, whom God be-stows On sin-ners and on just,
2. Re-mem-ber, Ma-ry, Vir-gin fair, It nev-er yet was told
3. O Moth-er blest, for me ob-tain, Un-grate-ful though I be,
1. What joy, what hope thou giv-est those Who in thy mer-cy trust.
2. That he who hum-bly sought thy care De-part-ed un-con-soled.
3. To love that God Who first could deign To show such love to me.
Refrain
Most ho-ly Ma-ry, at thy feet Thy chil-dren bend a sup-pliant knee; Dear Moth-er of my God, Do thou re-mem-ber me.

O PUREST OF CREATURES

FREDERICK W. FABER, *d. 1863,*
& FR. IRVIN, O.F.M. CAP.

Paderborn Gesangbuch, 1765, alt.
(H.W.)

1. O pur - est of crea - tures, sweet Moth - er, sweet Maid, The
2. O fair - est of vir - gins, sweet Moth - er, sweet Maid, Whom
3. Oh, may thy pure light on our souls ev - er shine; And
1. one spot - less womb where - in Je - sus was laid, All
2. God in His good - ness with beau - ty ar - rayed. He
3. keep them un - sul - lied and sin - less as thine, Till
1. lost in the dark - ness we call up - on thee, And
2. lov - ing - ly chose thee His moth - er to be; He
3. af - ter this ex - ile u - nit - ed we be, Through
1. look to thy shin - ing, bright Star of the Sea.
2. shone in thy shin - ing, bright Star of the Sea..
3. a - ges un - end - ing, in glo - ry with thee.

THE LORD WHOM EARTH AND STARS

Quem terra, pontus, sidera.
Ascribed to VENANTIUS FORTUNATUS, *d. 609.*
Tr. EDWARD CASWALL, *d. 1878, alt.*

'Cantarium S. Galli', 1845.
(C.O'S.)

1. The Lord Whom earth and stars and sea With one adoring voice resound, Who rules them all in majesty, In Mary's heart a cloister found.
2. O Mother, blessed by God's command, The Lord Who made the earth and sky And holds the world within His hand, Within your body deigned to lie.
3. O Mother by the angel blessed, Made fruitful by the Spirit's grace, Within your womb He took His rest, Awaited by the human race.
4. Eternal glory to the Son Who came to earth through Mary pure, With Father and with Spirit one, While endless ages yet endure.

THE FIVE LESSER JOYS OF MARY

EDWARD C. CURRIE.

Traditional Irish Melody.
(E.C.C.)

1. When Ma - ry, im - mac - u - late, ten - der and mild, Could find but a man - ger as crib for her Child,
2. When Ma - ry saw Je - sus, her ba - by, a - sleep, His pil - low, the straw in a sta - ble for sheep,
3. When Ma - ry thought sad - ly that Christ, the great King, Had none but poor shep - herds their hom - age to bring,
4. When Ma - ry lost Je - sus and sought in de - spair, She looked in the tem - ple and lo, He was there.
5. When Ma - ry saw Je - sus on Cal - va - ry's hill, The cru - ci - fied Vic - tim, o - bey - ing God's will,

THE FIVE LESSER JOYS OF MARY

1. Her— pure heart re - joiced in the—
2. Her— sor - row was— great when, be -
3. Then— kings from the— O - ri - ent—
4. The— heart of the— moth - er was—
5. A— sword pierced her— heart, yet she—
1. In - fant so fair, Pro - tec - ted
2. hold from the sky, Bright— choirs of
3. came to a - dore, And— Ma - ry,
4. filled with great joy To— find midst
5. knew, though she wept, That— Christ, our
1. by— Jo - seph, the— ho - ly one, near.
2. God's an - gels brought joy from on high.
3. His— moth - er, was— joy - ful once more.
4. the— doc - tors her— well - be - loved Boy.
5. Re - deem - er, was— God's prom - ise kept.

THOU THAT ART SO FAIR AND BRIGHT

Anon., 13th Cent.
After a Melody of JOSEPH POTHIER, O.S.B., d. 1923. (E.C.C.)
1. Thou that art so fair and bright, Ve - lut ma - ris stel - la,
2. All this world was so for - lorn, E - va pec - ca - tri - ce,
3. La - dy, flow'r of ev - 'ry - thing, Ro - sa si - ne spi - na,
1. Bright - er than the day is light, Pa - rens et pu - él - la,
2. Till our Lord was in it born, De te ge - ne - trí - ce;
3. Gave us Je - sus, heav - en's King, Grá - ti - a di - ví - na;
1. I cry to thee, look thou on me, La - dy, pray thy Son for me,
2. With A - ve, sor - row went a - way, Dark - est night to bright - est day,
3. Of ev - 'ry - one thou bear'st the prize, La - dy, Queen of Par - a - dise,
1. Tam_ pi - a, So that I might come to thee, Ma - rí - a.
2. Sa - lú - tis, From thee came the sav - ing ray, Vir - tú - tis.
3. E - lé - cta, Maid - en mild and Moth - er wise, Es ef - fé - cta.

ALMA REDEMPTORIS MATER*

Ascribed to
HERMANNUS CONTRACTUS, *d. 1054.*

Simple Tone, Mode 5.
(J.H.D.)

Al - - ma * Red - em - ptó - ris Ma - ter,
quae pér - vi - a cae - li por - ta ma - nes,
Et stel - la ma - ris, suc - cúr - re ca - dén - ti
súr - ge - re qui cu - rat pó - pu - lo:

* From Vespers of Saturday before the first Sunday of Advent until Second Vespers of the Purification, February 2.

ALMA REDEMPTORIS MATER

Tu quae ge - nu - í - sti, na - tú - ra mi - rán - te,
tu - um san - ctum Ge - ni - tó - rem:
Vir - go pri - us ac po - sté - ri - us,
Ga - bri - é - lis ab o - re su - mens
il - lud A - ve, pec - ca - tó - rum mi - se - ré - re.

AVE, REGINA CAELORUM*

Anon., 12th Cent.

Simple Tone, Mode 6.
(J.H.D.)

A - ve, Re - gí - na cae - ló - rum, * A - ve,

Dó - mi - na an - ge - ló - rum: Sal - ve ra - dix,

sal - ve por - ta, Ex qua mun - do lux est or - ta:

Gau - de, Vir - go glo - ri - ó - sa, Su - per

o - mnes spe - ci - ó - sa: Va - le, O val - de

de - có - ra, Et pro no - bis Chri-stum ex - ó - ra.

*From Compline of February 2 until Compline of Wednesday in Holy Week.

SALVE, REGINA*

Ascribed to
HERMANNUS CONTRACTUS, *d. 1054.*

Simple Tone, Mode 5.
(J.H.D.)

Sal - ve, Re - gí - na, * Ma - ter mi - se - ri - cór - di - ae:
Vi - ta, dul - cé - do, et spes no - stra, sal - ve.
Ad te cla - má - mus, éx - su - les, fí - li - i He - vae.
Ad te su - spi - rá - mus, ge - mén - tes et flen - tes
in hac la - cri - má - rum val - le. E - ia er - go,

* From First Vespers of the Feast of the Trinity until None on Saturday before the first Sunday of Advent.

SALVE, REGINA

Ad - vo - cá - ta no - stra, il - los tu - os
mi - se - ri - cór - des ó - cu - los ad nos con - vér - te.
Et Je - sum, be - ne - dí - ctum fru - ctum
ven - tris tu - i, no - bis post hoc ex - sí - li - um
o - stén - de. O cle - mens, O pi - a,
O dul - cis Vir - go Ma - rí - a.

 CONSECRATION TO OUR LADY

ALL OF SEEING, ALL OF HEARING

FR. M. J., O.C.S.O.
A MONK OF GETHSEMAN
1. All of see - ing, all of hear - ing, Ev - 'ry fra - grance
2. All the heart can know of sad - ness, Ev - 'ry thing it
3. All the soul can claim of wis - dom, All it stores in
4. All our hearts per - ceive as lof - ty, All that moves our
1. we per - ceive, All our touch and all our tast - ing,
2. knows of joy, Ev - 'ry thing it feels as fear - some,
3. mem - o - ry, All the sci - ence that we mas - ter,
4. will to love, Ev - 'ry gift that makes us Christ - like,
1. In thy Heart we con - se - crate. In its cool - ing
2. In thy Heart we con - se - crate. In its no - ble
3. In thy Heart we con - se - crate. In its hum - ble
4. In thy Heart we con - se - crate. In its liv - ing
1. fire, Ma - ry, All our sen - ses im - mo - late.
2. fire, Ma - ry, All our pas - sions el - e - vate.
3. fire, Ma - ry, All our know - ledge ded - i - cate.
4. fire, Ma - ry, All our be - ing con - sum - mate.

OUR LADY OF LOURDES

IMMACULATE MARY

Traditional.

Lourdes 'Ave Maria' Tune. (E.C.C.)

1. Im - ma - cu - late Ma - ry, thy prais - es
2. In heav - en, the bles - sed thy glo - ry
3. Thy name is our pow - er, thy vir - tues
4. We pray for our moth - er, the Church up -
1. we__ sing, Who reign - est in splen - dor with
2. pro - claim; On earth, we thy chil - dren in -
3. our__ light, Thy love is our com - fort, thy
4. on__ earth; And bless, dear - est La - dy, the
Refrain
1. Je - sus, our__ King.
2. voke thy fair__ name.
3. plead - ing our__ might.
4. land of our__ birth.
A - ve, A - ve, A - ve, Ma -
ri - a! A - ve, A - ve, Ma - ri - - - - a!

145 THE ANNUNCIATION

HAIL MARY, FULL OF GRACE

After BEDE CAMM, O. S. B.
Adapted by M. O. L.
HEALEY WILLAN
1. Hail Ma - ry, full of grace, Hail, flow'r of A - dam's race, Who gave the Son of God a dwell - ing; He found a place of rest With - in your sin - less breast: Oh, won - der - ful be - yond all tell - ing!
2. Hail Queen en-throned a - bove, Hail, mir - a - cle of love And wond - rous work of God's per - fec - tion; O love - ly morn - ing star Clear shin - ing from a - far, We sin - ners hope for your pro - tec - tion.
3. Through you all gra - ces flow To men on earth be - low; Through you is ev - 'ry fa - vor giv - en; Help us to con - quer sin That we may en - ter in Through you, O bles - sed gate, to heav - en.

IN THIS YOUR MONTH, CREATION'S QUEEN

FR. M. A., O. C. S. O. A MONK OF GETHSEMANI.

1. In this your month, cre - a - tion's Queen, When fields have blos-somed
2. O Moth - er, you who ruled the House At Naz - a - reth up -
3. We pray you, then, to set up - on Your chil - dren cor - o -
4. And as we spread be - fore your eyes These paths of_ praise with

1. and the_ trees, The di - a - dem of__ flow'rs we bring With
2. on the_ hill, Your Son has set up - on your brow A
3. nals of__ grace To bright - en joy of__ in - no - cence Or
4. blos - soms strown, We ask that you, when time shall cease, Will

1. your great maj - es - - ty a - grees, For Sol - o - mon, in__
2. crown of__ stars so you may still Rule o - ver_ an - gels_
3. tears of__ sad - ness to ef - face, That all may_ cel - e -
4. call us_ as Christ's ver - y__ own, To stand be - side the_

1. all his state, Was_ not ar - rayed as__ one of these.
2. and the earth, And_ see that_ all things do His will.
3. brate your love When we shall see you_ face to face.
4. Crys - tal Sea And_ cast our_ crowns be - fore His throne.

147

QUEEN OF THE WORLD

QUEEN, WHEN THE WORLD WAS FIRST HURLED INTO SPACE

Rerum supremo in vertice.
Hymn at Vespers, 1955.
Tr. M. O. L.

CARROLL T. ANDREWS

1. Queen, when the earth was first hurled in - to space;
2. Queen, who was des - tined to bear as a Son,
3. Queen, when your on - ly Son hung on the tree,
4. Queen, when the morn - ing stars burst in - to song;
1. Queen, when the stars were first sped on their race;
2. Him by whose will all the plan - ets are spun;
3. Steeped in the pur - ple of blood roy - al - ty;
4. Queen, when the sons of God shout - ed a - long:
1. Vir - gin all love - ly, ex - al - ted on high,
2. You were the love - li - est work of His hands,
3. Shar - ing the suff - 'rings of His Pas - sion then,
4. Hear us your sons as we joy - ful - ly sing
1. Gate of the ci - ty of God in the sky.
2. Pass - ing in beau - ty the seas and the lands.
3. Queen you be - came of all suf - fer - ing men.
4. Prais - es of heav - en, its Queen and its King.

MEDIATRIX OF ALL GRACES
MARIA, MATER GRATIAE
O Mary, Mother Full of Grace

Quem terra, pontus, sidera.
Ascribed to VENANTIUS FORTUNATUS, *d. 609. Tr.* M. O. L.

A MONK OF GETHSEMANI.

1. Ma - rí - a, Ma - ter grá - ti - ae, Dul -
2. Je - su, ti - bi sit gló - ri - a, Qui
1. O Ma - ry, Moth - er full of grace, Moth -
2. E - ter - nal praise to Thee, O Lord, Born

1. cis pa - rens cle - mén - ti - ae, Tu
2. na - tus es de Vír - gi - ne, Cum
1. er of love and mer - cy, hear! Help
2. of a Vir - gin ev - er pure; Praise

1. nos ab ho - ste pró - te - ge, Et
2. Pa - tre et al - mo Spí - ri - tu, In
1. us our en - e - my to face, And
2. to the ho - ly Trin - i - ty While

1. mor - tis ho - ra sú - sci - pe.
2. sem - pi - tér - na saé - cu - la. A - men.
1. at the hour of death be near.
2. end - less a - ges yet en - dure. A - men.

MARY IMMACULATE, MOTHER AND MAID

EDWARD C. CURRIE.
From a Chorale by
J. C. KITTEL, d. 180
1. Ma - ry im - mac - u - late, Moth - er and Maid!
2. Vir - gin most pow - er - ful, hear as we pray!
1. Help of all Chris - tians who ask for your aid;
2. Ev - er be near to us, guard us each day.
1. Ref - uge of sin - ners and strength of the frail,
2. Guide us, O Ma - ry, un - til life is done;
1. Shield of the trou - bled heart when doubts as - sail.
2. Then at last may we find heav - en is won.

LADY OF THE VISITATION

Quo sanctus ardor te rapit?
JEAN-BAPTISTE DE SANTEÜIL, *d. 1697.*
Tr. M. O. L.

'Maintzisch Gesangbuch', 1661.
(G. C.)

1. La - dy of the Vis - i - ta - tion,
2. Christ it is you bear with - in you;
3. See, E - liz - a - - beth in greet - ing
4. 'Bles - sed is the fruit of thy womb',
5. Hon - or, glo - ry, praise and pow - er
1. Daugh - ter of a roy - al name,
2. Love it is that leads you on
3. Comes to meet you with the word:
4. So your cous - in claims her Lord,
5. Be to You, the Vir - gin's Son,
Where so quick - ly
To at - tend your
'Blest art thou a -
Him Who lies with -
With the Fa - ther
1. are you run - ning, Glow - ing with the Spir - it's flame?
2. ho - ly cous - in At the birth of John, her son.
3. mong all wom - en,' Words as wom - an nev - er heard.
4. in your bod - y, King Im - mor - tal, Christ a - dored.
5. and the Spir - it, While e - ter - nal a - ges run.

151 ASSUMPTION OF OUR LADY

CONCORDI LAETITIA

Anon., 13th Cent.

Mode 6.
PIERRE DE CORBEIL, *d. 1222*
(J.H.D.)

1. Con - cór - di lae - tí - ti - a, Pro - púl - sa mae -
2. Quam con - cén - tu pá - ri - li Cho - ri lau - dant
3. O Re - gí - na vír - gi - num, Vo - tis fa - ve
4. Glo - ri - ó - sa Trí - ni - tas, In - di - ví - sa

1. stí - ti - a, Ma - rí - ae prae - có - ni - a
2. caé - li - ci, Et nos cum cae - lé - sti - bus,
3. súp - pli - cum, Et post mor - tis stá - di - um,
4. U - ni - tas, Ob Ma - rí - ae mé - ri - ta,

1. Ré - co - lat Ec - clé - si - a: Vir - go Ma - rí - a.
2. No - vum me - los pán - gi - mus: Vir - go Ma - rí - a.
3. Vi - tae con - fer práe - mi - um: Vir - go Ma - rí - a.
4. Nos sal - va per saé - cu - la: Vir - go Ma - rí - a.

SOUNDS OF JOY HAVE PUT TO FLIGHT

Concordi laetitia.
Anon., 13th Cent.
Tr. M. O. L.

PIERRE DE CORBEIL, *d. 1222.*
(S.M.F.)

1. Sounds of joy have put to flight All the sad - ness of the night; Now a maid be - yond com - pare Hears her prais - es fill the air: Vir - go Ma - rí - a.
2. Who is she whom an - gels sing, Mak - ing all cre - a - tion ring? She it is who wins our praise, As on earth our voice we raise: Vir - go Ma - rí - a.
3. Queen of vir - gins, Maid - en mild, Hear me, take me for your child. Ev - er my pro - tec - tor be; Bring e - ter - nal life to me: Vir - go Ma - rí - a.
4. Might - y God - head, Three in One, While e - ter - nal a - ges run, Look to Ma - ry, full of grace, And for - give the hu - man race: Vir - go Ma - rí - a.

153

ASSUMPTION OF OUR LADY

HAIL, HOLY QUEEN ENTHRONED ABOVE

Salve Regina caelitum.
Tr. Traditional, adapted
by M. O. L.

Traditional Melod
(H.W.)

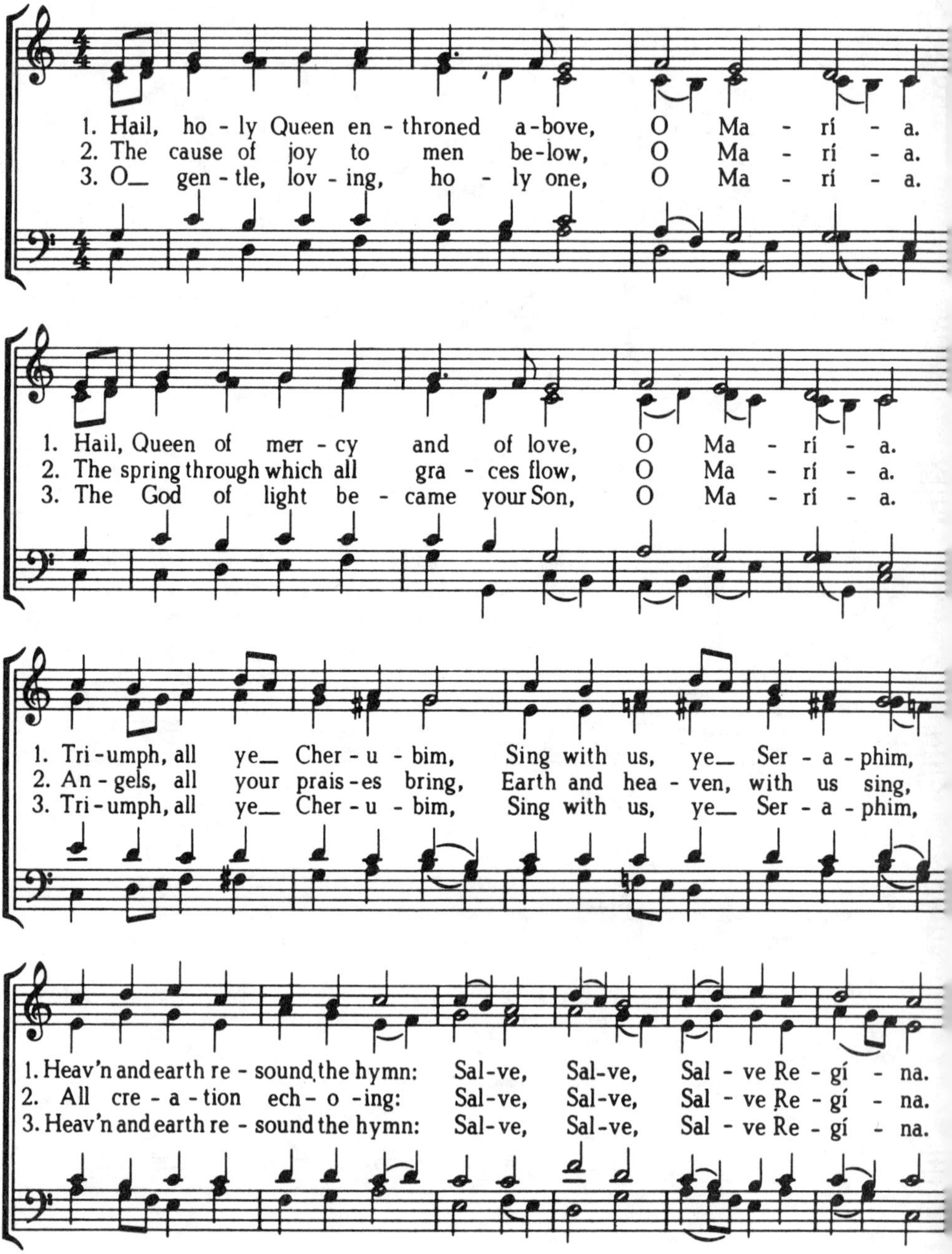
1. Hail, ho - ly Queen en - throned a-bove, O Ma - rí - a.
2. The cause of joy to men be-low, O Ma - rí - a.
3. O_ gen - tle, lov - ing, ho - ly one, O Ma - rí - a.
1. Hail, Queen of mer - cy and of love, O Ma - rí - a.
2. The spring through which all gra - ces flow, O Ma - rí - a.
3. The God of light be - came your Son, O Ma - rí - a.
1. Tri - umph, all ye_ Cher - u - bim, Sing with us, ye_ Ser - a - phim,
2. An - gels, all your prais - es bring, Earth and hea - ven, with us sing,
3. Tri - umph, all ye_ Cher - u - bim, Sing with us, ye_ Ser - a - phim,
1. Heav'n and earth re - sound the hymn: Sal-ve, Sal-ve, Sal - ve Re - gí - na.
2. All cre - a - tion ech - o - ing: Sal-ve, Sal-ve, Sal - ve Re - gí - na.
3. Heav'n and earth re - sound the hymn: Sal-ve, Sal-ve, Sal - ve Re - gí - na.

O HEART OF MARY, PURE AND FAIR

Anon., alt.

T. WORSLEY STANIFORTH, *d. 1909.* (C.T.A.)

1. O heart of Ma - ry, pure and fair, And
2. As some fair lil - y grown in thorns, Your
3. The Heart of Christ, by God's de - cree, Was
4. You kept His words with - in your heart And
1. free from sin's do - main, In A - dam's fall you
2. heart so full of grace With spot - less pur - i -
3. formed be - neath your heart; We long to love you
4. gave them ven - er - a - tion; Give us the grace which
1. had no share, In you there is no stain.
2. ty a - dorns Our sin - ful fal - len race.
3. just as He,— In your love give us part.
4. they im - part; Give us their con - so - la - tion.

HOLY NAME OF MARY

I'LL SING A HYMN TO MARY

JOHN WYSE, *d. 1898.*

Traditional German Melod
(H.W.)

1. I'll sing a hymn to Ma - ry, The Moth - er of my
2. The saints are high in glo - ry, With gol - den crowns so
1. God, The Vir - gin of all vir - gins, Of Da - vid's roy - al
2. bright; But bright - er far is Ma - ry Up - on her throne of
1. blood. Oh, teach me, ho - ly Ma - ry, A
2. light. Oh, that which God did give thee, Let
1. lov - ing song to frame, When wick - ed men blas -
2. mor - tal ne'er dis - claim; When wick - ed men blas -
1. pheme thee, To love and bless thy name.
2. pheme thee, I'll love and bless thy name.

QUEEN OF THE HOLY ROSARY 156

AVE, REGINA SACRATISSIMI ROSARII

Glorious Mary

From the Litany of Loreto.
English adapted by P.E.S.

SR. M. FLORIAN, S.S.J.

A - ve, Re - gí - - na Sa - cra - tís - si - mi
Glo - ri - ous Ma - ry, Queen and Giv - er of

Ro - sá - ri - i, O - ra pro no - bis.
the Ro - sa - ry, Pray for us, your chil - dren.

Fine

A - ve Re - gí - na Sa - cra - tís - si - mi
In your most ho - ly joys, in your sor - rows and

Ro - sá - ri - i, O - ra pro no - bis.
your glo - - ries, You, our Queen, we hon - or.

D. C.

157 QUEEN OF THE HOLY ROSARY

O QUEEN OF THE HOLY ROSARY

EMILY M. SHAPCOTE, *d. c. 1906,*
& FR. IRVIN, O.F.M. CAP.

Wirtemburg Gesangbuch, 1784
(T.C.K.)

1. O Queen of the Holy Rosary, Oh, bless us as we pray, And offer thee our roses In garlands day by day, While from our Father's garden With loving hearts and bold, We gather to thine honor Buds white and red and gold.

2. O Queen of the Holy Rosary, Each myst'ry blends with thine The sacred life of Jesus In ev'ry step divine. Thy soul was His fair garden, Thy virgin breast His throne, Thy thoughts His faithful mirror Reflecting Him alone.

3. O Queen of the Holy Rosary, We share thy joy and pain, And long to see the glory Of Christ's triumphant reign. Oh, teach us holy Mary, To live each mystery, And gain by patient suff'ring The glory won by thee.

WHAT MORTAL TONGUE CAN SING YOUR PRAISE

Quis te canat mortalium?
JEAN-BAPTISTE DE SANTEÜIL, *d. 1697.*
Tr. EDWARD CASWALL, *d. 1878, alt.*

Adapted from a Traditional Melody.
(C.O'S.)

1. What mor - tal tongue can sing your praise, Dear
2. O Vir - gin, say what force was it That
3. In - stead, it was your low - li - ness, Well
1. Moth - er of the Lord? To an - gels on - ly
2. from the Fa - ther's throne Drew forth His co - e -
3. pleas - ing to the Lord, That made you wor - thy
1. it be - longs Your glo - ry to re - cord. Who
2. ter - nal Son To be your ver - y own. Not
3. to be - come The Moth - er of the Word. Praise
1. born of man can un - der - stand Your soul's maj - es - tic grace?
2. on - ly your un - bound-ed faith Has raised you o - ver all;
3. to the Fa - ther with the Son And Ho - ly Ghost, through Whom
1. Who can your might - y gifts un - fold, Or all your hon - ors trace?
2. Not your de - vot - ed love a - lone Could earn you heav-en's call.
3. The Word e - ter - nal was con-ceived With - in the Vir - gin's womb.

159

OUR LADY OF VICTORY

O QUEEN OF PEERLESS MAJESTY

O Königin voll Herrlichkeit.
WILHELM MOLITOR, *pub. 1861.*
Tr. Traditional, alt.

Melody by JOHANN B. BENZ, *pub. 1861.* (H.W.)

1. O Queen of peer-less maj-es-ty, Ma-rí - - a!
2. O morn-ing star that scat-ters night, Ma-rí - - a!
3. O heav-en's por-tal, Vir-gin pure, Ma-rí - - a!
1. Thou glo-rious Queen of vic-to-ry, Ma-rí - - a!
2. Up-on our dark-ness spread thy light, Ma-rí - - a!
3. An en-trance safe for us pro-cure, Ma-rí - - a!
1. All to thee sub-ject-ed lies, All cre-a-tion lifts its eyes:
2. When we toss on storm-y waves, Thou the star that leads and saves:
3. Show us mer-cy when we die, Lead us to thy Son on high:
Refrain
O stand be-side us, Pro-tect and guide us In
death and life, In ev-'ry strife, Ma-rí - - - a!

O VIRGIN ALL LOVELY

O Vierge très belle.
F. LE DORZ.
Tr. SR. MARY GERTRUDE, C.S.J.

F. BRUN, *d. 1943.*
(E.C.C.)

1. O Vir - gin all love - ly, O Moth - er all gra - cious, O
2. O Dwel - ling of glo - ry, Thou Whit - er than i - v'ry, O
3. O Vir - gin all ho - ly, Thy soul filled with gra - ces, O

1. Daugh - ter of God. O Star bright - ly shin - ing, O
2. House all of gold. The Word there re - si - deth; Thy
3. Moth - er of God. Be near us in dan - ger; To

Refrain

1. Rose sweet - ly fra - grant, O Lil - y pure.
2. God thou a - dor - est In joy - ous love. Joy - ous we
3. us make pro - pi - tious Thy Son, our Judge.

praise thee, Vir - gin all love - ly, O Daugh - ter of God.

OUR LADY OF FATIMA

NOW THE WORLD IS SAVED FROM DARKNESS

M. OWEN LEE, C.S.B.

Ascribed to JAKOB HINTZE, *d. 1702.*
Altered from the version of
JOHANN S. BACH, *d. 1750.* (P.E.S.)

1. Now the world is saved from dark - ness:
2. La - dy, we of ev - - 'ry na - tion
1. Ma - ry's e - ra is be - gun;
2. Hum - bly come be - - fore your face,
1. See, her sign ap - pears in heav - en:
2. Of - fer - ing our rep - - a - ra - tion;
1. Fat - i - ma's re - splend - ent sun.
2. Take us to the throne of grace.

NOW THE WORLD IS SAVED FROM DARKNESS

1. La - dy, with the sun for rai - ment,
2. End the wars that rage a - round us,
1. Come to us, dis - - pel our night;
2. In our weak - ness prove your might;
1. As at Fat - i - ma you prom - ised,
2. Fat - i - ma will mean for - give - ness,
1. Be our La - dy of the light.
2. You, its Queen, will be our light.

OUR LADY OF GUADALUPE

BECAUSE YOU LIVE AGAIN, O ROSE

Adapted from the Ancient 'Abatal', 1532.
SR. M. FRANCIS, P. C. & M. OWEN LEE, C.S.B.

Traditional French Melody.
(E.C.C.)

1. Be - cause you live a - gain, O Rose
2. O Vir - gin, Rose in bram - bles grown,
3. God made you love - ly past com - pare,
4. We pray, pro - tect us as your own

1. Who bloomed in Gua - da - lu - pe's snows,
2. Who chose this peo - ple for your own,
3. Your life was one un - fold - ing prayer;
4. And in - ter - cede at Heav - en's throne;

1. In this your im - age, flow - 'ring fair,
2. Your flow - 'ring im - age glo - ri - fies
3. And then He fash - ioned you__ a - gain,
4. While here we kneel be - fore your face,

1. Our songs as flow - ers fill the air.
2. The tan - gled brush - wood of our lives.
3. An im - age which__ He gave to men.
4. Send down a ray__ of sav - ing grace.

163

DEAR ANGEL, EVER AT MY SIDE

FREDERICK W. FABER, *d. 1863, alt.*

Adapted from Day's Psalter, 1563. (E.C.C.)

1. Dear an - gel, ev - er at my side, How
2. Your beau - ti - ful and shin - ing face Is
3. My eyes see on - ly here be - low, But
4. My guard - ian an - gel, help me now To
1. lov - ing you must be To leave your home in
2. al - ways ver - y near; The mus - ic of your
3. you are by my side, And you have God be -
4. give to God my love, To serve Him in this
1. heav'n to guide A lit - tle child like me!
2. guid - ing voice Is ev - er in my ear.
3. fore your eyes; I need you for my guide.
4. world be - low And come to Him a - bove.

164 SAINT MICHAEL AND ALL ANGELS

MICHAEL, PRINCE OF ALL THE ANGELS

M. OWEN LEE, C.S.B.
WILLIAM J. MARSH.
1. Mi - chael, prince of all the__ an - gels,
2. Might - y champ - ion of the__ wom - an,
3. Ga - briel, mes - sen - ger to__ Ma - ry,
1. While your le - gions fill the sky,
2. Might - y ser - vant of her Lord,
3. Raph - ael, heal - er, friend and guide,
1. All vic - to - rious o - ver__ Sa - tan,
2. Come with all your myr - iad__ war - riors,
3. All you hosts of guard - ian__ an - gels
1. Lift your flam - ing sword on high;
2. Come and save us with your sword;
3. Ev - er stand - ing by our side,

MICHAEL, PRINCE OF ALL THE ANGELS

1. Shout to all the seas and heav - ens:
2. En - e - mies of God sur - round us:
3. Vir - tues, Thrones and Dom - i - na - tions,
1. Now the morn - ing is be - gun;
2. Share with us your burn - ing love;
3. Raise on high your joy - ful hymn,
1. Now is res - cued from the drag - on
2. Let the in - cense of our wor - ship
3. Prin - ci - pal - i - ties and Pow - ers,
1. She whose gar - ment is the sun!
2. Rise be - fore His throne a - bove!
3. Cher - u - bim and Ser - a - phim!

SAINT PATRICK

WHEN GREAT SAINT PATRICK RAISED THE CROSS

Anon. THOMAS C. KELLY.

1. When great Saint Pat - rick raised the Cross Where
2. Be - hold, his bles - sed al - tars stood Where
3. All praise to God Whose good - ness gave The
1. pa - gan wor - ship long held sway, And bade the peo - ple
2. once had flared the Dru - id fires, While up to heav - en's
3. sav - ing truths Saint Pat - rick taught; And praise to Him for
1. lift their eyes From dark - ness un - to
2. vault a - rose A thou - sand cross - crowned
3. all the deeds That dear Saint Pat - rick

WHEN GREAT SAINT PATRICK RAISED THE CROSS

1. day: The light of faith on Er - in's hills Then
2. spires. And from God's sa - cred tem - ples rang The
3. wrought; All thanks for faith's bright bea - con set To
1. dawned in splen - dor bright and clear, And all her ver - dant
2. peal - ing bells, the call to prayer, And o'er the land from
3. guide us pil - grims home-ward bound, And lead us to that
1. val - leys felt The Lord's own_ pres - ence near.
2. end to end Came peace and_ bles - sings rare.
3. host in bliss, Saint Pat - rick's chil - dren crowned.

166 SAINT PATRICK

PATRICK, THEE ADDRESSING

M. OWEN LEE, C.S.B.

Gaelic Hymn to St. Patrick
(E.C.C.)

1. Pat - rick, thee ad - dress - ing, We to - geth - er pray:
2. Pat - rick, our be - liev - ing All is owed to thee:
3. Pat - rick, wis - dom - bear - ing, Fear - less, God - in - spired:
1. Raise thy hand in bless - ing O - ver us this day.
2. Grant that, grace re - ceiv - ing, We may ho - ly be.
3. In thy ar - dor shar - ing, By thy vir - tue fired,
1. By God's in - spi - ra - tion, Cam - est thou a - flame,
2. We were wrapped in blind - ness, Lost in end - less night,
3. We in ven - er - a - tion Kneel with one ac - cord.
1. Charged to teach our na - tion His most Ho - ly Name.
2. Till with lov - ing kind - ness Thou didst bring us light.
3. Teach thy cho - sen na - tion! Show us Christ, our Lord!

SALVE, PATER SALVATORIS

Anon. 1874. CARROLL T. ANDREWS.

1. Sal - ve, pa - ter Sal - va - tó - ris, Sal - ve, cu - stos
2. Je - sum ó - cu - lis vi - dí - sti Et in brá - chi -
3. O fe - lí - cem et be - á - tum, Cu - sto - dí - ri
1. Red - em - ptó - ris, Jo - seph ter a - má - bi - lis.
2. is tu - lí - sti, O dul - cis fe - lí - ci - tas;
3. qui est da - tum Tu - o sub prae - sí - di - o,
1. Sal - ve, spon - se Ma - tris De - i, Sal - ve, ho - spes
2. Ge - nis ge - nas ad - mo - ví - sti, Ó - scu - la dans
3. Et qui mé - ru - it ha - bé - re Te pa - tró - num
1. Je - su me - i, Jo - seph ter mi - rá - bi - lis.
2. ac - ce - pí - sti, O fe - lix su - á - vi - tas.
3. et gau - dé - re Tu - o pa - tro - cí - ni - o.

168

SAINT JOSEPH

TE, JOSEPH, CELEBRENT

Anon. 1670.

Mode 1.
(J.H.D.)

1. Te, Jo - seph, cé - le - brent ág - mi - na caé - li - tum:
2. Post mor - tem ré - li - quos sors pi - a cón - se - crat,
3. No - bis, sum - ma Tri - as, par - ce pre - cán - ti - bus:
1. Te cun - cti ré - so - nent chri - stí - a - dum cho - ri,
2. Pal - mám - que e - mé - ri - tos gló - ri - a sú - sci - pit:
3. Da, Jo - seph mé - ri - tis, sí - de - ra scán - de - re
1. Qui cla - rus mé - ri - tis, jun - ctus es ín - cly - tae
2. Tu vi - vens, sú - pe - ris par, frú - e - ris De - o,
3. Ut tan - dem lí - ce - at nos ti - bi pér - pe - tim
1. Ca - sto foé - de - re Vír - gi - ni.
2. Mi - ra sor - te be - á - ti - or.
3. Gra - tum pró - me - re cán - ti - cum. A - men.

GUARDIAN OF VIRGINS

Virginum Custos et Pater.
Anon. 19th Cent. Prayer.
English adapted by S. C. M.

SR. CECILIA MIRIAM, S. N. J. M.

1. Guard - ian of vir - gins and ho - ly fa - ther, Jo - seph,
2. Most lov - ing fa - ther,— save us from all er - ror;

1. To whose care were trust - ed Je - sus and Ma - ry,
2. Aid us war - ring with the dread pow'rs of dark - ness.

1. We pray thee, help us serve these lov - ing pledg - es With
2. Thou, strong pro - tec - tor, who didst res - cue Je - sus, Now

1. pure mind and bod - y all the days of our lives.
2. guide us that we may win a glo - ri - ous crown.

170 SAINT JOSEPH

GREAT SAINT JOSEPH, SON OF DAVID

Du aus David's Stamm.
Tr. LOUIS C. CASARTELLI, *d. 1925.*

A. GEREON STEIN, *pub. 1852.*
(T.B.M.)

1. Great Saint Jo - seph, son of___ Da - vid,
2. Three long days, in grief, in___ an - guish,
3. Clasped in Je - sus' arms and___ Ma - ry's,

1. Fos - ter - fa - ther___ of our Lord,
2. With that moth - er sweet and mild,
3. When death gent - ly came at last,

1. Spouse of___ Ma - ry, ev - er___ vir - gin,
2. Ma - ry,___ Vir - gin, didst thou___ wan - der,
3. Thy pure___ spir - it, sweet - ly___ sigh - ing,

1. Keep - ing o'er them___ watch and ward:
2. Seek - ing her be - - lov - ed Child.
3. From its earth - ly___ dwell - ing passed.

GREAT SAINT JOSEPH, SON OF DAVID

1. In the sta - ble thou didst guard them
2. In the tem - ple thou didst find Him:
3. Dear Saint Jo - seph, by that pas - sing
1. With a fa - ther's lov - ing care;
2. Oh, what joy then filled thy heart!
3. May our death be like to thine,
1. Thou by God's com - mand didst save them
2. In thy sor - rows, in thy glad - ness,
3. And with Je - sus, Ma - ry, Jo - seph,
1. From the cru - el Her - od's snare.
2. Grant us, Jo - seph, to have part.
3. May our souls for - - ev - er shine.

171

SAINT JOSEPH

HAIL, HOLY JOSEPH, HAIL

FREDERICK W. FABER *d. 1863, alt.*

ROBERT L. DE PEARSALL, *d. 1856*
in 'Katholisches Gesangbuch', S. Gallen, 1863.

1. Hail, ho - ly Jo - seph, hail! Chaste spouse of Ma - ry, hail! Pure as the lil - y flow - er In E - den's peace - ful vale! Hail, ho - ly Jo - seph, hail! You were God's cho - sen one: To you the Word made flesh Was sub - ject as a Son.
2. Hail, ho - ly Jo - seph, hail! O friend of an - gels, hail! As - sist the hearts that faint And guide the steps that fail. Hail, ho - ly Jo - seph, hail! Prince of the house of God, May His best gra - ces be By your dear hands be - stowed.
3. Hail, ho - ly Jo - seph, hail! Teach us our flesh to tame. And, Ma - ry, keep the hearts That hon - or Jo - seph's name; He loved you with a love Of ho - ly pur - i - ty; We pray that we may be As pure in love as he.

SAINT BENEDICT

O BLESSED BY GOD*

ROGER SCHOENBECHLER, O.S.B.

Traditional Chant from Monte Cassino. (C. O'S.)

1. O blessed by God, Saint Ben - e - dict,
2. Saint Ben - e - dict, to thee we turn,
3. God taught thee to re - ject the wiles
4. In won - drous ray of God's own light
5. Praise, hon - or, glo - ry be to Thee,
1. Let sad - ness not our hearts af - flict, As we our year -
2. The se - crets of God's grace to learn, Oh, guide us by
3. Of sin - ful world, which men be - guiles; Then, like a star
4. The world ap-peared be - fore thy sight; Then thou the emp -
5. Most bles - sed, ho - ly Trin - i - ty, Thy love un - bound -
1. ly trib - ute bring, Thy saint - ly life and glo - ries sing.
2. thy wise de - crees That God a - lone we seek to please.
3. that glit - ters bright, God made of thee a ho - ly light.
4. ti - ness didst see Of earth - ly things what - e'er they be.
5. ed didst im - part Un - to our Saint's en - rap - tured heart.

* Stanza One is sung only on the feast.

173 SAINT ANTHONY

IF, NOW, THOU SEEKEST MIRACLES

Si quaeris miracula.
From a Franciscan Manual.
Tr. Anon.

Vehe's 'Gesangbüchlein', 153
(H.W.)

1. If, now, thou seek - est mir - a - cles: Death, er - ror, all— ca -
2. All dan - gers van - ish from our path, Our dir - est needs do
1. lam - i - ties, The lep - ro - sy and de - mons flee, The
2. quick - ly flee; Let those who know re - peat— the theme, Let
1. sick, by him made whole, a - rise.
2. Chris - tians praise Saint An - tho - ny.
Refrain
The sea with-draws and
fet - ters break; The with - ered limbs he doth re - store, While
treas - ures lost are found a - gain, When young or old his help im - plore.

SAINT BASIL THE GREAT **174**

HAIL, GLORIOUS APOSTLE

AMES B. DOLLARD, d. 1946.
HEALEY WILLAN.
1. Hail,_ glo - rious a - pos - tle, Saint Ba - sil the Great,
2. Des - troy - er of er - ror, strong cham - pion of right,
3. Thou wert zeal - ous and pow'r - ful of work and of word;
1. The stu - dent's pure mod - el, com - pan - ion of youth;
2. Saint Ba - sil, we hail thee and call on thy name;
3. The God - head of Christ thou didst teach and main - tain;
1. We_ greet thee and pray that from heav - en's high state,
2. Through Pon - tus and A - sia shone out thy blest light;
3. To His love by thy preach - ing the mul - ti - tudes stirred,
1. We may share in thy ho - li - ness, vir - tue and truth.
2. Cae - sa - re - a's great pon - tiff, all_ earth knew thy fame.
3. Pro - claimed 'Christ is King, in our_ hearts let Him reign.'

175

SAINT ANNE

GOD MOST TRULY HONORED THEE

EDWARD C. CURRIE.

JAMES E. DALEY, C.S.
(C. O'S.)

1. God most tru - ly hon - ored thee,
2. Thine the child of all our race,
3. Pray for us, O saint - ly Anne:

1. When He willed that thou should'st bear Ma - ry
2. Free from Ad - am's pri - mal stain— Sa - tan's
3. God will ev - er heed thy prayer! Aid us

1. pure be - yond com - pare,— Ho - ly Anne.
2. wiles a - gainst her vain,— Ho - ly Anne.
3. with thy lov - ing care, Good Saint Anne.

SAINT ANNE

LADY IN SORROW

FR. M. J., O.C.S.O. A MONK OF GETHSEMANI.

1. La - dy in sor - row, si - lent thy womb, Pure faith il - lu - mines the dark of thy room, Prom - ise from heav - en re - plies to thy hope. Mid - night Moth - er, stars for thy feet; Ma - ry laughs out in her ho - ly re - treat.
2. Moth - er in glad - ness, mel - o - dies bloom, Fil - ling with sweet-ness the space of thy womb; Grate - ful be, An - na, thou graced from on high! Noon - day Moth - er, cease now thy larms; Ma - ry comes forth to re - pose in thy arms.
3. Moth - er of Ma - ry, Moth - er of grace, Keep us, thy off - spring be - got - ten in faith. Teach us, thy chil - dren, re - joice - ment in God. Eve - ning Moth - er, An - na most dear, Guide us to heav - en and vi - sion all clear.

SAINT DOMINIC

DOMINIC, OUR LADY'S CHAMPION

M. OWEN LEE, C. S. B.

JOHN GOSS, *d. 188*

1. Dom - i - nic, our La - dy's cham - pion, Charged to pub - lish wide her fame, Sent to men to sound her A - ve And to speak her glo - rious name; With the grace of God with - in you, Like a he - ro lord you came.
2. Stain - less as a bur - nished chal - ice, Shin - ing as a fier - y brand, Dom - i - nic, you came to help us, Came to do your Lord's com - mand, With the grace of God with - in you And the ro - sary in your hand.
3. Now a - gain we need your good - ness: Be our pa - tron and our guide. Save us from all sin and er - ror, From our blind - ness and our pride; With the grace of God with - in us, May we stand close by your side.

SAINT FRANCIS XAVIER **178**

GLORIOUS SAINT WHOSE DEEDS IMMORTAL

JOHN DRISCOLL, S. J., *d. 1940.*
'Darmstadt Gesangbuch', 1698.
1. Glo - rious Saint whose deeds im - mor - tal We ex - tol and
2. Beau - ti - ful those feet that car - ried News of God's re -
3. Great thy la - bors in the vine - yard, Great the har - vest
4. Fa - ther, may we share thy tri - umphs, Join thee hence-forth
1. mag - ni - fy, Ra - diant star, whose ris - ing splen - dor
2. demp - tive plan, Cross - ing lands and fur - thest o - ceans,
3. gath - ered in, Great - er still thy soul's - am - bi - tion
4. in the fight, May our lives be flam - ing torch - es,
1. Set a - blaze the o - rient sky; Oh, how bright to -
2. Bring - ing peace to fal - len man, Her - ald who with
3. Fur - ther_ con - ti - nents to win; But God willed thy
4. Pure and_ ho - ly, burn - ing bright, Driv - ing hence the
1. day thy_ shin - ing 'Midst the saints of God on high!
2. torch up - lift - ed Realms of dark-ness o - ver - ran.
3. great - est_ con - quests Should hence - forth in heav'n be - gin.
4. pow'rs of_ dark - ness, Lead - ing to e - ter - nal light.

BLESSED FRANCIS, HOLY FATHER

From a Franciscan Manual. SR. M. THEOPHANE, O.S.F

1. Bles - sed Fran - cis, ho - ly fa - ther,
2. By the love so deep and burn - ing
3. Teach us al - so, dear Saint Fran - cis,
1. Now our hearts to thee we raise,
2. For thy Sav - ior cru - ci - fied;
3. How to mourn for ev - 'ry sin;
1. As we gath - er here be - fore thee,
2. By the tok - ens which He gave thee
3. May we walk in thy dear foot - steps
1. Pour - ing forth our hymn of praise.
2. On thy hands, and feet and side:
3. Till the crown of life we win.

BLESSED FRANCIS, HOLY FATHER

1. Bless thy chil - dren, ho - ly Fran - cis,
2. Bless thy chil - dren, ho - ly Fran - cis,
3. Make us love each price - less vir - tue
1. Who thy might - y help im - plore,
2. With those wound - ed hands of thine,
3. By our hid - den God es - teemed;
1. For in heav - en thou re - main - est
2. From thy glo - rious throne in heav - en,
3. Make them val - ued, ho - ly Fran - cis,
1. Still the fa - ther of the poor.
2. Where re - splend - ent - ly they shine.
3. By the souls of the re - deemed.

APOSTLES

EXSULTET ORBIS GAUDIIS

Let All on Earth Their Voices Raise

Anon., 10th. Cent.
Tr., after RICHARD MANT, *d. 1848.*

PETER E. SHEEHAN, C.S.B.

1. Ex - súl - tet or - bis gáu - di - is, Cae - lum re -
2. Vos, sae - cu - ló - rum jú - di - ces, Et ve - ra
3. Qui tem - pla cae - li cláu - di - tis Se - rás - que
1. Let all on earth their voi - ces raise, Re - sound - ing
2. Thou, at Whose word they bore the light Of Gos - pel
3. Thou, at Whose will to them was giv'n To bind and
1. súl - tet láu - di - bus: A - po - sto - ló - rum
2. mun - di lú - mi - na, Vo - tis pre - cá - mur
3. ver - bo sól - vi - tis, Nos a re - á - tu
1. heav - en's joy - ful praise To Him Who gave th'A -
2. truth to hea - then night, To us that heav'n - ly
3. loose in earth and heav'n, Our chains un - bind, our
1. gló - ri - am Tel - lus et a - stra cón - ci - nunt.
2. cór - di - um: Au - dí - te vo - ces súp - pli - cum.
3. nó - xi - os Sol - vi ju - bé - te, quaé - su - mus.
1. pos - tles grace To run on earth their glo - rious race.
2. light im - part, Make glad our eyes and cheer our heart.
3. sins un - do, And in our hearts Thy grace re - new.

DEUS, TUORUM MILITUM

O God, Thy Soldiers' Faithful Lord

Ambrosian, 6th Cent.
Tr. J. MASON NEALE, *d. 1866, alt.* A MONK OF GETHSEMANI.

1. De - us, tu - ó - rum mí - li - tum Sors
2. Ob hoc pre - cá - tu súp - pli - ci Te
3. Laus et per - én - nis gló - ri - a Pa -
1. O God, Thy sol - diers' faith - ful Lord, Their
2. We hum - bly pray Thee, Lord of love, Re -
3. All praise to God the Fa - ther be; All
1. et co - ró - na, praé - mi - um, Lau - des ca - nén - tes
2. pó - sci - mus, pi - ís - si - me, In hoc tri - úm - pho
3. tri sit, at - que Fí - li - o, San - cto si - mul Pa -
1. por - tion and their great re - ward, From all trans-gres - sions
2. gard us from Thy throne a - bove; On this Thy mar - tyr's
3. praise, e - ter - nal Son, to Thee; Whom with the Spir - it
1. már - ty - ris Ab - sól - ve ne - xu crí - mi - nis.
2. már - ty - ris, Di - mít - te no - xam sér - vu - lis.
3. rá - cli - to, In sem - pi - tér - na saé - cu - la.
1. set us free Who sing Thy mar - tyr's vic - to - ry.
2. tri - umph day, Wash ev - 'ry stain of sin a - way.
3. we a - dore For - ev - er and for - ev - er - more.

ISTE CONFESSOR DOMINI

This is the Day

Anon., 8th Cent.
Tr. JOHN O'CONNOR, *d. 1952.*

A MONK OF GETHSEMANI

1. I - ste Con - fés - sor Dó - mi - ni, co - lén - tes
2. No - ster hinc il - li cho - rus ob - se - quén - tem
3. Sit sa - lus il - li, de - cus at - que vir - tus,
1. This is the day where - on the Lord's true wit - ness,
2. Where - fore to him we raise the sol - emn cho - rus,
3. Heal - ing and pow - er, grace and beau - teous hon - or
1. Quem pi - e lau - dant pó - pu - li per or - bem, Hac di - e
2. Cón - ci - nit lau - dem ce - le - brés-que pal - mas, Ut pi - is
3. Qui su - per cae - li só - li - o co - rú - scans, Tó - ti - us
1. Whom all the na - tions lov - ing - ly do hon - or, Wor - thy at
2. Chant - ing his praise and his sur - pass - ing tri - umph; So may his
3. Al - ways be His Who, shin - ing in the high - est, Rul - eth and
1. lae - tus mé - ru - it su - pré - mos Lau - dis ho - nó - res.
2. e - jus pré - ci - bus ju - vé - mur O - mne per ae - vum.
3. mun - di sé - ri - em gu - bér - nat, Tri - nus et u - nus.
1. last was found to wear for - ev - er Glo - ry trans - cen - dent.
2. plead - ing help us in the bat - tle All through the a - ges.
3. keep - eth all the world's vast or - der, One God, three Per - sons.

VIRGINIS PROLES

Child of a Virgin

Anon., 8th Cent.
Tr. LAURENCE HOUSMAN.
THOMAS B. MAILLOUX, C. S. B.
1. Vír - gi - nis Pro - les, O - pi - féx - que Ma - tris, Vir - go quem
2. Hu - jus o - rá - tu, De - us al - me, no - bis Dé - bi - tas
3. Sit de - cus Pa - tri, ge - ni - taé - que Pro - li, Et ti - bi,
1. Child of a Vir - gin, Mak-er of Thy Moth - er, Thou, Rod and
2. Foun - tain of mer - cy, hear the prayers she of - fers; Purge our of -
3. Thou, the All - Fa - ther, Thou the One-Be - got - ten, Thou Ho - ly
1. ges - sit, pe - pe - rít - que Vir - go, Vír - gi - nis fe - stum
2. poe - nas scé - le - rum re - mít - te, Ut ti - bi pu - ro
3. com - par u - tri - ús - que vir - tus, Spí - ri - tus sem - per,
1. Blos - som from a stem un - stain - èd, Now, while a vir - gin
2. fen - ses, par - don our trans - gres - sions, So that here - af - ter
3. Spir - it, three in one co - e - qual, Glo - ry be hence-forth
1. cá - ni - mus be - á - tae; Ác - ci - pe vo - tum.
2. re - so - né - mus al - mum Pé - cto - re car - men.
3. De - us u - nus, o - mni Tém - po - ris ae - vo.
1. fair of fame we ho - nor, Hear our de - vo - tion.
2. we to Thee may ren - der Praise with thanks - giv - ing.
3. Thine through all the a - ges, World with - out end - ing. A - men.

FORTEM VIRILI PECTORE

The Praises of that Saint We Sing

SILVIO ANTONIANO, *d. 1603.*
Tr. ATHELSTAN RILEY, *d. 1909.*

Adapted from a French Melody
(W.J.M.)

1. For - tem vi - rí - li pé - cto - re Lau -
2. Rex Chri - ste, vir - tus fór - ti - um, Qui
3. De - o Pa - tri sit gló - ri - a, E -
1. The prais - es of that Saint we__ sing, To
2. King Christ, from Whom all vir - tue__springs, Who
3. All praise to God the Fa - ther__ be; All
1. dé - mus o - mnes fé - mi - nam, Quae san - cti - tá - tis
2. ma - gna so - lus éf - fi - cis, Hu - jus pre - cá - tu,
3. jús - que so - li Fí - li - o, Cum Spí - ri - tu Pa -
1. whom all lands their trib - ute bring, Who with in - dom - i -
2. on - ly do - est won - drous things, As now to Thee she
3. praise, e - ter - nal Son, to Thee; Whom with the Spir - it
1. gló - ri - a U - bí - que ful - get ín - cly - ta.
2. quaé - su - mus, Au - di be - ni - gnus súp - pli - ces.
3. rá - cli - to, Nunc et per o - mne saé - cu - lum.
1. ta - ble heart Bore through - out life true wom - an's part.
2. kneels in prayer, In mer - cy our pe - ti - tions hear.
3. we a - dore For - ev - er and for - ev - er - more.

O CHRIST, THY GUILTY PEOPLE SPARE

Placare, Christe, servulis.
Ascribed to RABANUS MAURUS, *d. 856.*
Tr. EDWARD CASWALL, *d. 1878.*

Adapted from a Melody by
H. WHITEHEAD, O. P.
(T.B.M.)

1. O Christ, Thy guilty people spare: For, kneeling at Thy gracious throne, The Virgin Mother pours her prayer, Imploring pardon for her own.
2. Ye angels happy evermore, Who in your circles nine ascend, As ye have guarded us before, So still from harm our steps defend.
3. Ye prophets and apostles high, Behold our penitential tears, And plead for us when death is nigh And our all-searching Judge appears.
4. Ye martyrs all, a purple band, Confessors too, a white-robed train, Oh, call us to our native land, From this our exile back again.
5. And all ye choirs of virgins chaste, Receive us to the realm above, Where hermits old from desert waste Unite to praise the God of love.

HELP, LORD, THE SOULS

Dutch Melody, 1500.
(C. O'S.)
JOHN H. NEWMAN, d. 1890.
1. Help, Lord, the souls which Thou hast made, The souls to Thee so dear, In pris - on for the debt un - paid Of sins com - mit - ted here.
2. For dai - ly falls, for par - doned crime, They joy to un - der - go The sha - dow of Thy cross sub - lime, The rem - nant of Thy woe.
3. Good Je - su, help, sweet Je - su, aid The souls to Thee most dear, In pris - on for the debt un - paid Of sins com - mit - ted here.

O LORD, REPRIEVE THE LONELY STATE

EDWARD C. CURRIE.

Ancient Irish Melody.
(E.C.C.)

1. O Lord, re - prieve the lone - ly state Of
2. Their yearn - ing for Thee, Lord, re - quite, And
3. By Cross and Pas - sion Thou hast borne, O
4. O Fa - ther, Son and Spir - it blest, We
1. those who on Thy_ mer - cy wait, To end their long - ing
2. let them come be - fore Thy sight, Re - leased from pur - ga -
3. Christ, re - lease those souls for - lorn, That they in Thee may
4. pray Thee, help these souls pos - sessed With love and long - ing
1. des - o - late.__ Mi - se - ré - re, Dó - mi - ne.
2. to - ry's night.__ Mi - se - ré - re, Dó - mi - ne.
3. be re - born.__ Mi - se - ré - re, Dó - mi - ne.
4. for Thy rest.__ Mi - se - ré - re, Dó - mi - ne.

188

OUT OF THE DEPTHS

After Ps. 129: De profundis clamavi.
Tr. Anon.

JOHN E. RONAN.

1. Out of the depths to Thee, O Lord, I cry, Lord
2. Oh, hear our prayers and sighs, Re - deem - er blest, And
3. To be ap - peased in wrath, dear Lord, is Thine; Thou
4. This God Him - self shall come from heav'n a - bove, The

1. gra - cious, turn Thine ear to sup - pliant sigh; If
2. grant Thy ho - ly souls e - ter - nal rest, And
3. mer - cy with Thy jus - tice canst com - bine; Thy
4. Christ, the God of mer - cy and of love. He

1. sins of man Thou scan - nest, who may stand That
2. let per - pet - ual light up - on them shine; For,
3. blood our count-less stains shall wash a - way: This
4. comes, He comes: the God In - car - nate He; And

1. search - ing eye of Thine and chast - 'ning hand?
2. though not spot - less, still these souls are Thine.
3. is Thy law, our hope and stead - fast stay.
4. by His glo - rious death makes all men free.

JUST FOR TODAY

SR. M. XAVIER, S.N.D. JOHN LEE.

1. Lord, for to - mor-row and its needs I do not pray;
2. Let me be slow to do my will, Prompt to o - bey;
3. Let me in sea-son, Lord, be grave, In sea-son gay;
1. Keep me, my God, from stain of sin, Just for to - day.
2. Help me to sac - ri - fice my - self, Just for to - day.
3. Let me be faith - ful to Thy grace, Just for to - day.
1. Let me both dil - i - gent - ly work And du - ly pray;
2. Let me no wrong or i - dle word Un - think-ing say;
3. So for to - mor-row and its needs I do not pray;
1. Let me be kind in word and deed, Just for to - day.
2. Set Thou a seal up - on my lips, Just for to - day.
3. But keep me, guide me, love me, Lord, Just for to - day.

190

MORNING

WHEN MORNING FILLS THE SKY

Beim frühen Morgenlicht.
'Katholisches Gesangbuch', Würzburg, 1828.
Tr. EDWARD CASWALL, *d. 1878, alt.*

Adapted from a Traditional German Melody. (E.C.C.)

1. When morn - ing fills the sky, Our hearts a - wak - ing
2. While work - ing through the day, May ev - 'ry ac - tion
3. Let all the earth a - round Ring joy - ous with the
1. cry: May Je - sus Christ be praised, May Je - sus
2. say: May Je - sus Christ be praised, May Je - sus
3. sound: May Je - sus Christ be praised, May Je - sus
1. Christ be praised! Our eyes a - bove we raise, And
2. Christ be praised! Our morn - ing_ off - 'ring be This
3. Christ be praised! Let air and_ sea and sky From
1. sing in_ joy - ful praise: May Je - sus_ Christ be praised!
2. song of_praise to Thee: May Je - sus_ Christ be praised!
3. depth to_height re - ply: May Je - sus_ Christ be praised!

PRAYER FOR A HOLY DEATH*

Benedictine 'Ultima'.
Tr. R. S.

Mode 1.
(P.E.S.)

Úl - ti - ma in mor - tis ho - ra,
At our life's last mo - ment fleet - ing,
Fí - li - um pro no - bis o - ra!
Thine own Son for us en - treat - ing,
Bo - nam mor - tem ím - pe - tra,
May we Christ with thee em - brace;
Vir - go Ma - ter Dó - mi - na!
Vir - gin Moth - er, grant this grace!

* For use in schools: this Prayer can appropriately be sung before or after class and at the end of the school day.

192 CHRIST, THE GLORY OF THE SKY

Aeterna caeli gloria.
Ambrosian, 5th Cent.
Tr. ROBERT CAMPBELL, *d. 1868.*

From a Chorale in Johann Scheffler's 'Heilige Seelenlust', 1657.
(E.C.C.)

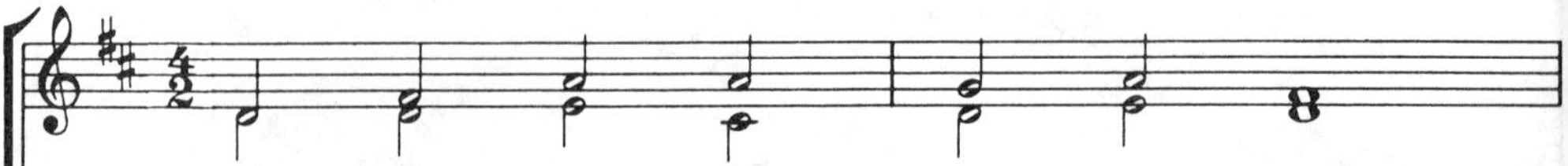

1. Christ, the glo - ry of the sky,
2. Pur - est Light, with - in us dwell,
3. Faith in Him Whose name we bear
4. Praise the Fa - ther, praise the Son;

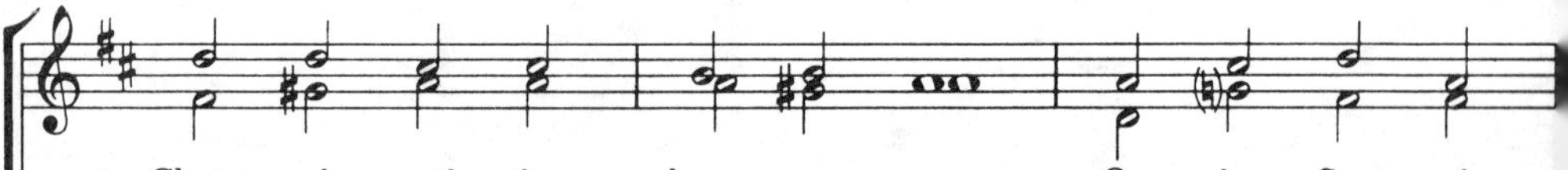

1. Christ, of earth the hope se - cure, On - ly Son of
2. Nev - er from our souls de - part; Come, the shades of
3. Ev - er in our hearts a - bound. Hope, thy bright - est
4. Spir - it blest, to Thee be praise; To the God - head

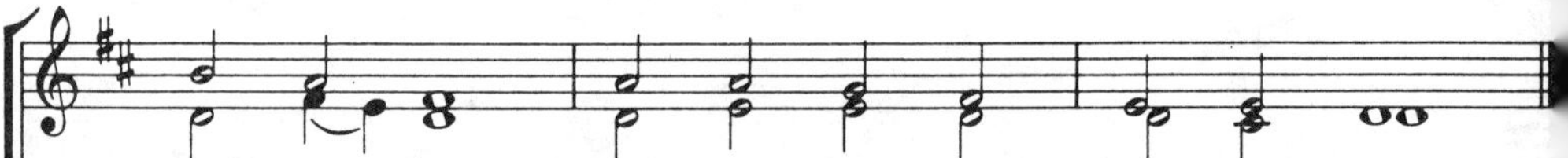

1. God most high, Off - spring of a maid - en pure!
2. earth dis - pel, Fill and pur - i - fy the heart.
3. torch pre - pare; All with ho - ly love be crowned.
4. three in one, Glo - ry be through end - less days.

IN MANUS TUAS, DOMINE

Mode 6.
(J.H.D.)

Short Responsory at Compline.

In ma - nus tu - as, Dó - mi - ne, *
Com - mén - do spí - ri - tum me - um.
Repeat: In manus.
V. Red - e - mí - sti nos, Dó - mi - ne, De - us ve - ri - tá - tis. *
Com-mén - do spí - ri - tum me - um. V. Gló - ri - a Pa - tri,
et Fí - li - o, et Spi - rí - tu - i San - cto.
Repeat: In manus.

JESUS, WHEN WE GO TO REST

Laba Nakti Jezau.
Tr. E.C.C.

Traditional Lithuanian Evening Hymn
(E.C.C.)

Je - sus, when we go to rest,
Grant that Thy pro - tect - ing grace
May our sleep by Thee be blest: - Je - sus,
Hold us in its safe em - brace; Keep us
Lord of light, Bless our sleep this night;
close to Thee, From all e - vil free.
Je - sus, lov - ing Sav - ior, be near.

SWEET SAVIOR, BLESS US ERE WE GO

FREDERICK W. FABER, *d. 1863.*

HENRY LAWES, *d. 1662.* (E.C.C.)

1. Sweet Sav - ior, bless us ere we go, In - to our
2. The day is done, its hours have run, And Thou hast
3. Grant us, O Lord, from e - vil ways True ab - so -
4. Sweet Sav - ior, bless us, night is come; Ma - ry and
1. minds Thy word in - still, And make our luke-warm hearts to glow
2. ta - ken count of all: What mea - ger tri-umphs grace hath won,
3. lu - tion and re - lease; More than the past, may com - ing days
4. Jo - seph, near us be; Good an - gels, watch a - bout our home,—
Refrain
1. With low - ly love and fer - vent will.
2. The bro - ken vow, the fre - quent fall.
3. Bring pur - i - ty and in - ward peace.
4. And we are one day near - er Thee.
Through life's long
day and death's dark night, O gen - tle Je - sus, be our light.

HOLY GOD, WE PRAISE THY NAME

Grosser Gott, wir loben dich.
IGNAZ FRANZ, *1771.*
Tr. CLARENCE A. WALWORTH, *d. 1900.*

'Katholisches Gesangbuch',
Vienna, c. 1774.
(T.C.K.)

1. Ho - ly God,_ we praise Thy Name! Lord of
2. Hark! the loud_ ce - les - tial hymn An - gel
3. Ho - ly Fa - ther, Ho - ly Son, Ho - ly
1. all,_ we bow_ be - fore Thee; All on earth Thy scep - ter
2. choirs a - bove are rais - ing; Cher - u - bim_ and Ser - a -
3. Spir - it, Three we name Thee, While in es - sence on - ly
1. 'claim, All in heav-en a - bove a - dore Thee; In - fi - nite Thy
2. phim In un - ceas - ing cho - rus prais - ing, Fill the heav'ns with
3. One, Un - di - vid - ed God we 'claim Thee, And a - dor - ing
1. vast do - main, Ev - er - last - ing is_ Thy reign.
2. sweet ac - cord: Ho - ly, ho - ly, ho - ly Lord!
3. bend the knee, While we own the mys - ter - y.

MY GOD, HOW WONDERFUL THOU ART

FREDERICK W. FABER, *d. 1863.*

Ascribed to WILLIAM CROFT, *d. 1727.*
(T.C.K.)

1. My God, how won - der - ful Thou art! Thy
2. How dread are Thine e - ter - nal years, O
3. How won - der - ful, how beau - ti - ful The
4. Oh, how I fear Thee, liv - ing God, With
1. Maj - es - ty how bright! How beau - ti - ful Thy
2. ev - er - last - ing Lord, By pros - trate spir - its
3. sight of Thee must be, Thine end - less wis - dom,
4. deep - est, ten - d'rest fears And wor - ship Thee with
1. mer - cy seat In depths of burn - ing light!
2. day and night Un - ceas - ing - ly a - dored!
3. bound - less power And aw - ful pur - i - ty!
4. trem - bling hope And pen - i - ten - tial tears!

NOW THANK WE ALL OUR GOD

Nun danket alle Gott.
MARTIN RINKART, *d. 1649.*
Tr. CATHERINE WINKWORTH, *d. 1878, alt.*

Melody by JOHANN CRÜGER, *d. 1662.*
Harmony: F. MENDELSSOHN BARTHOLDY, *d. 1847.*

1. Now thank we all our God, With heart and hands and voi - ces,
2. Oh, may this boun-teous God Through all our life be near us,
3. All praise and thanks to God The Fa - ther now be giv - en,

1. Who won-drous things hath done, In Whom His world re - joi - ces;
2. With ev - er joy - ful hearts And bles - sed peace to cheer us;
3. The Son, and Him Who reigns With Them in high - est heav - en,

1. Who from our moth - er's arms Hath blessed us on our way
2. And keep us in His grace, And guide us when per - plexed,
3. E - ter - nal Three in One Whom earth and heav'n a - dore;

1. With count - less gifts of love, And still is ours to - day.
2. And free us from all ills In this world and the next.
3. For thus it was, is now, And shall be ev - er - more.

PRAISE TO THE HOLIEST

'The Dream of Gerontius'.
JOHN H. NEWMAN, *d. 1890.*

THOMAS TALLIS, *d. 1585.*

1. Praise to the Ho - liest in the height, And in the depth be praise: In all His words most won - der - ful; Most sure in all His ways!
2. O lov - ing wis - dom of our God! When all was sin and shame, A sec - ond A - dam to the fight And to the res - cue came.
3. O wis - est love! that flesh and blood Which did in A - dam fail, Should strive a - fresh a - gainst the foe, Should strive and should pre - vail;
4. And that a high - er gift than grace Should flesh and blood re - fine, God's pres - ence and His ver - y Self, And Es - sence all di - vine.

HOLY CHURCH NOW STANDS TRIUMPHANT

T. AUBREY DE VERE, *d. 1902, alt.* RICHARD R. TERRY, *d. 1938*

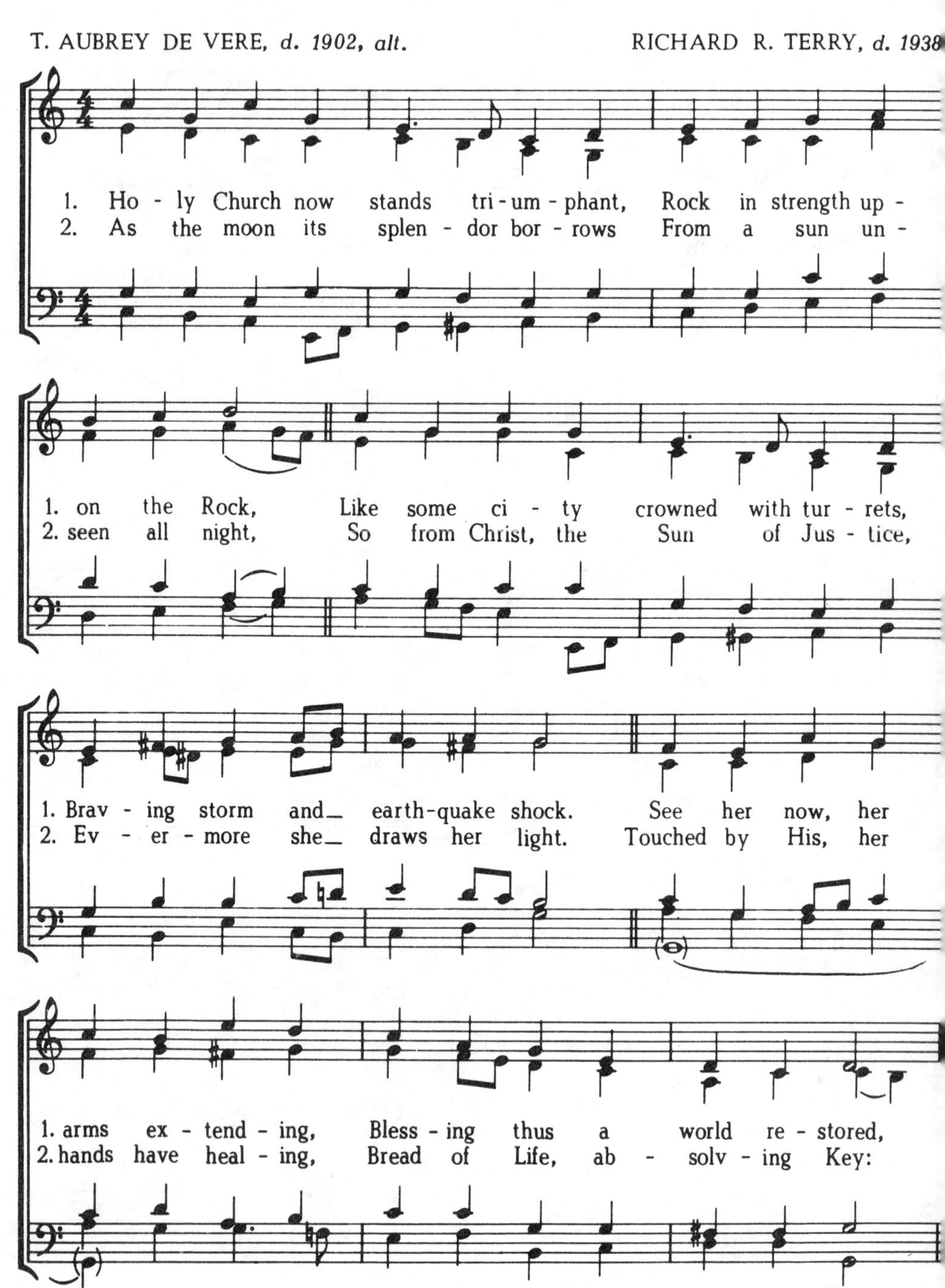
1. Ho - ly Church now stands tri - um - phant, Rock in strength up - on the Rock, Like some ci - ty crowned with tur - rets, Brav - ing storm and earth - quake shock. See her now, her arms ex - tend - ing, Bless - ing thus a world re - stored,
2. As the moon its splen - dor bor - rows From a sun un - seen all night, So from Christ, the Sun of Jus - tice, Ev - er - more she draws her light. Touched by His, her hands have heal - ing, Bread of Life, ab - solv - ing Key:

HOLY CHURCH NOW STANDS TRIUMPHANT

1. All the an - thems of cre - a - tion Lift - ing to Cre -
2. Christ In - car - nate is her Bride-groom; God is hers, His
Refrain
1. a - tion's Lord.
2. tem - ple_ she.
Hers the king - dom, hers the scep - ter;
Fall, ye na - tions, at her feet,
Hers the truth whose
fruit is free - dom, Light her yoke, her_ bur - den sweet.

201 FOR THE HOLY FATHER

OREMUS PRO PONTIFICE

Mode [illegible]
(J.H.D.)

V. O - ré - mus pro Pon - tí - fi - ce no - stro
[Pi - o]
R. Dó - mi - nus con - sér - vet e - um,
et vi - ví - fi - cet e - um, et be - á - tum
fá - ci - at e - um in ter - ra, et non tra - dat e - um
in á - ni - mam in - i - mi - có - rum e - jus.

ON THIS DAY, THE FIRST OF DAYS

Die parente temporum.
Le Mans Breviary, 1748.
Tr. HENRY W. BAKER, *d. 1877.*

JOHANN A. FREYLINGHAUSEN, *d. 1739,*
in 'Neues Geistreiches Gesangbuch',
Halle, 1704.

1. On this day, the first of days,
2. On this day th'e - ter - nal Son
3. Fa - ther, Who didst fash - ion me
4. Ho - ly Je - sus, may I be
5. Thou, Who dost all gifts im - part,
1. God the Fa - ther's Name we praise, Who, cre - a - tion's
2. O - ver death His tri - umph won; On this day the
3. I - mage of Thy - self to be, Fill me with Thy
4. Dead and bur - ied here with Thee, And, by love in -
5. Shine, Thou Spir - it, in my heart; Best of gifts, Thy -
1. Lord and Spring, Did the world from dark - ness bring.
2. Spi - rit came With His gifts of liv - ing flame.
3. love di - vine, Let my ev - 'ry thought be Thine.
4. flamed, a - rise Un - to Thee a sac - ri - fice.
5. self, be - stow; Make me yearn Thy love to know.

INTROIT: BRINGING OUR PRAISE, WE KNEEL BEFORE THY ALTAR

SR. M. FRANCIS, P.C.
SR. M. FRANCIS, P.
(E.C.C.)
1. Bring - ing our praise, we kneel be - fore Thy al - tar,
2. Praise to Thy Name, O God of end - less pow - er;
3. Glo - ry be Thine, our cause and our be - gin - ning;
1. Ask - ing Thy grace, Thy mer - cy when we fal - ter;
2. Thanks be to Thee with ev - 'ry dawn - ing hour;
3. Glo - ry be Thine for res - cue from our sin - ning;
1. Mer - cy re - veals the splen - dor of Thy glo - ry:
2. Now we a - dore and sing Thy an - cient glo - ry,
3. Thou Who dost call each man to share Thy glo - ry,
1. Thine be our praise, O God; be - stow on us Thy mer - cy.
2. Christ, we be - seech Thee, hear and save us with Thy mer - cy.
3. Grant us Thy crea - tures, Lord, the sol - ace of Thy mer - cy.

INTROIT: CHRIST IS OUR HEAD

quam juvat fratres, Deus.
HARLES COFFIN, d. 1749.
r. L. H. BUNN.
Melody from
'La Scala Santa', 1681.
1. Christ is our Head, our strength, our life, Our
2. Me - lo - dious let our min - gled praise From
3. Let here tran - quil - li - ty a - bound, As
4. Yet un - to those who love Thee, Lord, All
5. Here, then, O Trin - i - ty most blest, The
1. on - ly and suf - fi - cient good; Then, Lord, let u - ni -
2. this fair house to Thee as - cend; And our pe - ti - tions,
3. all in lov - ing con - cord strive; No bit - ter seed of
4. things to - geth - er work for good: From in - ju - ries we
5. hum - ble grace to each be giv'n To love his neigh - bour
1. ty in - spire And aid our com - mon broth - er - hood.
2. strong as deeds, In Thine ap - prov - ing pres - ence blend.
3. en - mi - ty Un - to a bale - ful har - vest thrive.
4. gain a spur, A crown by ag - o - ny and blood.
5. as him - self, Till Thou en - throne us all in heav'n.

OFFERTORY: REX SUMMAE MAJESTATIS

O King of Might and Splendor

A Ratisbon Manual of Chant. JOSEPH MOHR, S. J., *d.* 18
Tr. A. GREGORY MURRAY, O. S. B. (F.J.G.)

1. Rex sum - mae ma - je - stá - tis, Cre -
2. Tu cor - pus tra - di - dí - sti, O
1. O King of might and splen - dor, Cre -
2. Thy Bod - y Thou hast giv - en, Thy
1. á - tor hó - mi - num, Te so - lum his ob -
2. Je - su Dó - mi - ne, Tu sán - gui - nem fu -
1. a - tor most a - dored, This sac - ri - fice we
2. Blood Thou hast out - poured, That sin might be for -
1. lá - tis Fa - té - mur Dó - mi - num. Sint
2. dí - sti Pro mun - di crí - mi - ne: Dum
1. ren - der To Thee, our sov - 'reign Lord. May
2. giv - en, O Je - su, lov - ing Lord. As

OFFERTORY: REX SUMMAE MAJESTATIS

1. do - na ti - bi gra - ta Quae
2. tu - ae ce - le - brá - mus Mor -
1. these, our gifts, be pleas - ing Un -
2. now with love most ten - der Thy
1. nunc of - fé - ri - mus Et dé - le - ant pec -
2. tis_ me - mó - ri - am, Nos ip - sos con - se -
1. to_ Thy maj - es - ty, Man - kind from sin re -
2. death we cel - e - brate, Our lives in self - sur -
1. cá - ta Quis te of - fén - di - mus.
2. crá - mus In vi - vam_ hó - sti - am.
1. leas - ing Which has of - fend - ed Thee.
2. ren - der To Thee we_ con - se - crate.

206

OFFERTORY: ACCEPT, KIND FATHER, BREAD AND WINE

SR. M. FRANCIS, P. C. — THOMAS C. KELLY

1. Ac - cept, kind Fa - ther, bread and wine In
2. As wa - ter min - gled with the wine, Let
1. to - ken of that Gift di - vine Once of - fered Thee on
2. our poor lives be lost in Thine. Let mis - er - y be
1. Cal - v'ry's hill, Re - newed up - on our al - tars
2. drowned in grace That we may see Thy sav - ing
Refrain
1. still.
2. Face.
Thou Who hast worn our low hu - man - i -
ty, Give us to share Thy bright di - vin - i - ty.

SANCTUS: HOLY IS GOD

SR. M. FRANCIS, P. C.
EDWARD C. CURRIE.
1. Ho - ly is God! The light and dark-ness praise Him.
2. Ho - ly is God, Who lis - tens when we praise Him!
1. Ho - ly His Name! The sun and stars de - clare.
2. Ho - ly His Name, Who deigns to hear our prayer!
1. God of strength and pow - er, Lord of grace and mer - cy;
2. Lord of love and pi - ty, God of truth and jus - tice;
1. Ho - ly! Ho - ly! Ho - ly— is His Name!
2. Ho - ly! Ho - ly! Ho - ly— is His Name!

COMMUNION PROCESSIONAL

SR. M. FRANCIS, P. C. RICHARD KEYS BIGGS

1. Be - cause Thou hast made char - i - ty the sign
2. Take from our hearts the dark - ness which im - pedes
3. Make of our sep - 'rate lives a sin - gle bread,
1. Of those who are Thine own and fol - low Thee,
2. The splen - dor of Thy love that makes us one;
3. Merge all our life - blood in - to one pure wine,
1. Free us, O Lord, from ha - tred's cold de - sign
2. Pit - y our weak - ness, Lord, who come to plead
3. Who at Thy ban - quet ta - ble, Lord, are fed,
1. And make us all one soul, one heart in Thee.
2. Now with a sin - gle voice be - fore Thy throne.
3. Who hope to share th'e - ter - nal Feast Di - vine.
Refrain
Let Thy living love flow in - to us, Make Thy life of love shine out in us.

COMMUNION: I LOVE THEE, O THOU LORD MOST HIGH

O Deus, ego amo te, nam prior.
Psalteriolum Cantionum Catholicarum', Cologne, 1710. Tr. EDWARD CASWALL, *d. 1878.*

'Symphonia Sirenum', Cologne, 1695.
(F.J.G.)

1. I love Thee, O Thou Lord most high, Because Thou first hast loved me; I seek no other liberty Than that of being bound to Thee.
2. May memory no thought suggest But shall to Thy pure glory tend; May understanding find no rest, Except in Thee, its only end.
3. All mine is Thine: say but the word, What-e'er Thou willest shall be done; I know Thy love, all gracious Lord, I know it seeks my good alone.
4. Apart from Thee, all things are naught; Then grant, O my all-perfect Bliss, Grant me to love Thee as I ought; Thou givest all in giving this.

RECESSIONAL: TO GOD OUR FATHER

SR. M. FRANCIS, P. C. ARTHUR C. BECKER

1. To God our Fa - ther, Build-er and Cre - a - tor,
2. To God our Sav - ior, Son and Judge, Re - deem - er,
3. May God the Spir - it, Worker, Sanc - ti - fi - er,
1. Be praise and glo - ry giv - en ev - er - more.
2. Let hymns of joy___ be raised e - ter - nal - ly.
3. Be praised, bright Art - ist of the Trin - i - ty,
1. Mak - er of all that is, or was, or will be,
2. Washed in Thy sav - ing Blood, we sing Thy mer - cy
3. Flam-ing down up - on our world; we will thank Thee
1. Ev - er we'll thank Thee, ev - er Thee a - dore.
2. Who bought us at great_ price up - on the tree.
3. Through time, and then through all e - ter - ni - ty. A - men.

211

LITURGICAL DIRECTIONS

nly Latin may be used during the High Mass; that is, from the Introit to the Dismissal. he Proper and Ordinary of the Mass must be sung in their entirety.

The *Proper* consists of the *Introit, Gradual Section, Offertory* and *Communion.* These parts are changeable; that is, each day and feast has its own Proper.

The *Ordinary* consists of the *Kyrie, Gloria, Credo, Sanctus-Benedictus,* and *Agnus Dei.* These parts do not change (except the *Agnus Dei* in Requiem Masses and on Holy Thursday).

he organ may accompany the singing, and may also be played during the parts when o singing is required, but care should be taken not to delay the Mass.

he organ must never accompany any of the priest's chants at the altar — *Preface, Pater oster, etc.* It is desirable that the choir responses be unaccompanied, but this is not equired.

uring Lent and Advent and at Requiem Masses, the organ may be used only as an ccompaniment for the voices. It may not be used as a solo instrument either before, uring or after the Mass. It is strictly forbidden to use the organ at all, even to accom- any the voices, on the last three days of Holy Week.

HIGH MASS **212**

(Sung Mass or Missa Cantata)

PROCESSIONAL: As the procession of clergy and servers leaves the sacristy r Mass, any hymn may be sung in Latin or in English, preferably one appropriate to e season or the day. The *Introit* of the Mass may be used, provided there will be no spersion before the Mass.

ASPERSION: On Sundays only, the High Mass frequently is preceded by the rinkling of the people with holy water. The *Asperges me* is intoned by the priest and ntinued by the choir. From Easter until Pentecost inclusive, the *Vidi aquam* is used place of the *Asperges me.* After the choir has completed the singing, there are ver- cles and choir responses with an oration sung by the priest, concluding with the oir's *Amen.*

he celebrant then changes vestments for Mass. If he remains in the sanctuary to ange, the *Introit* may be sung immediately. If he returns to the sacristy, the *Introit* ay not begin until he returns to the church for Mass.

INTROIT *(Proper)*: If aspersion has preceded Mass, and the priest has remained the sanctuary to change vestments, begin the *Introit* immediately while priest is anging.

no aspersion precedes the Mass, the *Introit* may be sung as the priest enters the urch.

KYRIE *(Ordinary)*: Sing immediately after the *Introit.* (Be sure that the priest as begun the Mass.)

GLORIA *(Ordinary)*: Intoned by the celebrant. Do not repeat the Intonation. O certain days the *Gloria* is omitted.
Versicle: *Dóminus vobíscum.* Response: *Et cum spíritu tuo.*
Then *Collects* are sung by the celebrant, concluding with the choir's *Amen. The Epistl* is read in audible voice by the celebrant.

GRADUAL *(Proper)*: Sung as soon as the celebrant has completed reading th *Epistle.*

ALLELUIA *(Proper)*: Follows the *Gradual* immediately.

SEQUENCE *(Proper)*: Follows the *Alleluia* and *Verse* immediately. (Found i only five Masses of the year.)
N.B. On certain days and in certain seasons there is a *Gradual* and *Tract* – or n *Gradual* but double *Alleluias* with *Verses*, and various other combinations of thes which are clearly indicated in all books of Propers. This is called the *Gradual Sectio* of the Mass, and is sung as one entity regardless of the given combination.
The *Gospel,* sung by the celebrant, is preceded by the following versicles and response

V. *Dóminus vobíscum.* R. *Et cum spíritu tuo.*
V. *Sequéntia sancti Evangélii . . .* R. *Glória tibi, Dómine.*

CREDO *(Ordinary)*: Intoned by the priest. Do not repeat the intonation. On ce tain days, the *Credo* is omitted.
Versicle and Choir response, followed by the priest's *Oremus.*

OFFERTORY *(Proper)*: Begun immediately after the priest's *Oremus.* If tim permits after the Proper *Offertory* is completed, a short Latin hymn or motet may b sung. It should end in good time for the *Preface* versicles and responses.
The *Preface,* sung by the celebrant, is preceded by the following versicles an responses:

V. *Per ómnia saécula saeculórum.* R. *Amen.*
V. *Dóminus vobíscum.* R. *Et cum spíritu tuo.*
V. *Sursum corda.* R. *Habémus ad Dóminum.*
V. *Grátias agámus Dómino Deo nostro.* R. *Dignum et justum est.*

SANCTUS *(Ordinary)*: Immediately after the *Preface.* This is followed short by the Consecration. *The Sanctus-Benedictus may also be sung as a unit before th Consecration.*

BENEDICTUS *(Ordinary)*: Sung immediately after the *Consecration.*
Versicle and response – then the *Pater Noster* is sung by the priest with its cho response *Sed líbera nos a malo* concluding. This is later followed by other versicl and choir responses up to *Pax Dómini sit semper vobíscum* and the choir response *cum spíritu tuo.*

AGNUS DEI *(Ordinary)*: Follows immediately.
If Holy Communion is distributed a Latin hymn in honor of the Blessed Sacrament m be sung, if time permits.

COMMUNION *(Proper)*: Sung as the celebrant is purifying the chalice aft Communion.
Priest sings the *Post-Communion* and versicles with choir responses. He then sings t dismissal *Ite missa est,* or if there was no *Gloria, Benedicámus Dómino,* to which, either case, the choir responds *Deo grátias.* This dismissal varies with the season with the Mass sung. See pages 252 & 253.
The dismissal is followed immediately by the last *Blessing* and the last *Gospel.*

RECESSIONAL: Any hymn in Latin or English may be sung as the procession clergy and servers returns to the sacristy.

SOLEMN MASS 213

ll as for High Mass above, except the following:
ıe altar is incensed at the *Kyrie* and at the *Offertory*.
ıe *Epistle* is sung by the sub-deacon.
ıe *Gospel* is first read by the celebrant and then sung by the deacon.
Holy Communion is distributed, the deacon may sing the *Confiteor* before the stribution.

REQUIEM MASS 214

ll as for High Mass or Solemn Mass, except the following:
o *Gloria* is sung.
EQUENCE: *Dies irae* following the *Tract* is sung only at Funerals and on All ouls' Day.
GNUS DEI: Different text.
ISMISSAL: *Requiéscant in pace. Amen.*
ıe altar is incensed at Solemn Requiem Mass only at the *Offertory*. The organ at equiem Masses is tolerated only if it is needed to accompany the voices. It may not be ed as a solo instrument.

PONTIFICAL MASS 215

ll as for Solemn Mass except the following:
fter the *Gloria*, the Bishop sings *Pax vobis* to which the choir responds *Et cum spiritu o.*
ıe *Epistle* is sung by the sub-deacon as usual. Then the Bishop reads it; hence, the *radual Section* should not begin until the Bishop has read the *Epistle*.
Holy Communion is distributed, the deacon sings the *Confiteor* before the distri-ıtion.
t the last blessing the Bishop sings the *Pontifical Blessing*. See page 282.
is customary to sing either *Ecce Sacerdos Magnus* or *Sacerdos et Pontifex* as a pro-ssional. See pages 280 & 282. Any appropriate hymn of the season or feast, however, ay be used either in Latin or English. There is no Aspersion at Pontifical Mass. Fre-ıently the Bishop vests and unvests at the throne or faldstool. While this takes place, usic may be supplied according to the seasonal rules.

FIRST SOLEMN MASS OR JUBILEE OF A PRIEST 216

ll as for High Mass or Solemn Mass whichever the case may be.
ıere is no special Mass for these occasions. The Mass of the day, or a Votive Mass the priest's discretion may be used. The Pastor should be consulted in advance to certain which Mass will be celebrated.
is suggested that supplementary festive hymns and motets suitable to the occasion sung, such as *Juravit Dominus, Jam non dicam, Haec dies*, etc.

AT NUPTIAL MASS 217

ıere should be no music during the marriage ceremony itself. After the *Pater Noster* ıd before the *Post-Communion*, the priest reads a blessing over the couple. It would better not to have music at these particular times.

ASPERGES ME, DOMINE

*Sung before the Parochial Mass on Sundays outside of Paschal Time.**

Ps. 50, v. 8, 1.

13th Cent.
Mode 7. (J.H.D

A - spér - ges me, * Dó - mi - ne, hys - só - po,
et mun-dá - bor: la - vá - bis me, et su - per
ni - vem de - al - bá - bor. Ps. 50. Mi - se - ré - re me - i,
De - us, * se - cún - dum ma - gnam mi - se - ri -

* On the two Sundays of the Passion, the *Gloria Patri* is not sung, but the antiphon *Asperg me* is repeated immediately after the Psalm.
See p. 245 for versicles and responses which conclude the aspersion.

ASPERGES ME, DOMINE

cór - di - am tu - am.
Gló - ri - a Pa - tri, et
Fí - li - o, et Spi - rí - tu - i San - cto. *
Si - cut e - rat in prin - cí - pi - o, et nunc,
et sem - per,
et in saé-cu - la sae - cu - ló-rum. A - men.

Repeat: *Asperges me.*

219

VIDI AQUAM

Sung before the Parochial Mass from Easter Sunday until Pentecost inclusive.

10th Cent.
Mode 8. (J.H.D.)

Vi - di a - quam * e - gre - di - én - tem de
tem - plo, a lá - te - re dex - tro,
al - le - lú - ia: et o - mnes ad quos
per - vé - nit a - qua i - sta,
sal - vi fa - cti sunt, et di - cent,
al - le - lú - ia, al - le - lú - ia.

VIDI AQUAM

Ps.117. Con - fi - té - mi - ni Dó - mi - no quó - ni - am bo - nus: *
quó - ni - am in saé - cu - lum mi - se - ri - cór - di - a — e - jus.
Gló - ri - a — Pa - tri, et Fí - li - o, et Spi - rí - tu - i
San - cto. * Si - cut — e - rat in prin - cí - pi - o et — nunc,
et sem - per, et — in — saé - cu - la sae - cu - ló - rum. A - men.
Repeat: *Vidi aquam.*

V. Osténde nobis, Dómine, misericórdiam tuam. (In Paschal Time, add: *Allelúia.*)

R. Et salutáre tuum da nobis. (In Paschal Time, add: *Allelúia.*)

V. Dómine, exáudi oratiónem meam.

R. Et clamor meus ad te véniat.

V. Dóminus vobíscum.

R. Et cum spíritu tuo.

Orémus *(Prayer)*

Exáudi nos, Dómine . . . . *R.* Amen.

220

KYRIE, ELEISON

Orbis Factor

Mass XI.
Mode 1.
(J.H.D.)

Ký - ri - e, * e - - - - - - - lé - i - son. iij.
Chri-ste, e - - - - - - lé - i - son. iij.
Ký - ri - e, e - - - - - - - lé - i - son. ij.
Ký - ri - e, *
e - - - - - - - - - - - lé - i - son.

GLORIA*

Mode 2.
(J.H.D.)
Gló - ri - a in ex - cél - sis De - o. Et in ter - ra pax
ho - mí - ni - bus bo - nae vo-lun - tá - tis. Lau - dá - mus te.
Be - ne - dí - ci - mus te. A - do - rá - mus te.
Glo - ri - fi - cá - mus te. Grá - ti - as á - gi - mus ti - bi
pro - pter ma-gnam gló - ri - am tu - am. Dó - mi - ne De - us,

* An alternate *Gloria* is given on page 254

GLORIA

Rex cae - lé - stis, De - us_ Pa - ter o - mní - po - tens.
Dó - mi - ne_ Fi - li u - ni - gé - ni - te,
Je - su_Chri - ste. Dó - mi - ne_ De - us, A - gnus De - i,
Fí - li - us_ Pa - tris. Qui tol - lis pec - cá - ta mun - di,
mi - se - ré - re_ no - bis. Qui tol - lis pec - cá - ta mun - di,
sú - sci - pe de - pre - ca - ti - ó - nem_ no - stram.

Qui se - des_ ad déx - te-ram Pa - tris, mi - se - ré - re_ no - bis.
Quó-ni - am_ tu___ so - lus san - ctus. Tu_ so - lus Dó - mi - nus.
Tu so - lus Al - tís - si - mus, Je - su___ Chri - ste.
Cum San - cto_ Spí - ri - tu in gló - ri - a___
De - i Pa - - - - - - tris._ A - men._

SANCTUS & BENEDICTUS

Mode 2.
(J.H.D.)

San - ctus, * San - ctus, San - ctus Dó - mi - nus
De - us Sá - ba - oth. Ple - ni sunt cae - li
et ter - ra gló - ri - a tu - a. Ho - sán - na
in ex - cél - sis. Be - ne - dí - ctus qui ve - nit
in nó - mi - ne Dó - mi - ni.
Ho - sán - na in ex - cél - sis.

Mode 1.
(J.H.D.)
A - gnus De - i, * qui tol - lis pec - cá - ta
mun - di: mi - se - ré - re no - bis.
A - gnus De - i, * qui tol - lis pec - cá - ta
mun - di: mi - se - ré - re no - bis.
A - gnus De - i, * qui tol - lis pec - cá - ta
mun - di: do - na no - bis pa - cem.

THE DISMISSAL

(J.H.D
From the Easter Vigil until Saturday after Easter.
Mode
De - o grá - ti - as, al - le - lú - ia, al - le - - lú - ia.
On Solemn Feasts.
Mode
De - o
grá - - - ti - as.
Mass of the Angels (VIII).
Mode
De - - - o

THE DISMISSAL

grá - ti - as.
On Feasts of the Blessed Virgin Mary (IX).
Mode 1.
De - - - - o grá - ti - as.
On Sundays throughout the year (XI).
Mode 1.
De - o grá - - - - - - - ti - as.
On Sundays of Advent and Lent (XVII).
Mode 6.
De - o grá - - - - - - - - ti - as.

225

GLORIA

In the Ambrosian Style

Mode 4
(J.H.D.

Gló - ri - a in ex - cél - sis De - o. Et in ter - ra pax
ho - mí - ni - bus bo - nae vo - lun - tá - tis. Lau - dá - mus te.
Be - ne - dí - ci - mus te. A - do - rá - mus te.
Glo - ri - fi - cá - mus te. Grá - ti - as á - gi - mus
ti - bi pro-pter ma-gnam gló-ri - am tu - am.

Dó - mi - ne De - us, Rex cae - lé - stis, De - us Pa - ter
o - mní - po - tens. Dó - mi - ne Fi - li u - ni - gé - ni - te,
Je - su Chri - ste. Dó - mi - ne De - us,
A - gnus De - i, Fí - li - us Pa - tris. Qui tol - lis pec - cá - ta
mun - di, mi - se - ré - re no - bis.
Qui tol - lis pec - cá - ta mun - di,

sú - sci - pe de - pre - ca - ti - ó - nem no - stram.
Qui se - des ad déx - te - ram Pa - tris, mi - se - ré - re no - bis.
Quó - ni - am tu so - lus san - ctus. Tu so - lus Dó - mi - nus.
Tu so - lus Al - tís - si - mus, Je - su Chri - ste.
Cum San - cto Spí - ri - tu in gló - ri - a De - i Pa - tris.
** A - men.

CREDO

(III)

17th Cent.
Mode 5.
(J.H.D.)

Cre - do in u - num De - um. Pa - trem o - mni - po - tén - tem,
fa - ctó - rem cae - li et ter - rae, vi - si - bí - li - um
ó - mni - um, et in - vi - si - bí - li - um.
Et in u - num Dó - mi - num Je - sum Chri - stum,
Fí - li - um De - i u - ni - gé - ni - tum. Et ex Pa - tre na - tum

an - te ó - mni - a sáe - cu - la. De - um de De - o,
lu - men de lú - mi - ne, De - um ve - rum de De - o ve - ro.
Gé - ni - tum, non fa - ctum, con - sub - stan - ti - á - lem Pa - tri:
per quem ó - mni - a fa - cta sunt. Qui pro - pter nos hó - mi - nes,
et pro - pter no - stram sa - lú - tem de - scén - dit de cae - lis.

CREDO

Et in - car - ná - tus est de Spí - ri - tu San - cto
ex Ma - rí - a Vír - gi - ne: Et ho - mo fa - ctus est.
Cru - ci - fí - xus ét - i - am pro no - bis: sub Pón - ti - o
Pi - lá - to pas - sus et se - púl - tus est.
Et re - sur - ré - xit tér - ti - a di - e, se - cún - dum Scri - ptú - ras.

Et a - scén-dit in cae - lum: se-det ad déx-te-ram Pa - tris.
Et í - te - rum ven - tú - rus est cum gló - ri - a,
ju - di - cá - re vi - vos et mór - tu - os: cu - jus re - gni
non e - rit fi - nis. Et in Spí - ri - tum San-ctum, Dó - mi-num,
et vi - vi - fi - cán-tem: qui ex Pa - tre Fi - li - ó - que
pro - cé - dit. Qui cum Pa - tre et Fí - li - o si - mul

a - do - rá - tur, et con - glo - ri - fi - cá - tur: qui lo - cú - tus
est per Pro - phé - tas. Et u - nam san-ctam ca - thó - li - cam
et a - po - stó - li - cam Ec - clé - si - am. Con - fí - te - or
u - num ba - ptís - ma in re - mis - si - ó - nem pec - ca - tó - rum.
Et ex - spé - cto re - sur - re - cti - ó - nem mor - tu - ó - rum.
Et vi - tam ven - tú - ri saé - cu - li. A - - - - - - - men.

227

MASS OF SAINT TERESA

KYRIE, ELEISON

Andante ♩ = 120
HEALEY WILLA
mf
VOICES
ORGAN
mf
Ký - ri - e, e - lé - i - son. Ký - ri - e, e - lé - i - son.
Ký - ri - e, e - lé - i - son. Chri - ste, e - lé - i - son. Chri - ste, e -
lé - i-son. Chri - ste, e - lé - i - son. Ký - ri - e, e - lé - i - son.
poco rall.
Ký - ri - e, e - lé - i - son. Ký - ri - e, e - lé - i - son
poco rall.

Allegro moderato ♩ = 132
mp
Et in ter-ra pax ho - mí - ni-bus bo-nae vo-lun -
mp
f
tá - tis. Lau-dá-mus te. Be-ne - dí - ci-mus te. A-do -
f
rá-mus te. Glo - ri-fi-cá - mus te. Grá-ti-as á-gi-mus
ti - bi pro-pter ma-gnam gló-ri-am tu-am. Dó-mi-ne De - us, Rex cae-

GLORIA

poco rall.
lé - stis, De - us Pa - ter o - - - mní - po - tens.
poco rall.
Moderato ♩ = 112
mf
Dó - mi - ne Fi - li u - ni - gé - ni - te, Je - su
mf
Chri - ste. Dó - mi - ne De - us, A - gnus
De - i, Fí - li - us Pa - tris. Qui tol - lis pec - cá - ta

mun - di, mi - se - ré - re no - bis.
Qui tol - lis pec - cá - ta mun - di, sú - sci - pe
de-pre-ca - ti - ó - nem no-stram. Qui se - des ad déx - te-ram
poco rall.
Pa - tris, mi - se - ré - re no - - bis.
poco rall.

Tempo primo
f
Quó - ni - am tu so - lus_ san - ctus. Tu so - lus
f
Dó - mi - nus. Tu so - lus Al - - tís - si - mus, Je - su
Chri - ste. Cum Sancto Spí - ri - tu in gló - ri - a De - i Pa - tris.
f
f
cresc. e rall.
A - men, a - - - - - - - me
cresc. e rall.

Andante moderato ♩= 100
p
mp
San - - - - - ctus, San - - - - - - ctus,
mf
cresc.
San - - - - - - - - - - ctus Dó - mi-nus De - us
Sá - ba-oth. Ple - ni sunt cae - li et ter - ra gló - ri - a
f
animato e cresc.
tu - a. Ho - sán - na in ex - cél - sis.

230 BENEDICTUS

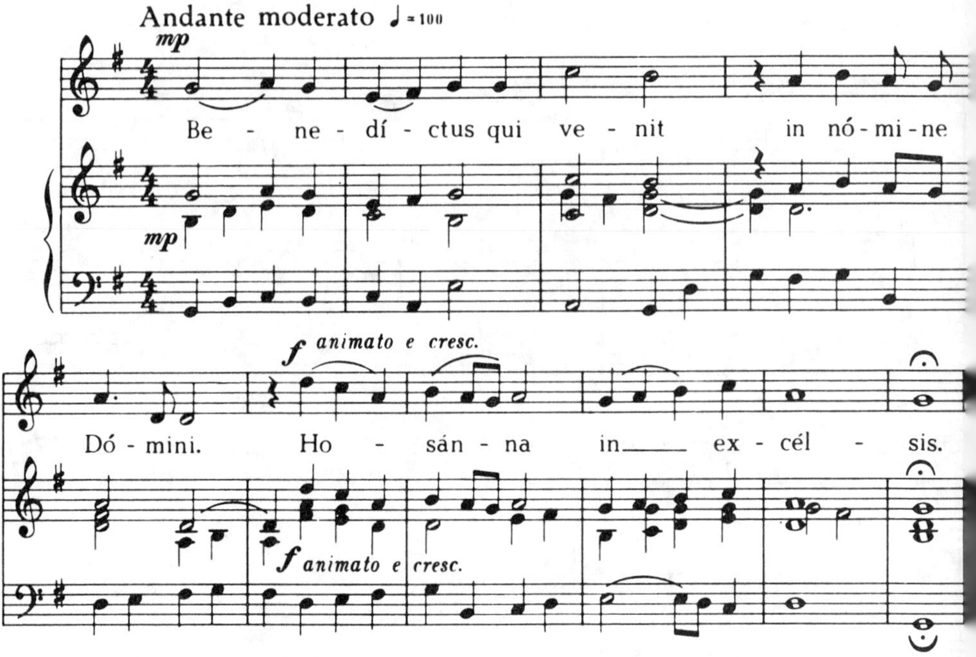
Andante moderato ♩ = 100
mp
Be - ne - dí - ctus qui ve - nit in nó - mi - ne
mp
Dó - mini. Ho - sán - na in ex - cél - sis.
f animato e cresc.
f animato e cresc.

231 AGNUS DEI

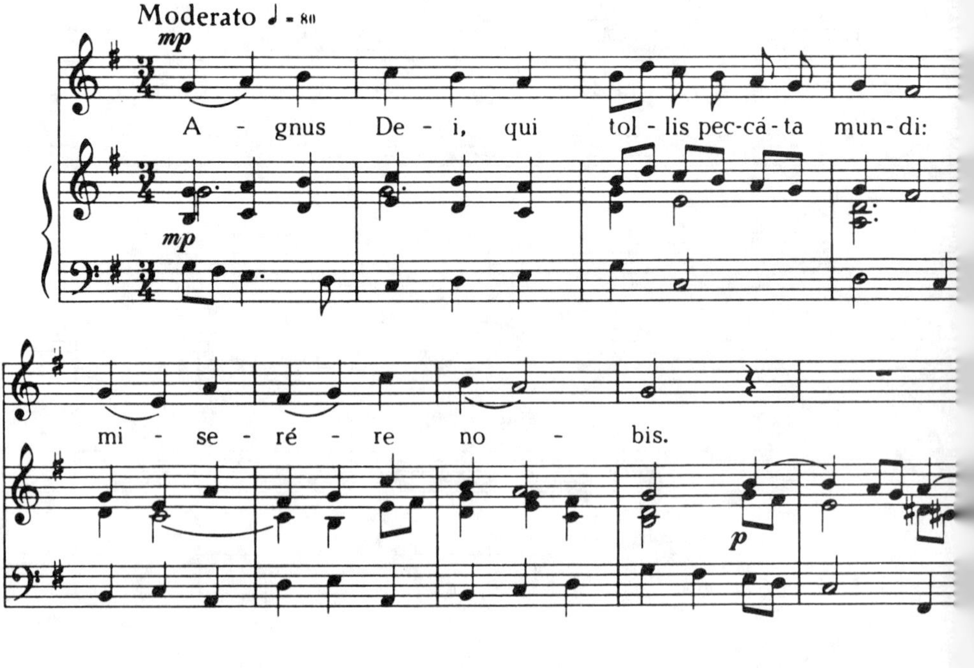
Moderato ♩ = 80
mp
A - gnus De - i, qui tol - lis pec-cá - ta mun - di:
mp
mi - se - ré - re no - bis.
p

AGNUS DEI

mp
A - gnus De - i, qui tol - lis pec - cá - ta
mp
mun - di: mi - se - ré - re no - bis.
p
mf
A - gnus De - i, qui tol - lis pec - cá - ta
mf
mp
rall. e dim.
mun - di: do - na no - bis pa - cem.
mp
rall. e dim.

FIRST DAY: EXPOSITION

MASS: Votive Mass of the Blessed Sacrament (when permitted) with *Gloria* and *Cred*
There is no Sequence.

After Mass, the celebrant changes into cope and the procession is formed. When cele brant takes monstrance in his hands and turns to face the people for the beginning o the procession, sing *Pange lingua*. (Even if no procession is held, the *Pange lingua* mus be sung. In this case, it is begun as soon as the priest reaches the altar after changin into the cope.) If necessary, repeat stanzas 1, 2, 3, 4 until the celebrant has replace the monstrance on the altar. Then sing *Tantum ergo* (stanzas 5–6) after which the Litan of the Saints is sung, including Psalm 69. This is followed by versicles and response See pages 122 & 271.

SECOND DAY

MASS: Votive Mass for Peace (when permitted) with *Credo*, but no *Gloria*. (In som dioceses, other votive Masses are used. Consult the Pastor for verification.)

THIRD DAY: REPOSITION

MASS: Votive Mass of the Blessed Sacrament (when permitted) with *Gloria* and *Cred*
There is no Sequence.

In some places, the ceremonies of reposition are held immediately after the Mass. others, the ceremonies are held later in the day. In either event, the directions are th same.

The celebrant, vested in cope, kneels at the altar. The Litany of the Saints, includir Psalm 69, followed by versicles and responses up to and including *Domine, exau orationem meam* and *Et clamor meus ad te veniat* are sung.

Then follows the procession. All the rules for the procession of the first day are follo ed here. After the *Tantum ergo* is sung, the ceremony concludes with Benediction usual.

LITANY OF THE SAINTS*

The invocations are not doubled. The use of the accompaniment is optional. A change n the melody of the invocations is indicated by underlined syllables.

(J.H.D.)

Ký-ri-e, e-lé-i-son. Chri-ste, e-lé-i-son. Ký-ri-e, e-lé-i-son.
Chri-ste, au-di nos. Chri-ste, ex-áu-di nos.
Pater de cae- -lis, De-us, mi-se-ré-re no-bis.
Fili, Redémptor mun- di, De-us, mi-se-ré-re no-bis.
Spíritus San- -cte, De-us, mi-se-ré-re no-bis.
Sancta Trínitas, u- -nus De-us, mi-se-ré-re no-bis.

This form of the Litany is proper to the Forty Hours Adoration; it differs from that which sung on April 25, the Rogation Days, and during the Easter Vigil.

LITANY OF THE SAINTS

San - cta Ma - rí - a, o - ra pro no - bis.
Sancta Dei Gé - ni - trix, o - ra pro no - bis.
Sancta Virgo vír - gi - num, o - ra pro no - bis.
Sancte Mí - cha - el, o - ra pro no - bis.
Sancte Gá - bri - el, o - ra pro no - bis.
Sancte Rá - pha - el, o - ra pro no - bis.
Omnes sancti Ángeli et Arch - án - ge - li, o - rá - te pro no - bis.
Omnes sancti beatórum Spiritúum ór - di - nes, o - rá - te pro no - bis.
Sancte Joánnes Ba - ptí - sta, o - ra pro no - bis.
Sancte Jo - seph, o - ra pro no - bis.

LITANY OF THE SAINTS

mnes sancti Patriárchae et Prophétae,	oráte.
ncte Petre,	ora.
ncte Paule,	ora.
ncte Andréa,	ora.
ncte Jacóbe,	ora.
ncte Joánnes,	ora.
ncte Thoma,	ora.
ncte Jacóbe,	ora.
ncte Philíppe,	ora.
ncte Bartholomaée,	ora.
ncte Matthaée,	ora.
ncte Simon,	ora.
ncte Thaddaée,	ora.
ncte Matthía,	ora.
ncte Bárnaba,	ora.
ncte Luca,	ora.
ncte Marce,	ora.
mnes sancti Apóstoli et Evangelístae,	oráte.
mnes sancti Discípuli Dómini,	oráte.
mnes sancti Innocéntes,	oráte.
ncte Stéphane,	ora.
ncte Lauránti,	ora.
ncte Vincénti,	ora.
ncti Fabiáne et Sebastiáne,	oráte.
ncti Joánnes et Paule,	oráte.
ncti Cosma et Damiáne,	oráte.
ncti Gervási et Protási,	oráte.
Omnes sancti Mártyres,	oráte.
Sancte Silvéster,	ora.
Sancte Gregóri,	ora.
Sancte Ambrósi,	ora.
Sancte Augustíne,	ora.
Sancte Hierónyme,	ora.
Sancte Martíne,	ora.
Sancte Nicoláe,	ora.
Omnes sancti Pontífices et Confessóres,	oráte.
Omnes sancti Doctóres,	oráte.
Sancte Antóni,	ora.
Sancte Benedícte,	ora.
Sancte Bernárde,	ora.
Sancte Domínice,	ora.
Sancte Francísce,	ora.
Omnes sancti Sacerdótes et Levítae,	oráte.
Omnes sancti Mónachi et Eremítae,	oráte.
Sancta María Magdaléna,	ora.
Sancta Ágatha,	ora.
Sancta Lúcia,	ora.
Sancta Agnes,	ora.
Sancta Caecília,	ora.
Sancta Catharína,	ora.
Sancta Anastásia,	ora.
Omnes sanctae Vírgines et Víduae,	oráte.
Omnes Sancti et Sanctae Dei,	intercédite pro nobis.

Pro - pí - ti - us es - to, par - ce no - bis, Dó - mi - ne.
Pro - pí - ti - us es - to, ex - áu - di nos, Dó - mi - ne.

Ab omni malo,	líbera nos, Dómine.
Ab omni peccáto,	líbera nos, Dómine.
Ab ira tua,	líbera nos, Dómine.
Ab imminéntibus perículis,	líbera nos, Dómine.
A flagéllo terraemótus,	líbera nos, Dómine.
A peste, fame et bello,	líbera nos, Dómine.
A subitánea et improvísa morte,	líbera nos, Dómine.
Ab insídiis diáboli,	líbera nos, Dómine.
Ab ira et odio et omni mala voluntáte,	líbera nos, Dómine.
A spíritu fornicatiónis,	líbera nos, Dómine.
A fúlgure et tempestáte,	líbera nos, Dómine.
A morte perpétua,	líbera nos, Dómine.

Per mystérium sanctae incarnatiónis tuae,	lìbera nos, Dómine.
Per advéntum tuum,	lìbera nos, Dómine.
Per nativitátem tuam,	lìbera nos, Dómine.
Per baptísmum et sanctum jejúnium tuum,	lìbera nos, Dómine.
Per crucem et passiónem tuam,	lìbera nos, Dómine.
Per mortem et sepultúram tuam,	lìbera nos, Dómine.
Per sanctam resurrectiónem tuam,	lìbera nos, Dómine.
Per admirábilem ascensiónem tuam,	líbera nos, Dómine.
Per advéntum Spíritus Sancti Paráclìti,	líbera nos, Dómine.
In die judícii,	líbera nos, Dómine.

Pec - ca - tó - res, te ro - gá - mus au - di nos.

Ut nobis parcas,	te rogámus audi n
Ut nobis indúlgeas,	te rogámus audi n
Ut ad veram paeniténtiam nos perdúcere dignéris,	te rogámus audi n
Ut Ecclésiam tuam sanctam | régere et conserváre dignéris,	te rogámus audi n
*Ut (Domnum Apostólicum et) omnes ecclesiásticos órdines | in sancta religióne conserváre dignéris,	te rogámus audi n
Ut inimícos sanctae Ecclésiae | humiliáre dignéris,	te rogámus audi n
Ut régibus et princípibus christiánis | pacem et veram concórdiam donáre dignéris,	te rogámus audi n
Ut cuncto pópulo christiáno | pacem et unitátem largíri dignéris,	te rogámus audi n
Ut omnes errántes ad unitátem Ecclésiae revocáre, | et infidéles univérsos ad Evangélii lumen perdúcere dignéris,	te rogámus audi n
Ut nosmetípsos in tuo sancto servítio | confortáre et conserváre dignéris,	te rogámus audi n
Ut mentes nostras | ad caeléstia desidéria érigas,	te rogámus audi n
Ut ómnibus benefactóribus nostris | sempitérna bona retríbuas,	te rogámus audi n
Ut ánimas nostras | fratrum, propinquórum et benefactórum nostrórum | ab aetérna damnatióne erípias,	
Ut fructus terrae | dare et conserváre dignéris,	te rogámus audi n
Ut ómnibus fidélibus defúnctis | réquiem aetérnam donáre dignéris,	te rogámus audi n
Ut nos exaudíre, dignéris,	te rogámus audi n
Fili Dei,	te rogámus audi

*If the papacy is vacant, the invocation will be simply *Ut omnes ecclesiásticos, etc.*

LITANY OF THE SAINTS

A - gnus De - i, qui tol - lis pec - cá - ta
A - gnus De - i, qui tol - lis pec - cá - ta
A - gnus De - i, qui tol - lis pec - cá - ta
mun - di, par - ce no - bis, Dó - mi - ne.
mun - di, ex - áu - di nos, Dó - mi - ne.
mun - di, mi - se - ré - re no - bis.
Chri - ste, au - di nos. Chri - ste, ex - áu - di nos.
Ký-ri-e, e-lé-i-son. Chri-ste, e-lé-i-son. Ký-ri-e, e - lé - i - son.

LITANY OF THE SAINTS

The celebrant intones:

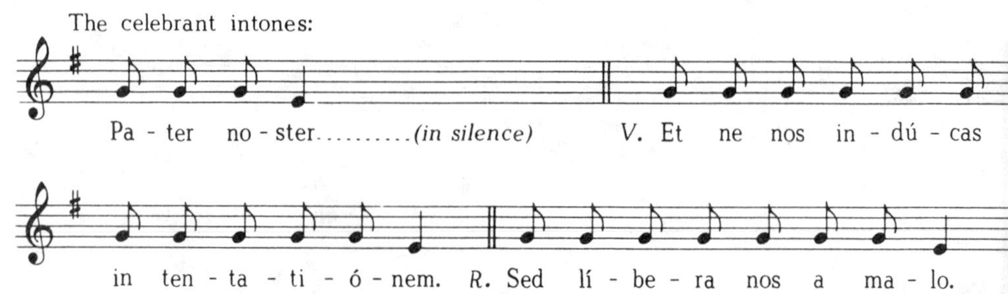
Pa - ter no - ster..........(in silence)
V. Et ne nos in - dú - cas
in ten - ta - ti - ó - nem.
R. Sed lí - be - ra nos a ma - lo.

The cantors intone:

Ps. 69. Deus in adjutórium me - um in - tén - de: * Dómine, ad adjuvándum me fe - stí - na.

2. Confundántur et revereántur, * qui quaerunt ánimam meam.
3. Avertántur retrórsum, et erubéscant, * qui volunt mihi mala.
4. Avertántur statim erubescéntes, * qui dicunt mihi: Éuge, éuge.
5. Exsúltent et laeténtur in te omnes qui quaerunt te: * et dicant semper: Magnificétu Dóminus: qui díligunt salutáre tuum.
6. Ego vero egénus et pauper sum: * Deus, ádjuva me.
7. Adjútor meus et liberátor meus es tu: * Dómine, ne moréris.
8. Glória Patri, et Fílio, * et Spirítui Sancto.
9. Sicut erat in princípio, et nunc, et semper, * et in saécula saeculórum. Amen

V. Sal - vos fac ser - vos tu - os.
R. De - us me - us spe - rán - tes in te.

V. Esto nobis, Dómine, turris fortitúdinis. *R.* A fácie inimíci.
V. Nihil profíciat inimícus in nobis.
R. Et fílius iniquitátis non appónat nocére nobis.
V. Dómine, non secúndum peccáta nostra fácias nobis.
R. Neque secúndum iniquitátes nostras retríbuas nobis.
**V.* Orémus pro Pontífice nostro [*Pio*].

*If the papacy is vacant, this versicle, *Oremus pro Pontifice, etc.*, together with i response, is omitted.

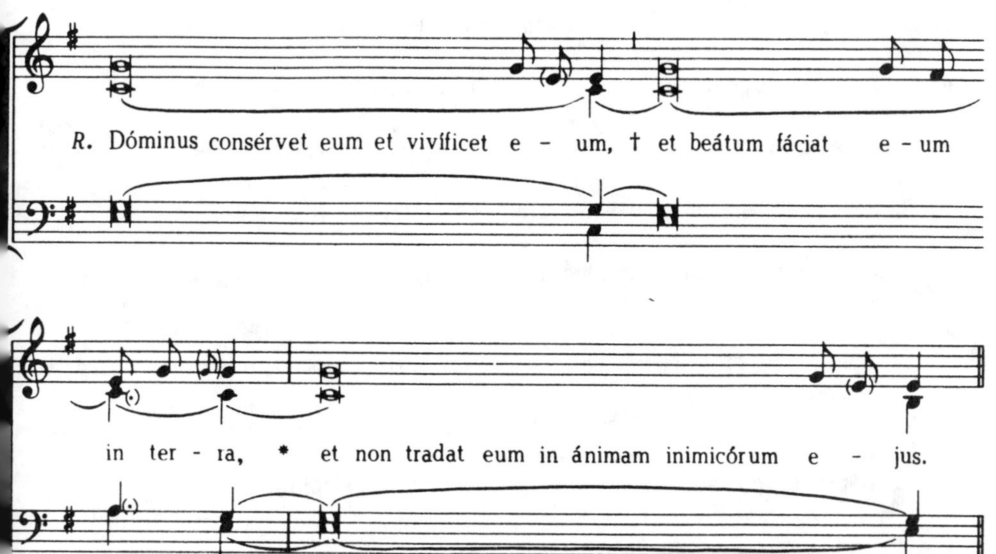
R. Dóminus consérvet eum et vivíficet e - um, † et beátum fáciat e - um
in ter - ra, * et non tradat eum in ánimam inimicórum e - jus.

V. Orémus pro benefactóribus nostris.
R. Retribúere dignáre, Dómine, † ómnibus nobis bona faciéntibus propter nomen tuum, * vitam aetérnam. Amen.
V. Orémus pro fidélibus defúnctis.
R. Réquiem aetérnam dona eis, Dómine, * et lux perpétua lúceat eis.
V. Requiéscant in pace. R. Amen.
V. Pro frátribus nostris abséntibus.
R. Salvos fac servos tuos, * Deus meus, sperántes in te.
V. Mitte eis, Dómine, auxílium de sancto. R. Et de Sion tuére eos.
V. Dómine, exáudi oratiónem meam. R. Et clamor meus ad te véniat.
V. Dóminus vobíscum. R. Et cum spíritu tuo.

Orémus: Deus, qui . . . . R. Amen.

V. Dómine, exáudi oratiónem meam.
R. Et clamor meus ad te véniat.
V. Exáudiat nos omnípotens et miséricors Dóminus.
R. Et custódiat nos semper. Amen.

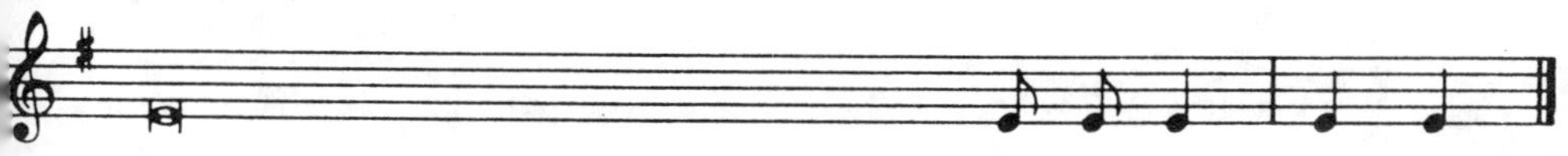

V. Fidélium ánimae per misericórdiam Dei requiéscant in pa - ce. R. A - men.

The only requirements for the choir are the singing of responses to any versicles and orations sung by the Bishop, and the singing of the antiphon *Confirma hoc Deus* as the Bishop washes his hands after the confirmation is completed.

The following is a suggested program, subject to local custom:

Entrance of the Bishop: sing *Ecce sacerdos magnus* or *Sacerdos et Pontifex*. See pages 280 & 282.
Bishop kneels at altar: sing *Veni, Creator Spiritus*. See page 134.

Bishop extends his hands and sings or recites versicles and orations. Make the following responses if above are sung:

V. Spíritus Sanctus supervéniat in vos, et virtus Altíssimi custódiat vos a peccátis
R. Amen.
V. Adjutórium nostrum in nómine Dómini. *R.* Qui fecit caelum et terram.
V. Dómine, exáudi oratiónem meam. *R.* Et clamor meus ad te véniat.
V. Dóminus vobíscum. *R.* Et cum spíritu tuo.

Orémus. *(Prayer.)*
Omnípotens sempitérne Deus,. . . . .*R.* Amen.

During anointing of candidates: sing either Latin or English hymns in honor of the Holy Spirit or Blessed Trinity or, less appropriately, hymns of the season.

As Bishop washes his hands: sing *Confirma hoc Deus*.

Ps. 67, 29, 30.
Mode 8
(J.H.D.
Con - fír - ma hoc De - us * quod o - pe - rá - tus es in no - bis,
a tem - plo san - cto tu - o, quod est in Je - rú - sa - lem.

V. Gló - ri - a Pa - tri, et Fí - li - o, et Spi - rí - tu - i San-cto.
R. Si - cut e - rat in prin - cí - pi - o, et nunc, et sem - per,
et in saé - cu - la sae - cu - ló - rum. A - men.

Repeat: *Confirma hoc.*

Bishop sings or recites versicles and orations: make proper responses if they are sung.

V. Osténde nobis, Dómine, misericórdiam tuam.	*R.* Et salutáre tuum da nobis.
V. Dómine, exáudi oratiónem meam.	*R.* Et clamor meus ad te véniat.
V. Dóminus vobíscum.	*R.* Et cum spíritu tuo.

Orémus *(Prayer.)*
Deus, qui Apóstolis tuis . . . . *R.* Amen.

Ecce sic benedicétur . . . . *R.* Amen.

At Benediction: observe the same directions, whether Bishop or priest celebrates. See page 121.

The Bishop's interrogation of the candidates may precede or follow the anointing. The Bishop may impart the Pontifical Blessing. (See page 282.) A sermon is sometimes given separately from the Bishop's remarks. The Pastor should be consulted in advance for the order of the service.

THE SOLEMN RECEPTION OF A BISHOP
ECCE SACERDOS MAGNUS*

A. GREGORY MURRAY, O.S.B.

On the Bishop's arrival, this responsory is sung. The antiphon *Sacerdos et Pontifex* may be sung in its place.

Ec - ce sa - cér - dos ma - gnus, qui in di -
é - bus su - is plá - cu - it De - o:
R. Í - de - o ju - re - ju - rán - do fe - cit il - lum
Dó - mi - nus cré - sce - re in ple - bem su - am.
V. Be - ne - di - cti - ó - nem ó - mni - um gén - ti - um de - dit il -

*If desired, the verses *Benedictionem* and *Gloria* may be sung in semi-chorus, with the refrain *Ideo* repeated by the full choir.

ECCE SACERDOS MAGNUS

li et te - sta - mén - tum su - um con - fir - má - vit su - per
ca - put e - - jus. V. Gló - ri - a Pa - tri, et
Repeat Ideo as above.
Fí - li - o, et Spi - rí - tu - i San - cto.
Repeat Ideo as above.

While the Bishop kneels before the altar, the priest sings the following versicles, to which the choir makes the proper responses:

V. Protéctor noster áspice Deus. *R.* Et réspice in fáciem Christi tui.
V. Salvum fac servum tuum. *R.* Deus meus sperántem in te.
V. Mitte ei, Dómine, auxílium de sancto. *R.* Et de Sion tuére eum.
V. Nihil profíciat inimícus in eo. *R.* Et fílius iniquitátis non appónat nocére ei.
V. Dómine, exáudi oratiónem meam. *R.* Et clamor meus ad te véniat.
V. Dóminus vobíscum. *R.* Et cum spíritu tuo.

Orémus *(Prayer.)*
Omnípotens sempitérne Deus,. . . . . . . *R.* Amen.

SACERDOS ET PONTIFEX

Mode 1.
(J.H.D.)

On the Bishop's arrival, the following antiphon is sung. The responsory *Ecce sacerdos magnus* may be sung in its place.

Sa - cér - dos et Pón - ti - fex ____ *et vir - tú - tum

ó - pi - fex, pa - stor bo - ne in pó - pu - lo, ____

sic __ pla - cu - í - sti ____ Dó - mi - no. *T. P.* Al - le - lú - ia.

237 THE PONTIFICAL BLESSING

The Bishop sings the following versicles and the choir responds.

V. Sit nomen Dómini bene - - dí - ctum. *R.* Ex hoc nunc et usque in

V. Adjutórium nostrum in nómine Dó - mi - ni. *R.* Qui fecit caelum et

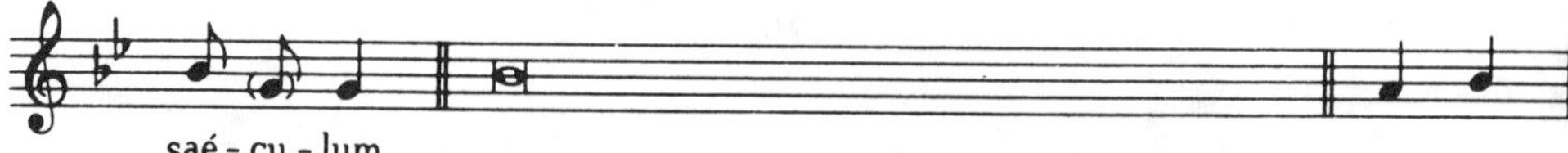
saé - cu - lum.
ter - ram. *V.* Benedícat vos omnípotens Deus. . . . . *R.* A - men.

TE DEUM

Early 5th Cent.

Simple Tone, Mode 3. (J.H.D.)

Te De - um lau - dá - mus:—* te Dó - mi - num con - fi - té - mur.
Te ae - tér - num Pa - trem o - mnis ter - ra ve - ne - rá - tur.
Ti - bi o - mnes Án - ge - li, ti - bi Cae - li et
u - ni - vér - sae Po - te - stá - tes: Ti - bi Ché - ru - bim et

Sé - ra - phim in - ces - sá - bi - li vo - ce pro - clá - mant:
San - ctus: San - ctus: San - ctus Dó - mi - nus
De - us Sá - ba - oth. Ple - ni sunt cae - li et ter - ra
ma - je - stá - tis gló - ri - ae tu - ae. Te glo - ri - ó - sus
A - po - sto - ló - rum cho - rus: Te Pro - phe - tá - rum

lau - dá - bi - lis nú - me - rus: Te Már - ty - rum
can - di - dá - tus lau - dat ex - ér - ci - tus. Te per or - bem
ter - rá - rum san - cta con - fi - té - tur Ec - clé - si - a:
Pa - - - trem im - mén - sae ma - je - stá - tis:
Ve - ne - rán - dum tu - um ve - rum et ú - ni - cum Fí - li - um:

San - ctum quo - que Pa - rá - cli - tum Spí - ri - tum.
Tu Rex gló - ri - ae, Chri - ste. Tu Pa - tris
sem - pi - tér - nus es Fí - li - us. Tu ad li - be - rán - dum
su - sce - ptú - rus hó - mi - nem, non hor - ru - í - sti
Vír - gi - nis ú - te - rum. Tu de - ví - cto mor - tis

a - cú - le - o, a - pe - ru - í - sti cre - dén - ti - bus
re - gna cae - ló - rum. Tu ad déx - te - ram De - i se - des,
in gló - ri - a Pa - tris. Ju - dex cré - de - ris es - se ven - tú - rus.
All kneel while this verse is sung.
Te er - go quaé - su - mus, tu - is fá - mu - lis súb - ve - ni,
quos pre - ti - ó - so sán - gui - ne red - e - mí - sti.

TE DEUM

Ae - tér - na fac cum san - ctis tu - is in gló - ri - a
nu - me - rá - ri. Sal - vum fac pó - pu - lum tu - um, Dó - mi - ne,
et bé - ne - dic hae - re - di - tá - ti tu - ae.
Et re - ge e - os, et ex - tól - le il - los
us - que in ae - tér - num. Per sín - gu - los di - es,

be - ne - dí - ci - mus te. Et lau - dá - mus no - men
tu - um in saé - cu - lum, et in saé - cu - lum saé - cu - li.
Di - gná - re, Dó - mi - ne, di - e i - sto__ si - ne pec - cá - to
nos cu - sto - dí - re. Mi - se - ré - re no - stri, Dó - mi - ne,
mi - se - ré - re no - stri. Fi - at mi - se - ri - cór - di - a tu - a,

TE DEUM

Dó - mi - ne, su - per nos, quem - ád - mo - dum

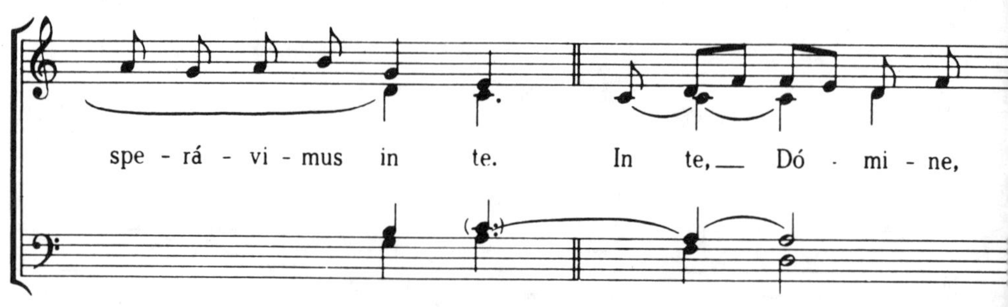
spe - rá - vi - mus in te. In te, Dó - mi - ne,

spe - rá - vi: non con - fún - dar in ae - tér - num.

V. Benedicámus Patrem et Fílium cum Sancto Spíritu.
R. Laudémus et superexaltémus eum in saécula.
V. Benedíctus es, Dómine, in firmaménto caeli.
R. Et laudábilis, et gloriósus, et superexaltátus in saécula.
V. Dómine, exáudi oratiónem meam. *R.* Et clamor meus ad te véniat.
V. Dóminus vobíscum. *R.* Et cum spíritu tuo.

Orémus *(Prayer.)*
Deus, cujus misericórdiae . . . . *R.* Amen.

INTROIT

Esdras 2, 34-35.
Mode 6.
(J.H.D.)
Ré - qui - em * ae - tér - - nam do - na
e - is, Dó - mi - - - - ne:
et lux per - pé - tu - a lú - ce - at
e - - - - is. Ps. 64. Te de - cet hy - mnus, De - us, in Si - on,
et ti - bi red - dé - tur vo - tum in Je - rú - sa - lem: *
ex - áu - di o - ra - ti - ó - nem me - am, ad te o - mnis ca - ro vé - ni - et.

Repeat *Requiem* as far as the Psalm.

240 KYRIE, ELEISON

Mode
(J.H.D

Ký - ri - e,___ * e - - - lé - i - son.
Ký - ri - e,___ e - - - lé - i - son.
Ký - ri - e,___ e - - - lé - i - son.
Chri - ste,___ e - - - lé - i - son.

KYRIE, ELEISON

Chri - ste, e - - - lé - i - son.
Chri - ste, e - - - lé - i - son.
Ký - ri - e, e - - - lé - i - son.
Ký - ri - e, e - - - lé - i - son.
Ký - ri - e, * e - - - lé - i - son.

GRADUAL

4 Esdras 2, 34 - 35.

Tone 'in directum'
(J.H.D.)

Réquiem aetér - nam do - na e - is, Dó - mi - ne: *
et lux perpétua lú - ce - at e - is.
V. In memória ae - tér - na e - rit ju - stus: *
ab auditióne mala non ti - mé - bit.

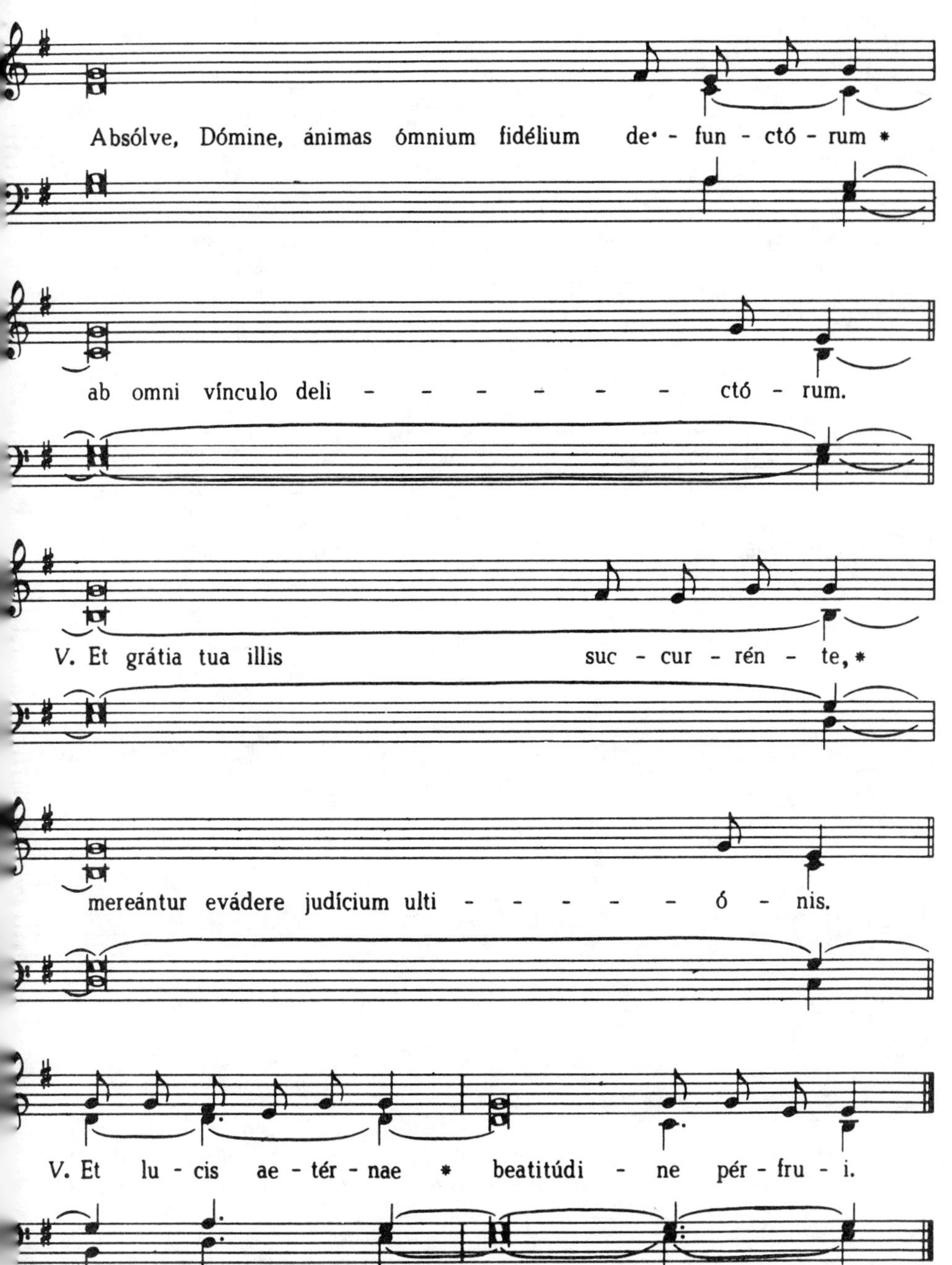
Absólve, Dómine, ánimas ómnium fidélium de - fun - ctó - rum *
ab omni vínculo deli - - - - - - ctó - rum.
V. Et grátia tua illis suc - cur - rén - te, *
mereántur evádere judícium ulti - - - - - ó - nis.
V. Et lu - cis ae - tér - nae * beatitúdi - ne pér - fru - i.

SEQUENCE: DIES IRAE

Ascribed to
THOMAS OF CELANO, O.F.M., *13th Cent.*

Mode
(J.H.D

1. Di - es i - rae, di - es il - la, Sol - vet_ sae - clum_
2. Quan - tus tre - mor est fu - tú - rus Quan - do_ ju - dex_

1. in fa - víl - la: Te - ste_ Da - vid_ cum Si - býl - la.
2. est ven - tú - rus, Cun - cta_ stri - cte_ di - scus - sú - rus!

3. Tu - ba mi - rum_ spar - gens so - num_ Per se - púl - cra
4. Mors stu - pé - bit_ et_ na - tú - ra,_ Cum re - súr - get

3. re - gi - ó - num Co - get_ o - mnes_ an - te thro - num.
4. cre - a - tú - ra, Ju - di - cán - ti_ re - spon - sú - ra.

▸ 296

5. Li - ber scri - ptus pro - fe - ré - tur, In quo to - tum
6. Ju - dex er - go cum se - dé - bit, Quid-quid la - tet
5. con - ti - né - tur, Un - de mun-dus ju - di - cé - tur.
6. ap - pa - ré - bit: Nil in - úl - tum re - ma - né - bit.
7. Quid sum mi - ser tunc di - ctú - rus? Quem pa - tró - num
8. Rex tre - mén-dae ma - je - stá - tis, Qui sal - ván - dos
7. ro - ga - tú - rus? Cum vix ju - stus sit se - cú - rus.
8. sal - vas gra - tis, Sal - va me, fons pi - e - tá - tis.

DIES IRAE

9. Re - cor - dá - re, Je - su pi - e, Quod sum cau - sa
10. Quae-rens me, se - dí - sti las - sus: Red - e - mí - sti
9. tu - ae vi - ae: Ne me per - das il - la di - e.
10. cru - cem pas - sus: Tan - tus la - bor non sit cas - sus.
11. Ju - ste ju - dex ul - ti - ó - nis, Do - num fac re
12. In - ge - mí - sco tam - quam re - us: Cul - pa ru - bet
11. mis - si - ó - nis An - te di - em ra - ti - ó - nis.
12. vul - tus me - us: Sup - pli - can - ti par - ce, De - us.

13. Qui Ma - rí - am ab - sol - ví - sti, Et la - tró - nem
14. Pre - ces me - ae non sunt di - gnae: Sed tu bo - nus
13. ex - au - dí - sti, Mi - hi quo - que spem de - dí - sti.
14. fac be - ní - gne, Ne per - én - ni cre - mer i - gne.
15. In - ter o - ves lo - cum prae - sta, Et ab hae - dis
16. Con - fu - tá - tis ma - le - dí - ctis, Flam - mis á - cri -
15. me se - qué - stra, Stá - tu - ens in par - te dex - tra.
16. bus ad - dí - ctis, Vo - ca me cum be - ne - dí - ctis.
17. O - ra sup - plex et ac - clí - nis, Cor con - trí - tum

17. qua - si ci - nis: Ge - re cu - ram me - i fi - nis.
18. La - cri - mó - sa di - es il - la, Qua re - súr - get
18. ex fa - víl - la 19. Ju - di - cán - dus ho - mo re - us:
19. Hu - ic er - go par - ce, De - us. 20. Pi - e Je - su
20. Dó - mi - ne, do - na e - is ré - qui - em. A - men.

OFFERTORY (1): DOMINE JESU

Mode 2.
(J.H.D.)

Dó - mi - ne Je - su Chri - ste, * Rex
gló - - - ri - ae, lí - be - ra á - ni - mas
ó - mni - um fi - dé - li - um de - fun - ctó - rum
de poe - nis in - fér - ni, et de pro - fún - do la - cu:
lí - be - ra e - as de o - re le - ó - - nis,
ne ab - sór - be - at e - as tár - ta - rus,

ne ca - dant in ob - scú - - - rum: sed
sí - gni - fer, san - ctus Mí - cha - el,
re - pre - sén - tet e - - as in lu - - cem
san - ctam: * Quam o - lim Á - bra - hae pro - mi - sí - sti
et sé - - - - - - mi - ni e - - jus.
V. Hó - sti - as et pre - ces ti - bi, Dó - mi - ne,

OFFERTORY (1)

lau - dis of - fé - ri - mus: tu sú - sci - pe
pro a - ni - má - bus il - lis, qua - rum hó - di - e
me - mó - ri - am fá - ci - mus: fac e - as, Dó - mi - ne,
de mor - te trans - í - re ad vi - tam.
* Quam o - lim Á - bra - hae pro - mi - sí - sti et sé -
- - - - - - - - - - - mi - ni e - - jus.

OFFERTORY (2): DOMINE JESU

Tone 'in directum'
(J.H.D.)

Dómine Jesu Christe, Rex gló - ri - ae, † líbera ánimas ómnium fidélium
de - fun - ctó - rum * de poenis inférni, et de pro - fún - do la - cu:
Líbera eas de o - re le - ó - nis, * ne absórbeat eas tárta - rus,
ne cadant in ob - scú - rum: Sed sígnifer, sanctus Míchael, represéntet eas

OFFERTORY (2)

lu-cem san-ctam: * Quam olim Ábrahae promisísti et sé - mi - ni e - jus.
V. Hóstias et preces tibi, Dómine, laudis offé - ri - mus: † tu súscipe pro a -
ni - má - bus il - lis, * quarum hódie memóriam fá - ci - mus:
Fac eas, Dómine, de morte trans - í - re ad vi - tam. *
Quam olim Ábrahae promisí - sti et sé - mi - ni e - jus.

SANCTUS & BENEDICTUS

Mode 2
(J.H.D.

San - ctus, * San - ctus, San - ctus Dó - mi - nus De - us
Sá - ba - oth. Ple - ni sunt cae - li et ter - ra gló - ri - a tu - a.
Ho - sán - na in ex - cél - sis. Be - ne - dí - ctus qui ve - nit
in nó - mi - ne Dó - mi - ni. Ho - sán - na in ex - cél - sis.

AGNUS DEI

Mode 8.
(J.H.D.)

A - gnus De - i, * qui tol - lis pec - cá - ta mun - di:

do - na e - is ré - qui - em. A - gnus De - i, *

qui tol - lis pec - cá - ta mun - di: do - na e - is

ré - qui - em. A - gnus De - i, * qui tol - lis pec - cá - ta

mun - di: do - na e - is ré - qui - em ** sem - pi - tér - nam.

COMMUNION: LUX AETERNA

4 Esdras 2, 34–35.

Mode 8
(J.H.D.)

Lux ae - tér - na * lú - ce - at e - is, Dó - mi - ne: *
Cum san-ctis tu - is in ae - tér - num, qui - a pi - us es.
V. Ré - qui - em ae - tér - nam do - na e - is, Dó - mi - ne,
et lux per - pé - tu - a lú - ce - at e - is *
Cum san-ctis tu - is in ae - tér - num, qui - a pi - us es.

Re - qui - é - scant in pa - ce. R. A - men.

BURIAL SERVICE 250

The rules for the burial service presume that the priest and singers go to the lace where the body is laid out, escort it in procession to the church, and, after the urch services, accompany it to the grave. In most parishes, this is no longer done; ence, many of the rules are slightly changed or omitted. In some places, it is allowed sing many of the chants in English. It is wise to consult the Pastor to determine the cal custom.

The following are the complete rules:

he body is blessed where it is laid out, and the *De profundis* is recited. The procession aves for the church and the *Miserere* is sung. As the body is taken down the aisle of e church, the *Subvenite* is sung.

he Office of the Dead is then sometimes sung.

equiem Mass follows and after that sometimes a eulogy is given.

fter Mass, and after the eulogy if there is one, the celebrant, vested in cope, ap- oaches the body and recites the prayer *Non intres*. The choir then sings the *Libera* hich may be intoned by the celebrant). The choir sings the *Kyrie, eleison; Christe, eison; Kyrie, eleison* at the end of the *Libera*. The celebrant then intones the *Pater oster* and it is recited by all silently as he sprinkles and incenses the body. He then tones *Et ne nos inducas in tentationem* along with several other versicles and an ation to which the choir makes the proper responses. (The second last versicle and sponse *Requiescat in pace. Amen,* are both sung by the choir.)

s the body is escorted down the aisle leaving the church, *In paradisum* is sung.

t the grave, the canticle *Benedictus* is sung, along with various versicles and respon- s, similar to those used at the absolution in church.

n the return to the church, the priest recites the *De profundis*.

Absolution (at the catafalque) when the body is not present:

l as when the body is present, except that the *Libera* is commenced immediately at e beginning, since the prayer *Non intres* is omitted.

MISERERE

Ps. 50. *Mode 1* (J.H.D.)

The priest intones the antiphon *Exsultabunt Domino;* the choir then continues with the psalm, concluding with the entire antiphon.

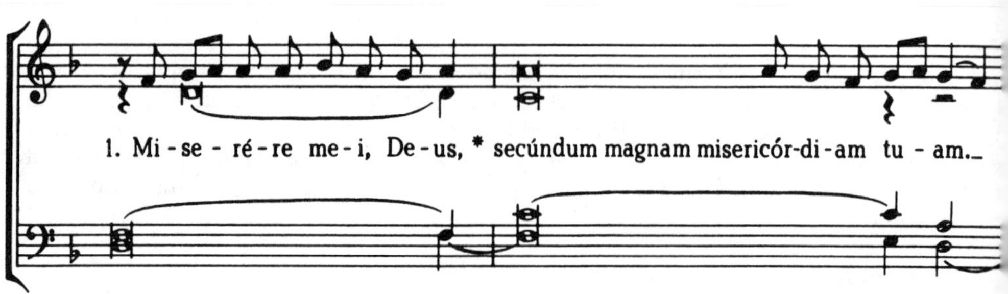
1. Mi - se - ré - re me - i, De - us, * secúndum magnam misericór-di - am tu - am.

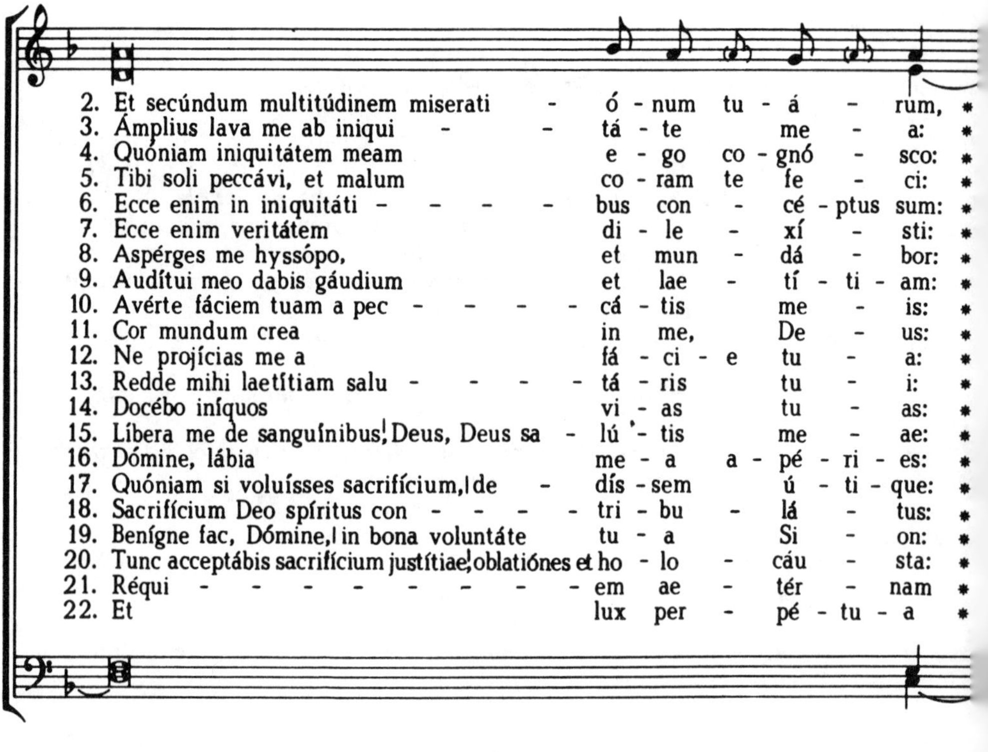

2. Et secúndum multitúdinem miserati - ó - num tu - á - rum, *
3. Ámplius lava me ab iniqui - - tá - te me - a: *
4. Quóniam iniquitátem meam e - go co - gnó - sco: *
5. Tibi soli peccávi, et malum co - ram te fe - ci: *
6. Ecce enim in iniquitáti - - - - - bus con - cé - ptus sum: *
7. Ecce enim veritátem di - le - xí - sti: *
8. Aspérges me hyssópo, et mun - dá - bor: *
9. Audítui meo dabis gáudium et lae - tí - ti - am: *
10. Avérte fáciem tuam a pec - - - - - cá - tis me - is: *
11. Cor mundum crea in me, De - us: *
12. Ne projícias me a fá - ci - e tu - a: *
13. Redde mihi laetítiam salu - - - - - tá - ris tu - i: *
14. Docébo iníquos vi - as tu - as: *
15. Líbera me de sanguínibus, Deus, Deus sa - lú - tis me - ae: *
16. Dómine, lábia me - a a - pé - ri - es: *
17. Quóniam si voluísses sacrifícium, de - dís - sem ú - ti - que: *
18. Sacrifícium Deo spíritus con - - - - - tri - bu - lá - tus: *
19. Benígne fac, Dómine, in bona voluntáte tu - a Si - on: *
20. Tunc acceptábis sacrifícium justítiae, oblatiónes et ho - lo - cáu - sta: *
21. Réqui - - - - - - - - - - - em ae - tér - nam *
22. Et lux per - pé - tu - a *

MISERERE

2. dele iniqui - - - - - - - - - - tá - tem me - am.
3. et a peccáto me - o mun - da me.
4. et peccátum meum contra me est sem - per.
5. ut justificéris in sermónibus tuis,|et vincas cum ju - di - cá - ris.
6. et in peccátis concépit me ma - ter me - a.
7. incérta et occúlta sapiéntiae tuae|manife - stá - sti mi - hi.
8. lavábis me, et super nivem de - al - bá - bor.
9. et exsultábunt ossa hu - - - - - - - - mi - li - á - ta.
10. et omnes iniquitátes me - as de - le.
11. et spíritum rectum ínnova in viscé - - - ri - bus me - is.
12. et spíritum sanctum tuum|ne áu - - - - fe - ras a me.
13. et spíritu principá - - - - - - - - - - li con - fír - ma me.
14. et ímpii ad te con - ver - tén - tur.
15. et exsultábit lingua mea justí - - - - - ti - am tu - am.
16. et os meum annuntiábit lau - dem tu - am.
17. holocáustis non de - le - ctá - be - ris.
18. cor contrítum et humiliátum,|Deus non de - spí - ci - es.
19. ut aedificéntur mu - - - - - - - - - ri Je - rú - sa - lem.
20. tunc impónent super altáre tu - um ví - tu - los.
21. dona e - i, Dó - mi - ne.
(e - is,)
22. lú - - - - - - - - - - - - - - ce - at e - i.
(e - is.)
Ant. Ex - sul - tá - bunt Dó - mi - no os - sa hu - mi - li - á - ta.

SUBVENITE

Mode 4
(J.H.D.

Sub - ve - ní - te, * San - cti De - i;
oc - cúr - ri - te, Án - ge - li Dó - mi - ni:
* Su - sci - pi - én - tes á - ni - mam e - jus:
† Of - fe - rén - tes e - am in con - spé - ctu
Al - tís - si - mi. V. Su - scí - pi - at

SUBVENITE

te Chri - stus, qui
vo - cá - vit te: et in si - num
Á - bra-hae Án-ge-li de - dú - cant te:
* Su - sci - pi - én - tes á - ni - mam e - jus:
† Of - fe - rén - tes e - am in con - spé - ctu

SUBVENITE

Al - - - - - tís - si - mi. V. Ré-qui-em
ae - tér - nam do - na e - - i, Dó - mi - ne:
et lux per - pé - tu - a lú - - - - ce - at
e - - - - i. † Of - fe - rén - tes e - am
in con - spé - ctu Al - - - - - - - tís - si - mi.

LIBERA ME, DOMINE

Mode 1.
Lí - be - ra me, Dó - mi - ne, * de mor - te ae - tér - na,
in di - e il - la tre - mén - da: * Quan - do cae - li
mo - vén - di sunt et ter - ra: † Dum vé - ne - ris
ju - di - cá - re saé - cu - lum per i - gnem.

LIBERA ME, DOMINE

V. Tre - mens fa - ctus sum e - go, et tí - me - o,
dum dis - cús - si - o vé - ne - rit, at - que ven - tú - ra i - ra.
* Quan - do cae - li mo - vén - di sunt et ter - ra.
V. Di - es il - la, di - es i - rae, ca - la - mi - tá - tis
et mi - sé - ri - ae, di - es ma - gna et a - má - ra val - de.

LIBERA ME, DOMINE

Dum vé - ne - ris ju - di - cá - re saé - cu - lum per i - gnem.
V. Ré - qui - em ae - tér - nam do - na e - is, Dó - mi - ne,
et lux per - pé - tu - a lú - ce - at e - is.
Repeat *Libera me* as far as the *V. Tremens.*
Ký - ri - e, e - lé - i - son. Chri - ste, e - lé - i - son.
The priest sings
Ký - ri - e, e - lé - i - son. Pa - ter no - ster.... *(in silence)*
V. Et ne nos in - dú - cas in ten - ta - ti - ó - nem.

R. Sed líbera nos a malo.

V. A porta ínferi. *R.* Érue, Dómine, ánimam ejus.

V. Requiéscat in pace. *R.* Amen.

V. Dómine, exáudi oratiónem meam. *R.* Et clamor meus ad te véniat.

V. Dóminus vobíscum. *R.* Et cum spíritu tuo.

Orémus *(Prayer.)*

Deus, qui próprium . . . . *R.* Amen.

254

THE RECESSIONAL

IN PARADISUM

Mode 7.
(J.H.D.)

In pa - ra - dí - sum * de - dú - cant te Án - ge - li:
in tu - o ad - vén - tu su - scí - pi - ant te
Már - ty - res, et per - dú - cant te in ci - vi - tá - tem
san - ctam Je - rú - sa - lem. Cho - rus An - ge - ló - rum
te su - scí - pi - at, et cum Lá - za - ro quon - dam
páu - pe - re ae - tér - nam há - be - as ré - qui - em.

BENEDICTUS

Canticle of Zachary. *Mode 2.*
Luke 1, 68-79. (J.H.D.)

The priest intones the antiphon *Ego sum*; the choir then continues with the canticle, concluding with the entire antiphon.

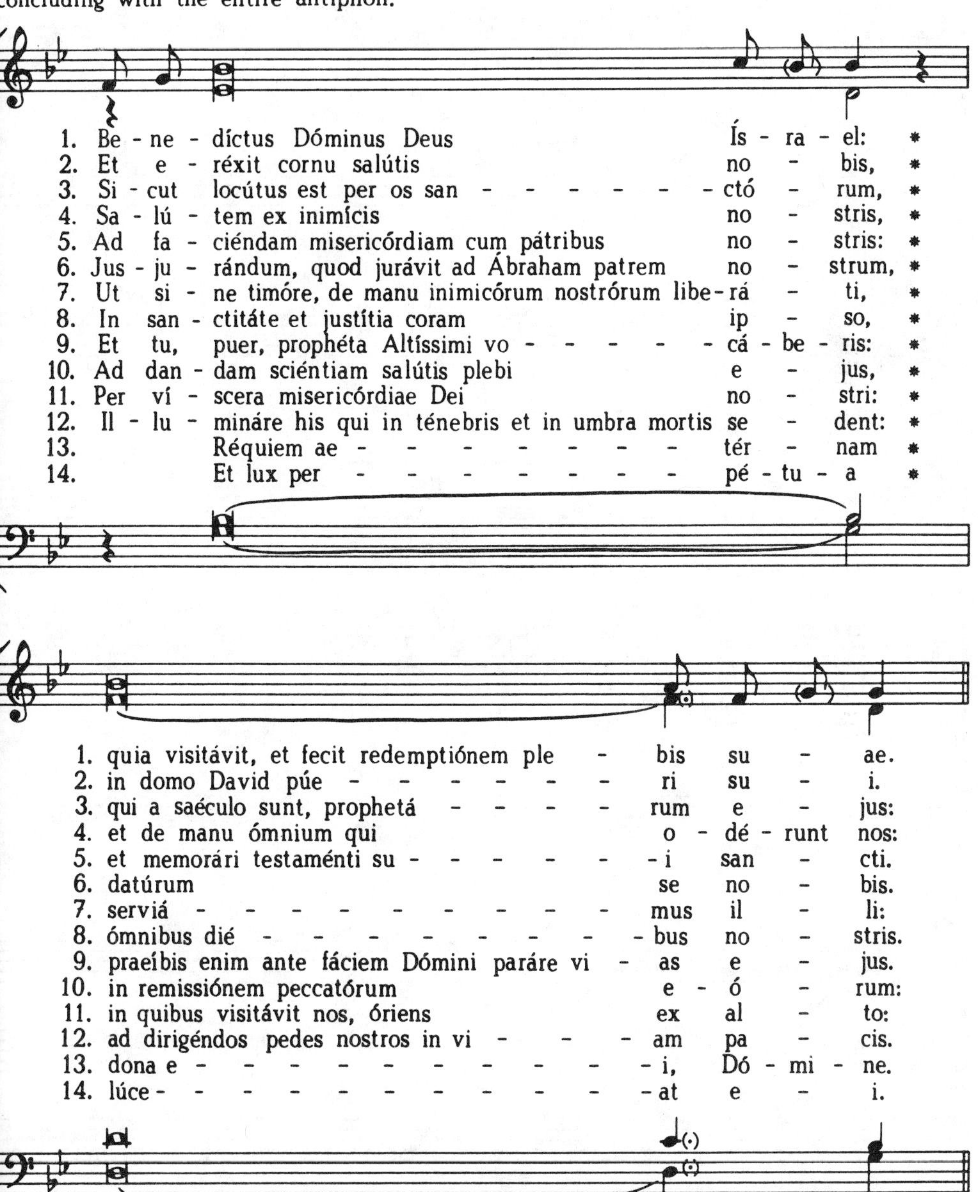
1. Be - ne - díctus Dóminus Deus Ís - ra - el: *
2. Et e - réxit cornu salútis no - bis, *
3. Si - cut locútus est per os san - - - - - - - ctó - rum, *
4. Sa - lú - tem ex inimícis no - stris, *
5. Ad fa - ciéndam misericórdiam cum pátribus no - stris: *
6. Jus - ju - rándum, quod jurávit ad Ábraham patrem no - strum, *
7. Ut si - ne timóre, de manu inimicórum nostrórum libe - rá - ti, *
8. In san - ctitáte et justítia coram ip - so, *
9. Et tu, puer, prophéta Altíssimi vo - - - - - - cá - be - ris: *
10. Ad dan - dam sciéntiam salútis plebi e - jus, *
11. Per ví - scera misericórdiae Dei no - stri: *
12. Il - lu - mináre his qui in ténebris et in umbra mortis se - dent: *
13. Réquiem ae - - - - - - - - - tér - nam *
14. Et lux per - - - - - - - - - pé - tu - a *
1. quia visitávit, et fecit redemptiónem ple - bis su - ae.
2. in domo David púe - - - - - - - - ri su - i.
3. qui a saéculo sunt, prophetá - - - - - rum e - jus:
4. et de manu ómnium qui o - dé - runt nos:
5. et memorári testaménti su - - - - - - - - i san - cti.
6. datúrum se no - bis.
7. serviá - - - - - - - - - - - - mus il - li:
8. ómnibus dié - - - - - - - - - - bus no - stris.
9. praeíbis enim ante fáciem Dómini paráre vi - as e - jus.
10. in remissiónem peccatórum e - ó - rum:
11. in quibus visitávit nos, óriens ex al - to:
12. ad dirigéndos pedes nostros in vi - - - - am pa - cis.
13. dona e - - - - - - - - - - - - - i, Dó - mi - ne.
14. lúce - - - - - - - - - - - - - - at e - i.

BENEDICTUS

Ant. E - go sum re - sur - ré - cti - o et vi - ta:
qui cre - dit in me, é - ti - am si mór - tu - us
fú - e - rit, vi - vet: et o - mnis qui vi - vit et
cre - dit in me, non mo - ri - é - tur in ae - tér - num.

BENEDICTUS

The priest sings: The choir sings:

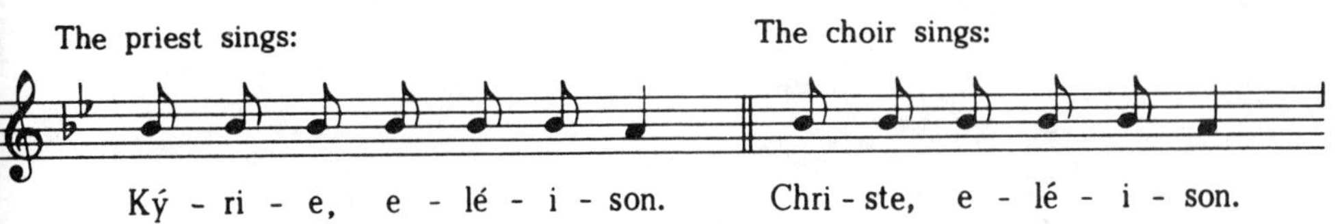

Ký - ri - e, e - lé - i - son. Chri - ste, e - lé - i - son.

The priest sings:

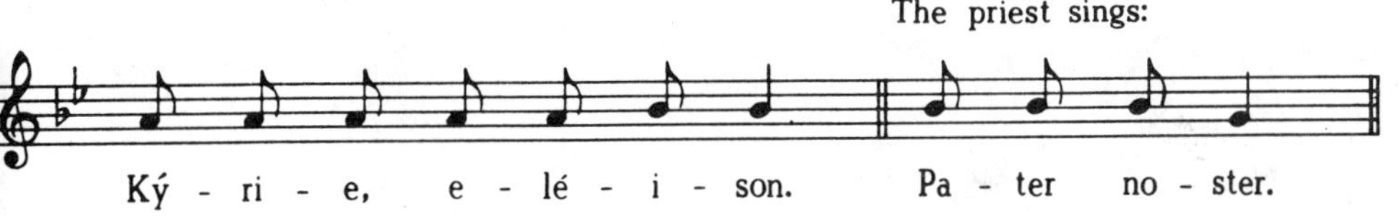

Ký - ri - e, e - lé - i - son. Pa - ter no - ster.

V. Et ne nos inducas in tentatiónem.	*R.* Sed lìbera nos a malo.
V. A porta ínferi.	*R.* Érue, Dómine, ánimam ejus.
V. Requiéscat in pace.	*R.* Amen.
V. Dómine, exáudi oratiónem meam.	*R.* Et clamor meus ad te véniat.
V. Dóminus vobíscum.	*R.* Et cum spíritu tuo.

Orémus *(Prayer.)*
Fac, quaésumus Dómine - - - - - - - - - - - - *R.* Amen.

V. Réquiem aeternam dona ei, Dómine. *R.* Et lux perpétua lúceat ei.

The cantors sing:

V. Re - qui - é - scat in pa - ce. R. A - men.

The priest sings:

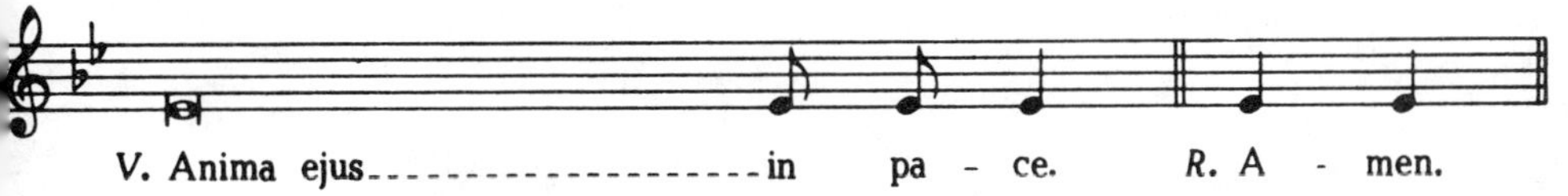

V. Anima ejus - - - - - - - - - - in pa - ce. R. A - men.

METRICAL INDEX OF TUNES

This list of the meters which recur throughout the hymnal will frequently enable choirmasters to select alternative tunes.

INDEX OF AUTHORS, TRANSLATORS AND SOURCES

The numbers in brackets indicate translations.

English Hymns

Latin Hymns

INDEX OF COMPOSERS, ARRANGERS AND SOURCES

The numbers in brackets indicate arrangements.

INDEX OF ORIGINAL FIRST LINES OF TRANSLATED HYMNS

GENERAL INDEX

English Hymns

Latin Hymns

Service Section

This First edition of The New Saint Basil Hymnal was designed by John C. Menihan of Rochester, New York. The engraving of the music and hymns was executed by Gregor & Zimmer in Hamburg, Germany. Introductory pages and indexes were set in Weiss types by Rochester Typographic Service, Inc., Rochester, New York.